INSIGHT CITY GUIDE

AMSTERDAM

Part of the Langenscheidt Publishing Group

✻ INSIGHT GUIDE
aMSTERDaM

Editor
Tom Le Bas
Art Director
Klaus Geisler
Picture Editor
Hilary Genin
Cartography Editor
Zoë Goodwin
Editorial Director
Brian Bell

Distribution

UK & Ireland
GeoCenter International Ltd
The Viables Centre, Harrow Way
Basingstoke, Hants RG22 4BJ
Fax: (44) 1256-817988

United States
Langenscheidt Publishers, Inc.
46–35 54th Road, Maspeth, NY 11378
Fax: (1) 718 784-0640

Canada
Thomas Allen & Son Ltd
390 Steelcase Road East
Markham, Ontario L3R 1G2
Fax: (1) 905 475 6747

Australia
Universal Publishers
1 Waterloo Road
Macquarie Park, NSW 2113
Fax: (61) 2 9888 9074

New Zealand
Hema Maps New Zealand Ltd (HNZ)
Unit D, 24 Ra ORA Drive
East Tamaki, Auckland
Fax: (64) 9 273 6479

Worldwide
Apa Publications GmbH & Co.
Verlag KG (Singapore branch)
38 Joo Koon Road, Singapore 628990
Tel: (65) 6865-1600. Fax: (65) 6861-6438

Printing

Insight Print Services (Pte) Ltd
38 Joo Koon Road, Singapore 628990
Tel: (65) 6865-1600. Fax: (65) 6861-6438

©2004 Apa Publications GmbH & Co.
Verlag KG (Singapore branch)
All Rights Reserved

First Edition 1991
Fourth Edition 2004

ABOUT THIS BOOK

This guidebook combines the interests and enthusiasms of two of the world's best-known information providers: Insight Guides, whose titles have set the standard for visual travel guides since 1970, and Discovery Channel, the world's premier source of nonfiction television programming.

The editors of Insight Guides provide both practical advice and general understanding about a destination. Discovery Channel and its Web site, www.discovery.com, help millions of viewers explore their world from the comfort of their own home.

How to use this book

The book is carefully structured both to convey an understanding of the city and its culture and to guide readers through its sights and activities:

◆ The Best Of Amsterdam section at the front of the guide helps you to prioritise what you want to see. Top family attractions, the best walks, markets, festivals, parks and cafés are listed, together with money-saving tips and a rundown of city's eccentricities.

◆ To understand Amsterdam, you need to know something of its past. The city's history and culture are described in lively, authoritative essays written by specialists with an intimate knowledge of its evolution and present-day challenges.

◆ The main Places section provides a full run-down of all the attractions worth seeing. The main places of interest are coordinated by number with full-colour maps.

◆ A list of recommended restaurants and cafés is included at the end of

each chapter in the Places section, and plotted on the pull-out restaurants map provided with the guide.

♦ Photographs throughout the book are chosen not only to illustrate geography and buildings but also to convey the moods of the city and the life of its people.

♦ The new-look Travel Tips listings section provides a point of reference for information on transport, accommodation, cultural attractions, shopping and other activities. There is also an A–Z directory of practical information, and a useful language guide. Information may be located quickly by using the index printed on the back cover flap – and the flaps are designed to serve as bookmarks.

♦ A detailed street atlas is included at the back of the book, complete with a full index.

The contributors

This new edition was re-written and updated by **George McDonald**, a former resident of Amsterdam currently living in Germany, but who takes every available opportunity to scoot along the rail line to Centraal Station in his favourite city. George expanded the Places section considerably for the new City Guide format, and provided all of the restaurant reviews that appear at the end of each chapter. He is also the author or co-author of various other Insight Guides covering the Netherlands, Belgium and Cyprus.

This revised City Guide builds on previous editions of the book. The original author, **Joan Gannij**, was assisted in her researches on the guide by **Frank Balleny**. **Stuart Ridsdale** contributed much of the text of the original Places chapters, while **Tim Harper** and **Michael Gray** wrote the majority of the original Features text. **Joan Corcoran-Lonis** contributed the essay on Anne Frank.

Prominent among the fine photographers whose work brings Amsterdam vividly to life are **Glyn Genin**, who returned to photography after many years as a national newspaper picture editor, and **Guglielmo Galvin**, an Insight regular.

Editor **Tom Le Bas** was ably assisted by **James Alexander** and **Pam Barrett**, who helped to get the book completed on time. Thanks also go to **Neil Titman** for proofreading and **Helen Peters** for indexing this new edition.

CONTACTING THE EDITORS

We would appreciate it if readers would alert us to errors or outdated information by writing to:

Insight Guides, P.O. Box 7910, London SE1 1WE, England. Fax: (44) 20 7403-0290. insight@apaguide.co.uk

www.insightguides.com

Maps

Travel Tips

THE BEST OF AMSTERDAM

Setting priorities, saving money, unique attractions...
here, at a glance, are our recommendations, plus some
tips and tricks even the locals won't always know

AMSTERDAM FOR FAMILIES

These six attractions are popular with children,
though not all will suit every age group.

- **NEMO Science and Technology Centre**. Part of the revitalised harbour, the NEMO centre has been a favourite with kids of all ages since it opened in 1997. *See page 182.*
- **Artis Zoo**. A fascinating animal habitat in the heart of the city. As well as the zoo, there's also an aquarium and planetarium on site. *See page 174.*
- **Tropenmuseum TM Junior**. Kids get a look in when it comes to life in the tropics at this section of the grown-ups' museum. *See page 175.*
- **Electrische Museum-tramlijn (Electric Museum Tram Line)**. It's far from leaden-footed, this moving "museum" that rolls out to the Amsterdamse Bos onboard antique trams. *See page 194.*
- **Madame Tussaud's**. Come face to face with life-size waxen effigies of Dutch and international famous faces at the Amsterdam branch of the famous London waxworks. *See page 82.*
- **Children's Farm**. Getting close to nature right in the city at this miniature waterfront farm on Bickers Island. *See page 186.*

ONLY IN AMSTERDAM

- **Canal-Boat Tours** Take a *rondvaart* tour and glide through the city's signature canals – and out onto the River Amstel – on a, yes, touristy excursion, but one that's really a "must-do" in Amsterdam. *See pages 113 and 214.*
- **Canal-Bike Tours** Cruising the canals on a pedalo (water-bike) is even more touristy, and even more looked down on by the natives, than going on the powered boats. But there's a certain satisfaction and fascination from gliding around, however slowly, on your own chosen route. *See page 215.*
- **Making a Hash of It** In a dope café, that is, otherwise known as a smoking coffee shop. You can puff your way through officially tolerated cannabis at one of these smoky dens, and no one will disturb the serenity of your slumbers. *See page 63.*
- **Paying Homage to Anne Frank** Visit the thought-provoking, sadness-inducing World War II canalhouse refuge on the Prinsengracht where Anne and her family hid for years from the Nazis, and wrote the famous diary. *See page 117.*
- **Admiring *The Night Watch*** The Rijksmuseum may have a truncated look while it undergoes a multi-year renovation and rebuilding, but Rembrandt's famous painting, the symbol of the Dutch Golden Age, still occupies the place of honour. *See page 150.*

LEFT: the NEMO Science and Technology Centre is the place to come for hands-on fun.

BEST WALKS

- **The Canal Ring**
You can choose one or more from the beautiful Singel, Herengracht, Keizersgracht and Prinsengracht canals, and walk the entire length from Brouwersgracht to the River Amstel (Muntplein in the case of Singel). Alternatively, choose a route that zigzags back and forth between the canals, using the many small streets that connect them. *See pages 111–142.*

- **The Old Centre**
About a quarter of the area around Nieuwmarkt is occupied by the Red Light District, but this is by no means the whole story of this beautiful part of the city. *See page 95.*
- **The Waterfront**
From the Western Islands to the Eastern Islands, a stroll through Amsterdam's old harbour on either side of Centraal Station provides fresh air and history in abundance. *See page 177.*

ABOVE: Amsterdam celebrates Koninginnedag (the Queen's birthday) on the 30th April.

BEST FESTIVALS AND EVENTS

- **Koninginnedag** 30 April. *See page 56.*
- **Holland Festival** June. *See page 56.*
- **Uitmarkt** End of August. *See page 56.*
- **Sint-Nicolaas** November. *See page 56.*

LEFT: restored ships recall the Golden Age outside the Scheepvaarthuis (Maritime Museum) on the waterfront.
BELOW: at Waterlooplein Flea Market.

BEST MARKETS

- **Waterlooplein Flea Market**
Everything and anything that's old – or new – and tatty makes its way onto the stalls of this age-old market in the Jewish Quarter. *See page 163.*
- **Albert Cuypmarkt**
The best street market in the city, covering food, clothes and many other items, ranges through a long street in Amsterdam South. *See page 190.*
- **Flower Market**
Often called the "floating" market (although it doesn't really float), this superb cluster of stalls on Singel is the best place in the city to buy flowers. *See page 92.*

BEST BARS

- **Brown Cafés**
Among the best of these atmospheric traditional (or old-looking) bars are: Hoppe *(see page 93)*, De Engelbewaarder *(see page 109)*, Café Chris, Café 't Smalle and Papeneiland *(all page 125)*, Het Molenpad *(see page 135)* and De Sluyswacht *(see page 175)*.

- **Grand Cafés**
Many fancy modern cafés have adopted this designation, and not all of them are truly grand. These ones are: Café Lux-embourg *(see page 93)*, Café Américain *(see page 135)* and Royal Café De Kroon *(see page 143)*.

- **Trendy Cafés**
In these cases, "trendy" does not necessarily signify a fickle, "here today, gone tomorrow" style: try De Jaren *(see page 109)*, Café Schiller *(see page 143)* and Kanis en Meiland *(see page 187)*.

- **Breweries**
Both of these small-scale breweries have great traditional bars attached: Brouwhuis Maximilaan *(see page 109)* and Bierbrouwerij 't IJ *(see page 175)*.

ABOVE & LEFT: hanging out in two of the city's many brown cafés. **BELOW LEFT:** Het Houten Huys at the Begijnhof, Amsterdam's oldest dwelling, dates from around 1470.

FREE AMSTERDAM

- **The Schuttersgalerij**. You have to pay to get into the Amsterdams Historisch Museum but not into its Schut-tersgalerij, a covered passageway that holds 15 Civic Guards paintings from the Dutch Golden Age. *See page 89.*

- **Harbour Ferries**. Ferries crossing the IJ channel between Cen-traal Station and Ams-terdam-Noord are free; a perfectly ac-ceptable short harbour cruise. *See page 178.*

- **The Begijnhof**. This oasis of tranquil-lity is one of the city centre's stellar sights and experiences. *See page 89.*

- **Lunchtime Concerts**. Both the Concertge-bouw and the Muziek-theater have free 30-minute rehearsal concerts once a week (on most weeks) from 12.30–1pm, the Concertgebouw on Wednesday and the Muziektheater on Tuesday. *See page 157.*

- **National Museum Weekend** On the last weekend in April, admission to many museums is free; oth-ers charge reduced fees. *See page 229.*

AMAZING AMSTERDAM

- The Koninklijk Palace on the Dam *(see page 79)* stands on 13,659 wooden pilings driven into the sandy Amsterdam soil.
- Rembrandt's famous painting *The Night Watch*, actually depicts a daytime scene, a fact that was uncovered only when renovations removed centuries of dirt and revealed the sunlight in the picture.
- Amsterdam has more than 1,200 bridges – more than Venice, but not as many as Hamburg.

- There are some 600,000 bicycles in Amsterdam, which works out at four bikes for ever five residents (or four-fifths of a bike per resident).
- The world's first fully legal same-sex marriage took place in Amsterdam in 2002.
- During the 17th-century "Tulipomania", when speculators drove the price for tulip bulbs to crazy levels (before the inevitable crash brough them back to earth), a record was reached of 30,000 florins (about €6 million) for three.

ABOVE: Amsterdam is a city of bicycles.
BELOW LEFT: giant waterlilies at the Hortus Botanicus (Botanical Gardens).
BOTTOM: there is plenty for children to see and do in the city.

TOP PARKS

- **Vondelpark**. For a taste of alternative Amsterdam, with its shirt off and its hair down (at least in summer), visit this green oasis that was the Hippie's stamping ground in the 1960s. *See page 158.*

- **Amsterdamse Bos**. For fresh air, open space and a place to escape from the crowds and irritations of the centre, Amsterdammers head out to this huge park on the city's southern edge. *See page 193.*

MONEY-SAVING TIPS

Amsterdam Pass Available for 1, 2 or 3 days, the pass gives good savings on public transport, museum entry and other expenses – but only if used to the best advantage. *See page 213.*

Strippenkaart For short-term, intermittent use of public transport around the centre, these multiple-use tickets can be better value than single tickets or day passes. *See page 213.*

Canal Boats Tickets for both the Museumboot (Museum Boat) and the

Canal Bus give reductions on certain museum entry prices, and using the boat trip as a substitute for a dedicated canal-boat tour only adds to the potential savings. *See page 214.*

Many Amsterdam hotels depend on tourist visitors. At times when tourist numbers are low, particularly in winter (and especially on week days in winter), outside of the Christmas and New Year period, rates are lower and good deals are often available. *See page 217.*

Hotels that are primarily oriented towards business visitors are likely to

offer deals aimed at tourists at times when business travel is reduced. Four- and five-star hotels may drop their rates by one or even two levels. It's always worth asking about this.

THE FREEWHEELING CITY

Behind the tourist clichés is a
cosmopolitan city with a village ambience
and a remarkable breadth of culture

Amsterdam, the city of water and brick, is unique for the way it balances past and present. Perhaps no community has ever had such a glorious explosion of wealth and culture as Amsterdam during the 17th century, the city's Golden Age. While the legacy of that period is pervasive, the city is hardly devoted to worship of the past. Instead, modern Amsterdam, from the titillation of the Red Light District to the vitality of the contemporary arts, from the energy of the entrepreneurs in their small shops to the fast-growing immigrant fringes of the city, offers a range of experiences that are the result of a remarkable human heritage.

Explore the less beaten paths away from Centraal Station and Damrak and discover the side streets adjacent to the canal circles, with their shops and friendly cafés. In strolling around Amsterdam – one of the best walking cities in the world – you are also reminded continually of how the city was built and how it thrives: on hard-headed business acumen and a sense of community that combines several qualities. Foremost among these, paradoxically, is the desire to be left alone and the willingness to leave others alone – that is, unless they need help. For while Amsterdam is, and always has been, a city of people pulling themselves up by their own bootstraps, it is also a city that believes in spreading its wealth. Money and comfort are important, but so is a happy, healthy society.

Amsterdam is intriguing in several respects. Its small size, in terms of both population and geography, make it intimate and accessible. It has the ambience of a cosmopolitan village rather than a European capital. English is becoming more and more of a second language; in fact many Amsterdammers speak at least three languages – few people plunge into conversation with strangers as readily as the Dutch – and this provides visitors with an opportunity to look beyond what they've read or heard about the city.

For Amsterdam, apparently so solid, as it sits astride its miles of canals, is really a city that is changing constantly. What's the latest trend in art? Where's the best place to go dancing this week? Who's saying what about the future of NATO and the EU? When is the next demonstration? How are the authorities getting along in their efforts to clean up the streets?

Amsterdam is a city of character and of characters. It is a freewheeling city – so feel free. ❏

PRECEDING PAGES: reflections on Prinsengracht; bicycle and tulips by the Singel canal.
LEFT: street theatre in the Rokin district.

EARLY YEARS TO THE GOLDEN AGE

From its origins as a 12th-century fishing village, Amsterdam
became a prosperous wool-trading centre, and a hotbed of
religious dissent. Its inexorable rise culminated in the 17th-
century Golden Age, when the city was the richest in Europe
and the trading heart of a great empire.

The herring fishermen who established a community at the mouth of the Amstel River at the end of the 12th century must have struggled to survive. As elsewhere along the North Sea coast, they pieced their huts together on top of mounds anchored by wooden stakes and piled up the mounds with seaweed and anything else dredged from the tidal flats that couldn't be put to a better use. Along with a few craftsmen, these early settlers had to devise a more reliable existence than living at the whim of the unpredictable tides that surged in from the Zuiderzee.

Yet the Amstel community grew, and the scattered huts became rows of timber-framed houses built on top of dykes by the river. Three of the old dykes are still visible today as Warmoesstraat, Nieuwendijk and Kalverstraat.

Damming the tides

With the excess soil from digging drainage canals, the level of the houses was raised about 70 cm (27 inches) above Normal Amsterdam Level (NAP; this is the standard "zero" measurement for the nation, not sea level – in Amsterdam and the whole of western Holland, sea level means knee-deep in water).

The first dam, intended to hold back the highest tides, was built around 1200 – most likely at the site of the present-day square called the Dam. It was probably nothing more than a sluice gate across the mouth of the

LEFT: *The Mill at Wijk bij Duurstede* by Jacob Ruysdael (1670), now in the Rijksmuseum.
RIGHT: *The Noorderkerk* by A. Beerstraten (1644).

Amstel, which would halt the inundation from the large tides; at low tide it could be opened to allow the river to flow into the sea.

By 1275, the peat bogs surrounding the hamlet known then as "Amestelledamme" had gradually attracted farmers, refugees and tradesmen who bolstered the population to the point where it might, generously, be called a town; even so, it was still very small by comparison with higher, drier European capitals.

From burg to city

According to a contemporary woodcut, the forerunner of the Oude Kerk (Old Church) had been erected near the site of today's church, on Oudekerksplein, along with about 600 houses. Surrounding the little burg was a moat, the remnants of which can be traced in the Oudezijds Voorburgwal and the Nieuwezijds Voorburgwal canals.

Amestelledamme, or Amstelredam (it did not become Amsterdam until the mid-16th century), then began making great strides – quickly enough, in fact, to find itself the prize in a battle for provincial fiefdoms between the Bishop of Utrecht and the Count of Holland towards the end of the 13th century. In the first recorded reference to the city, in 1275 Count Floris V granted the people of Amsterdam freedom from paying tolls on goods shipped along the waterways of Holland.

In 1300, Amsterdam was officially granted city status, receiving its charter from the Bishop of Utrecht. By this time the conflict between the bishop and the counts of Holland had been resolved, in typical medieval fashion. Count Floris V's heir defeated the old bishop and installed his brother as the new Bishop of Utrecht. When he died, the count of Holland duly inherited his brother's fiefdom, including the whole of the city of Amsterdam and the surrounding Amstelland.

Canals and commerce

The weirs and drainage ditches that had kept residents dry were proving an obstacle for shipping, and the canals were equally restrictive for population expansion. Locks were constructed to enable smaller vessels to move into the city, where they often sold their wares from the canalside. Shops sprang up beside the dykes and on the approaches to the big dam (Damrak). An agricultural market and town square evolved around the Waag (Weigh House) on the present-day Dam Square; this lasted until the French king of Holland removed the building in 1808, as it blocked his view.

Expansion would prove to be an eternal dilemma for the growing port. The first solution was to widen the tops of the dykes and embankments to enable them to become the main streets. Next, rows of warehouses and homes were extended over the water. Narrow alleys and tiny canals connected the principal canals to the Amstel. The next step was to dig more canals parallel to the dykes on either side of the river.

This process was repeated throughout the 15th century. An encircling series of canals and walls was built, and the city boundary from this time can still be traced today; the squat turret at the Nieuwmarkt is one of its remnants.

By 1420, Amsterdam was the largest city in the Netherlands and by the middle of the 1500s had a population of 30,000. Fuelling this growth was commerce, particularly with the coastal towns of the Baltic. Salt became crucial for cod and herring fishermen, who could preserve their catch by gutting and salting it and therefore stay longer at sea. Amsterdam was the perfect halfway point between southern Europe and the Baltic for salt from

Portugal, especially as the city benefited from the favourable tax status granted by its benefactor, the Count of Holland.

Clothing sweatshops were well established in Amsterdam by the late 14th century. Wool from England initially went to workshops in Leiden and Haarlem, but throughout the 16th century Amsterdam increasingly manufactured good-quality cloth, and eventually became the leading wool centre in the country.

Amsterdam's beer trade was equally vital to the medieval economy. Amsterdam was granted the sole right to import large quantities of hop beer from Hamburg. Eventually, Dutch brewers in Haarlem, Gouda, Delft and

Amsterdam abandoned their own grout-flavoured brew and began making a similar style of stronger-flavoured hop beer. These local breweries proved so successful that they were soon exporting their products through the free port of Amsterdam.

Grain for beer and bread also passed through the Baltic to Amsterdam. Spices, pitch, fur, timber and iron ore kept city warehouses full, and the principle of entrepôt was born; goods entering the city destined for another port could be stored without incurring tolls, taxes or duty. This principle, maintained through the centuries, remains today in the form of bonded warehouses.

Habsburg hands. Maximilian's son, Philip, who succeeded his father, married Joan ("the Mad") of Spain – a powerful and intolerant Catholic country, where the Inquisition had been introduced in 1478. With this dynastic marriage, Spain became a force in the region – a development that would have momentous repercussions for Amsterdam.

Until the repressions initiated by the fanatically Catholic Philip II of Spain in the 1560s, however, Amsterdam, with its flourishing economy, was a veritable pot-pourri of religious convictions, although not everyone could practise their beliefs openly. The fine line between religious orthodoxy and heresy

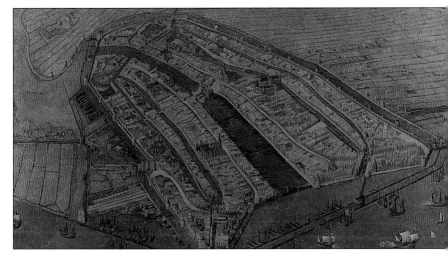

Religious divisions

Through a process of dynastic marriages and conquest, Amsterdam and the surrounding areas (the Netherlands, of which Holland and Zeeland were part) were controlled by the dukes of Burgundy from the 1430s. Charles the Bold was the last of the dukes to hold sway; when he died in 1477, he was succeeded by his daughter Mary, wife of the Habsburg Empire's Crown Prince, Maximilian of Austria. In this way the Burgundian lands passed into

was often drawn along political rather than religious grounds. Until the turbulent 1500s, Amsterdam's population was 98 percent Catholic. The city even had its own miraculous host, housed in a healing shrine that soon turned Amsterdam into an important destination for pilgrims *(see page 20)*. The church containing the shrine, at Nieuwzijds Voorburgwal, later became Protestant and was ultimately destroyed.

Erasmus of Rotterdam was the first of the religious reformers to challenge the established Catholic Church when he claimed man was the ideal creation rather than the root of sin. But Spanish and Catholic dominance of

LEFT: *Woman Spinning* by Van Heemskerck (1529).
ABOVE: Cornelius Anthoniszoon's well-known 1544 map of Amsterdam.

northern Europe really began to fragment after the Augustinian monk Martin Luther nailed his 95 points, condemning Church abuses, to the chapel door of Wittenberg Castle in 1517. Luther's translation of the Bible was first published in the Netherlands.

More popular in Amsterdam were the teachings of a French Protestant theologian, John Calvin, which leaned heavily on the doctrine of predestination. The Catholic Church urged punishment on the heretical followers of Calvin, but little was done in the city. The civic fathers were not going to shatter their prosperous co-existence with the Calvinists at the behest of Catholic bishops based in Brussels who, technically, held pastoral authority over the Netherlands.

This lax attitude was blamed for the Anabaptist uprising of 1535. These early Protestant charismatics were followers of a furrier named Melchior Hofmann, who imagined himself a Doomsday prophet. About 40 "Melchiorieten" worked themselves up into a religious frenzy, tore off their clothes and stormed the Town Hall, imitating an earlier uprising in Münster. Many rioters were arrested and executed on the Dam, and their heads placed on pikes at the city gates.

Strict Catholic leaders took control of the city and a period of anti-Protestant repression

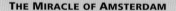

THE MIRACLE OF AMSTERDAM

The so-called Miracle of the Host occurred in 1345 when a dying man was given the last communion rites, but was unable to keep the host down; his vomit was thrown on the fire but the host refused to burn. A small shrine was built on the site of this miracle, and over the years other magical acts were attributed to it.

A century later, when the chapel burned down, the host was again miraculously spared. Pilgrims from far and wide would converge on Amsterdam for the annual procession parading the sacred relic. The ritual, the Stille Omgang (Silent Procession) is held to this day from Saturday to Sunday between 12 and 22 March.

followed. But when something is forbidden, curiosity to discover more about it increases exponentially. Calvinism was no exception; it soon gained support from wealthy city merchants, including some liberal Catholic mayors, who felt the city was being administered through corrupt measures.

Switching sides

By the 1560s, Protestant services were being held outside the city gates and outside the jurisdiction of the Catholic police. Religious tensions boiled over in the summer of 1566. In another episode of copy-cat violence, this time with inspiration from Antwerp, a Calvinist mob smashed their way through the altars and statuary of the Oude Kerk, a protest that became known as the "Iconoclasm". In the following months the rioters also turned their destructive attentions to the city's priories, hitting the wine cellars when they ran out of works of religious art to break upstairs.

In typical Amsterdam fashion, the city fathers chose to placate the rioters rather than confront the situation head on. In return for profitable peace they allowed the Calvinists to hold services openly in one of the Franciscan churches they had earlier looted. The Protestants accepted their lot and were quietened for a while.

But just two years later, in 1568, Philip II of Spain, champion of the Counter Reformation, initiated an anti-heresy campaign that triggered 80 years of war. Calvinism was outlawed, repression was ruthless and the Dutch rose up in revolt. Unlike most of the Netherlands, however, Amsterdam remained Catholic, choosing not to switch allegiance to the Protestant Prince William of Orange, leader of the Dutch revolt against Spain. Only in 1578, when it was obvious that the Spanish were in retreat and William's forces surrounded Amsterdam, did the city prudently and swiftly change sides – a process known as the Alteration.

The 1579 Treaty of Utrecht created the United Provinces, the foundation for the modern Netherlands, a loose alliance of seven northern provinces. More significantly for the development of a Dutch empire, the treaty gave the United Provinces shipping control of the lower Rhine, and allowed Amsterdam to eclipse its rival Antwerp as the region's principal commercial centre.

In Amsterdam, Catholic city officials were replaced by Protestant merchants and the city's churches became Calvinist. Wealthy Calvinist merchants fled to Amsterdam from the southern provinces, which had remained subject to Spain and evolved into modern Belgium and Luxembourg. Crucially, this influx of wealth helped the city to become a major trading centre: many of these men were to finance the Dutch merchant fleets and trading companies that were beginning to make huge profits from the new East Indies spice trade *(see page 23)*.

This industrious revolution was to some degree encouraged by the eight decades of strife with Spain. And as in most conflicts, money played a part – the Spanish had wanted not only to control religion but to restrain the increasingly vigorous Dutch economy which they perceived as a threat to their interests, particularly in terms of trade and the competition to control and profit from the newly opened sea routes.

Officially, freedom of belief was allowed in the United Provinces, but Catholics did not have freedom of worship, largely because Catholicism and Spanish sympathies were too closely interlinked. Many Amsterdammers remained Catholic and it was they who now had to worship secretly, in barns or in the hidden attics of their city homes. While traces do remain of other attic churches, only one, the Amstelkring, is today completely preserved, and serves as a museum *(see page 107)*.

An unofficial "pacification" evolved by 1630 under which the Catholic minority was quietly tolerated but barred from public office. The attic churches became an open secret,

FAR LEFT: the religious reformer John Calvin.
LEFT: the Anabaptist uprising of 1535.
RIGHT: the secret attic church that is now the Amstelkring Museum.

even though, for the next 200 years, Catholic worship was officially prohibited. Still fearful of papal influence, however, the authorities would not yet allow any of the Catholic churches to become "visible".

Once the Catholic threat was removed, however, it wasn't long before the Calvinist principle of "freedom of conscience" evolved into an ethos of religious tolerance. Citizens could choose their official religion at the time of marriage, a pragmatic decision that was often influenced by the power of different denominations to offer a secure guild job or large dowry.

Non-Christians had a far more more difficult time. Portuguese Sephardic and High

pastor even published a book denouncing his own church for its superstitious belief in witches and black magic. The church dismissed him, but the city mayors continued to pay his salary and held the official position vacant until his death.

This freedom of conscience was not without cultural and economic benefits. Over the next century, Amsterdam became a haven for intellectuals from across Europe who were unable to work in their native lands because of their religious beliefs. These included philosophers such as René Descartes and John Locke. Writers and Amsterdam printers used the city's liberal ethos to create

German Ashkenazi Jews enjoyed good relations with officialdom but suffered economic discrimination. Citizenship could not be inherited, and had to be purchased anew by each generation. Marriage with non-Jewish citizens was prohibited. With the exception of surgeons, brokers, printers and booksellers, Jews were barred from guild membership. This left street trading and diamond cutting, which had no guilds, as the preserve of the Jews.

A free press

Preoccupied with commerce, Amsterdam was practically the only city in Europe to have no form of censorship on publications. The city

publishing empires, the remnants of which are still important to the city's economy.

By the time aftershocks from the French Revolution hit Amsterdam in 1796, the religious make-up of the city clearly reflected the previous two centuries of tolerance. Only 22 percent of the population was now Catholic, compared to 98 percent 300 years earlier. The largest group was Calvinist (50 percent), and there were also sizeable Lutheran (16 percent) and Jewish (12 percent) communities. Already the city had developed a mixed character and was shortly to change again, as migrants arrived from far-flung parts of the mighty Dutch empire.

Trade and empire

During the 17th century, Amsterdam was the pre-eminent city in Europe. Although much smaller than its rivals – London, Paris and Rome – during that brief, shining moment in history known as the Golden Age of the Netherlands, it was very much the commercial and cultural capital of Europe.

Taking advantage of the discovery of the sea routes to the east, and resisting Spanish control of their economy, the Dutch began competing for trade across the seas in the latter part of the 16th century. The first Dutch ships landed in the East Indies (now Indonesia) in 1595, and the United East India Company (VOC) was formed in 1602, with a government-guaranteed monopoly on all trade east of the Cape of Good Hope. In an innovative move, the company sold shares, in effect allowing any daring Dutch investor to help finance voyages and reap the profits. This gave a far broader section of society an interest in the spread of the empire. The Bank of Amsterdam was formed in 1609 and quickly established fiscal policies that made the city the financial centre of Europe.

Eventually, the eastern Dutch empire included parts of Ceylon (now Sri Lanka), Tasmania and South Africa, but the heart of the company, and the empire, was the Dutch East Indies which included many of the islands of present-day Indonesia – Bali, Timor, Java, Sumatra, Borneo and New Guinea.

The West India Company (WIC) was founded in 1621. The company was modelled on its East Indies predecessor, but making a profit was secondary to fighting the Spanish, and it was never as financially successful as its East Indies counterpart. Nonetheless, the Dutch holdings eventually expanded to include Tobago, Cayenne, Bonaire, Curaçao, St Eustatius, St Martin, the Dutch Antilles, Aruba and Dutch Guyana (now Suriname). From the start of the 17th century the Dutch fleet was the largest in existence, their ship design the envy of the world. Tsar Peter the Great came to Holland to acquire knowledge for creating a new Russian navy.

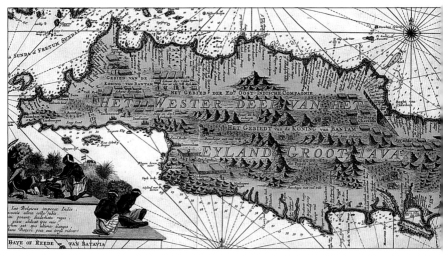

End of an era

The empire did not last, however. The home-loving Dutch were never very good colonists. They liked to conduct their trade and then go back home. Consequently, they did not put down the roots that were key to the longer-surviving European colonies. There were

LEFT: inside the Portuguese-Israelite Synagogue.
ABOVE: the Dutch East Indies as shown on a 17th-century map.

other more tangible reasons for the decline, too: one was that the end of the Thirty Years War – a conflict that had diverted the attention and resources of other European powers while the Dutch were busy empire-building – allowed the English, amongst others, to turn their attention towards the traders of Amsterdam. England wasted little time in initiating the first of several wars with the Dutch (1652–54) that resulted in the loss of significant chunks of East Indies trade. In the West Indies, war with Portugal cost the Dutch their holdings in Brazil.

Another contributory factor was that the Zuiderzee had begun silting up, making it dif-ficult for ships to reach the Amsterdam docks. Perhaps more significantly, many of the citizens living in their new canal houses no longer wanted ships sailing up to their front doors and unloading cargoes into the attic. By the mid-17th century, the lustre of the Golden Age was fading fast.

The Golden Age in the city

While it lasted, however, the Golden Age provided the prosperity that led to an unprecedented period of development in art, architecture and many related crafts. Besides the paintings of the Dutch Masters – of whom Rembrandt, Frans Hals and Jan Vermeer are

TULIPOMANIA

A strange phenomenon arose in Amsterdam in the 1630s – Tulipomania. The tulip had been brought to Europe from Turkey almost a century earlier, but it was in Holland that it became such a prized commodity, with bulbs, auctioned in winter while they were still in the ground, changing hands for outrageous sums of money. One bulb, of the rare Admiraal van Enkhuijsen variety, sold for 5,300 guilders – almost 15 times the average annual wage, and a sum that would certainly have paid for a coveted canal-side property.

Economists and historians have been fascinated by this mania, but no one has ever satisfactorily explained it. The tulip was rare and exotic, it's true, and the flowers could change colour from one year to the next – actually the result of a virus, although this was not known at the time. And there was a lot of money in Amsterdam in the mid-17th century, and those with new-found wealth always look for status symbols. But many played the market who could not afford to do so: people mortgaged properties to get into the game. At the height of the boom, a farmhouse is said to have changed hands for three tulip bulbs. Then, in 1637, the market collapsed as suddenly and dramatically as it began, leaving many people in debt, and some financially ruined.

the most prestigious – and the attendant "Little Masters", Amsterdam was the focus for developments in silver, porcelain, furniture, engraving, printing and various building skills.

The ultimate, lasting expression of the Golden Age in Amsterdam is the city itself, particularly the 17th-century design and construction of the concentric rings of canals linked by radial canals – a model much studied and admired by other cities. It is doubtful whether such a project could have been planned, much less completed, without the medieval-style city-state administration that prevailed in the city.

Because Amsterdam was its own master in the loose alliance with other Dutch city-states known as the United Provinces, the commercial middle classes were the driving force. They had no ruling monarchy over them and the other provinces had little say over the internal affairs of the city. Consequently, the usual vetoes were absent for such an ambitious and far-sighted project as the expansion of the city by building three new canal rings – Herengracht, Keizersgracht and Prinsengracht – outside the city walls *(see page 111)*.

Constructing the canals

Designed by municipal carpenter Hendrick Staets, the Herengracht is 3.5 km (2¼ miles) long, the Keizersgracht 4 km (2½ miles) and the Prinsengracht 4.5 km (2¾ miles). The three ring canals were built 2.1 metres (7 ft) deep and 25 metres (82 ft) wide to accommodate four lanes of medium-sized ships 6 metres (20 ft) wide. Ships frequently moored directly in front of a merchant's home and the cargo was unloaded directly into the fourth-storey storeroom/warehouse via the crane-hooks that still survive in the gables of most canal-house facades.

The combined 25 km (16 miles) of quayside on the three main canals provided enough space for some 4,000 ships to be moored at once, which resulted in a forest of masts that often obscured the views from the houses. The most prestigious residences were all to be built

on the three main ring canals, while smaller houses and shops would be fitted in along the radial canals.

The Jordaan area, a decidedly desirable part of the city today, was constructed (from 1612) to provide accommodation for local artisans and small factories, which included sugar refineries, potteries, printworks, ropeworks and glass factories, among others. The straight-sided sections of the large canals made it easier to lay out regular building plots for the fine houses, but precluded the sweeping canal vistas of cities such as Venice, Pisa and St Petersburg.

Many commentators have remarked on the fact that the physical layout of the ring canals

means they must be "enjoyed as scenes of individual vignettes", and that the only way to get an idea of the massive scale of the design is to walk all the canals and their numerous side streets. Thousands of trees were planted along the quays on either side of the three main canals. Originally, the quays were planted with elms and those that survive are diligently looked after by municipal tree surgeons. (Incidentally, Dutch elm disease got its name not because it originated in the Netherlands, but because the most comprehensive studies have been done here.)

This town plan, which has effectively left modern Amsterdam perched on 90 islands

LEFT: 17th-century Amsterdam as depicted by A. van Nieulandt. **RIGHT:** the Flower Market around 1670, by G.A. Berckheyde.

linked by 500 bridges, also provided the model for future municipal zoning. The city paid for the construction of the canals, which took most of the 17th century to complete, by selling off canal-side housing plots. House owners had to conform to a set of strict rules, including a requirement to pay for the maintenance of the quayside and footpath that lay in front of their homes. Although a few exceptions were made for some of the most influential and wealthy residents, most of the canal-side lots were sold with 30 metres (100 ft) of canal frontage.

Zoning laws also limited how deep the houses could be, and insisted on a certain

amount of clearance between the backs of houses on adjacent canals. Other rules specified that certain types of brick and stone should be used in the construction, and left only minor opportunities in the facades and gables for owners to express their individuality – sometimes these were embellished with flourishes or a sculptural relief to indicate the owner's occupation, such as cannons on a gunmaker's home.

The result is an attractive city of essentially similar buildings, but with a wide range of distinctive decorative elements. "Architectural good manners", today's critics sometimes call it.

Lasting monuments

The Trippenhuis, on Kloveniersburgwal, is an example of one of the very few Amsterdam houses that can be said to rival the palaces of Venice. It was built in 1662 by Justus Vingboons who, along with his brother, Philips, designed many of the large canal houses, which are often marked by their trademark pilaster gables.

Across the street from the palatial Trippenhuis is the narrowest house in Amsterdam. According to the story, the Trip family coachman was overheard complaining that he wished he could afford a canal house even if it was only as wide as the door of his master's home; so they built him exactly that at No. 26 – a house measuring just 2.5 metres (8¼ ft) across *(see page 100)*.

The wealth of the Golden Age also produced most of Amsterdam's best-known and most splendid public buildings and monuments, particularly the churches. The most prominent building, of course, is the Town Hall, now the Royal Palace, completed on the Dam in 1665 *(see page 79)*. Jacob van Campen, a Haarlem painter and architect, was given the job of designing the grandest town hall in all Europe, and he did – but only after managing to overcome the enormous technical difficulties of putting a building of such size on what was virtual swampland.

The building was eventually constructed on 13,659 pilings (essential because of the soft, porous top soil, a mixture of sand, peat and clay) dug 18 metres (60 ft) deep. Amsterdammers all know the number of pilings because a formula, drilled into them at school, goes: "Take the number of days in a year and add a 1 at the beginning and a 9 at the end."

Modern critics still marvel at the wealth of decoration on the Royal Palace. There are a number of specific features for visitors to note, including the plan of the building, constructed around two courtyards, with a huge central hall. The bronze gates are fitted with gunports for muskets, and the narrow staircases and hidden entrances were designed to allow officials to defend the building easily against mob attack. The weathervane represents one of the thousands of Dutch merchant ships that roamed the world and came home laden with riches. ❏

LEFT: an 18th century view along Oude Schans.

Art and the Golden Age

The rapid growth of the Dutch trading empire provided the prosperity that led to an unprecedented period of development in art. The wealth of the middle classes allowed the Dutch to indulge their love of art – probably for the first time anywhere in the world, ordinary citizens could afford to commission and buy paintings. Therefore, instead of being dependent on a few rich patrons demanding grand religious and historical works, artists in Amsterdam were able to diversify and experiment.

Art historians credit the Dutch artists of the Golden Age with launching the era of realism in painting, particularly with their landscapes and seascapes (as well as what have been whimsically termed "cowscapes" after the portraits commissioned by prosperous farmers of their favourite bulls and cows).

Frans Hals (1580–1666) is regarded as the founder of the Dutch School of realistic painting. Often called "the first modern painter", he introduced to fine art the emotion of the moment, a glance or a grimace that might be seen anywhere on the street but not in the posed, stilted portraiture seen in the past.

Jan Vermeer (1623–75) lived and worked in the nearby town of Delft. Although only 30 of his works are known, he is regarded as one of the great Dutch Masters. However, he did not achieve fame as an artist of great stature until the late 19th century, when a French writer and critic singled him out for his techniques in painting, use of light and talent for creating illusions. Most of his works are painted in bright tints that produce clearly defined forms, thus creating a strong feeling of reality. His *View of Delft*, for example, looks astonishingly vivid, as if a colour photograph had been reproduced. Among his best-known works are *Head of a Girl, The Lady Writing a Letter*, and *Young Woman with a Water Pitcher*.

Few, however, would doubt that the greatest Golden Age painter was Rembrandt van Rijn (1606–69), who started painting in his native Leiden but spent his most productive years living and working in Amsterdam. More than three centuries after his death, Rembrandt remains the most deeply loved of all the great masters of painting, his face so familiar from the self-portraits painted throughout his life, yet still so mysterious.

Like other leading members of the Dutch School, he broke new ground in

realism. One of his most daring, and most costly, paintings was his 1642 masterpiece *De Nachtwacht (The Night Watch)*, a study of the members of one of Amsterdam's volunteer civic guards. The large painting now has pride of place in the Rijksmuseum *(see page 151)*, but was ill-received at the time because it was regarded as too casual and haphazard. Critics did not like the fact that not all the faces of the guards could be seen clearly, demonstrating an insensitivity to factors that modern critics most admire – his realism in creating a crowded scene. ❑

RIGHT: detail of Rembrandt's most famous work, *The Night Watch*.

SLOW DECLINE AND RECOVERY

Amsterdam was the first capital of the independent Netherlands, a nation born out of European strife. After a period of decline its recovery from the devastating events of World War II is testament to the spirit of its citizens, and its liberal, open-minded reputation is well deserved

You can still see and touch the Golden Age legacy all around you in Amsterdam, even though the lustre has been dulled by the passage of four centuries. By the start of the 18th century, the reservoir of inspiration, confidence and wealth that was the wellspring of this gilded time had run dry. The second and third generations of the merchant families did not share their ancestors' zest for chasing the guilder to the ends of the earth; they were more interested in spending money than in garnering it. The merchant fleet was depleted, national debt grew, and peasants who had been wearing leather shoes went back to making wooden ones. The United Provinces went into a period of decline, losing commercial pre-eminence to England and France.

Troubled times

In 1688, in what Protestants called the "Glorious Revolution", England's Catholic monarch, James II, was deposed. In his place, William of Oranje-Nassau, Stadholder of Holland and Zeeland (the Stadholder's role was roughly that of a provincial governor), and his wife, the English princess Mary Stuart, were jointly crowned as William III and Mary II of England. William's wars against France, in opposition to Louis XIV's expansionist policies, strained the economy of the United Provinces, which went into steep decline.

The situation worsened when the United Provinces became embroiled in the War of the

LEFT: sleigh excursion on a frozen canal, 18th century.
RIGHT: *cloisonné* spice jar from the East Indies.

NEW YORK

A war with England erupted in 1664 over the New Netherlands in America and the harbour at Nieuw Amsterdam (now New York). The New Netherlands was founded in 1612, but there was no permanent settlement at Nieuw Amsterdam, the capital, until 1625. By 1626, when Peter Minuit, the Dutch governor, "bought" Manhattan Island from its Native American inhabitants for $24-worth of beads, the population was still fewer than 300. After the English seized the colony in 1664 and renamed it New York, the Dutch gave up claims on the New Netherlands in exchange for English promises not to take Dutch Guyana.

Spanish Succession, after the Habsburg Charles II of Spain died childless and the throne, and therefore control of the Spanish Netherlands (the southern provinces), passed to Philip of Anjou, grandson of Louis XIV. The war ended in 1713, and the Treaty of Utrecht brought the Bourbon Philip V to the Spanish throne.

William III died without an heir in 1702, and the Stadholdership was vacant until 1747 when William IV inherited it, unifying the republic under one leader for the first time. Between 1751 and 1788, the United Provinces were torn by civil strife between conservative supporters of the House of Orange and liberal

1810 Napoleon forced him to abdicate and incorporated the country into the French empire. Economic activity declined on a disastrous scale. The French requisitioned men and resources and the Dutch lost most of their overseas trade because of the British blockade. Napoleon's failed 1812 invasion of Russia and his crushing defeat at Leipzig in 1813 spelled the end of the Napoleonic adventure. Prince William VI of Orange returned from exile and was crowned King William I of the United Kingdom of the Netherlands in 1814, under the terms of the Congress of Vienna.

At the end of the Napoleonic era, therefore, the Netherlands was independent, and still

reformers, known as the Patriots, influenced by the new ideas of the Enlightenment, who demanded a more democratic system.

In 1795, a French revolutionary army invaded and (helped by the Patriots) replaced the political institutions of the United Provinces with the Batavian Republic, a unitary state with its own National Assembly. William V fled to England and the office of Stadholder was abolished.

In 1806, Napoleon Bonaparte took over the republic and proclaimed his brother Louis Napoleon King of the Netherlands, with Amsterdam as his capital. But Louis proved too sympathetic to his new subjects, and in

retained a good part of its empire. In 1815, however, the seat of government was transferred from Amsterdam to Den Haag; and in 1830 the southern provinces rebelled and proclaimed the separate kingdom of Belgium.

Positive developments

In 1848, a new constitution came into force, providing for a directly elected parliament. From around 1870, a period of rapid development saw improvements in education and public health provision. In 1876, the economy received a boost when the Noordzee Kanaal (North Sea Canal) opened, reviving Amsterdam's port and bringing fresh prosperity.

Bicycles appeared in 1880 – the start of a passionate romance with two-wheeled transport that continues unabated to this day. The first car put in an appearance in Amsterdam on 21 July 1897; a century later cars were regarded as guests who had over-stayed their welcome in the city of canals and narrow streets, and tough measures were put in force to control and, ultimately, banish them.

The 20th century

Economically, the Netherlands concentrated on trade and agriculture well into the 20th century, then developed a large-scale industrial base. Trade with member countries of the

completed in 1932, protecting Amsterdam from the constant danger of flooding, and creating the IJsselmeer lake. When it became obvious that Europe was heading back to war, the Netherlands hoped to retain its neutral status, but it was not to be. On 10 May 1940, German air and ground units invaded, plunging the nation into the darkest chapter in its history.

The Jews in Amsterdam

The first Jews came to Amsterdam in the 16th century, fleeing persecution in Portugal. The Netherlands had a reputation for tolerance but the Dutch, also excellent businessmen, were aware that many of the Jews were wealthy and

empire, in tin, quinine, coffee, timber and rubber remained an integral part of the Dutch economy until World War II.

Although the Netherlands remained neutral during World War I, it suffered severe food shortages. Then, after a brief period of prosperity in the 1920s during which Amsterdam embarked on innovative, low-cost housing schemes, the country was hit by the global economic depression. Despite this, the Afsluitdijk dam across the mouth of the Zuiderzee was

LEFT: Louis Napoleon Bonaparte.
ABOVE: Jewish deportations to the concentration camps began in 1941.

would bring their money and vital trade connections with them. Less affluent Jews ended up in ghettos, poor but safe. Despite a degree of economic discrimination, records show that the Jews lived peacefully in the city, experiencing little or no animosity. Therefore the revulsion felt by the Dutch when the first Nazi deportation of Jews from occupied Amsterdam got under way, was great.

Amsterdam's Raadhuisstraat, a street leading to the Dam, was lined with hundreds of silent Amsterdammers when the German convoy drove in during the first week of May 1940. One tenth of the population – the Jews – stayed at home. The crowd watched with fascinated horror. Many had read the red-bordered proclamation of power issued by the country's new ruler, Dr Arthur Seyss-Inquart, which was displayed around the city. The message was friendly in tone. "I have today taken over civilian authority in the Netherlands… The magnanimity of the Führer and the efficiency of German soldiers has permitted civil life to be restored quickly. I intend to allow all Dutch law and general administration to go on as usual."

Some people watching the triumphant arrival of the Germans actually allowed themselves to believe the message. But the city's Jews knew better, especially those who had

fled from Germany to Amsterdam to escape persecution in the 1930s.

Soon German military traffic signs went up and Nazi newspapers appeared on the streets, sold by members of the Dutch Nazi Party (NSB), which was now coming into its own. German marching songs, accompanied by hectoring voices and the sound of marching jackboots, were heard.

On 29 June 1940, the Dutch showed that, although they may have relinquished any thought of taking direct action against the occupiers, they had not abandoned hope. Thousands took to the streets wearing white carnations. It was Prince Bernhard's birthday

and the people were copying one of his best-known vanities as a symbol of passive resistance – he always wore a white carnation in the buttonhole of his tweeds.

Anti-Jewish measures

The noose was tightening for the Jews. From July 1940, the Germans started to issue more and more restrictive proclamations. Jews could not be employed in the Civil Service and those who were already there were to be sacked. Jews could not enter cinemas or travel on public transport and all Jewish-owned firms had to be reported for registration.

In February 1941 the Germans made their move – 425 Jewish men and youths were rounded up and herded into Jonas Daniël Meijerplein in the Jewish quarter. Photographs in the Jewish Historical Museum show them staring straight ahead, hands high, faces full of terror. They were kept in the square for hours before being moved into trucks lined up beside the Portuguese Synagogue. The trucks drove off; there was to be only one survivor.

Today a statue of a burly Amsterdam docker stands on the square, commemorating a general strike led by the city's dockers two days later. It was Amsterdam's first open gesture of rebellion. German retaliation was swift. Police patrolled the streets, arresting hundreds and shooting nine people dead. Notices were posted ordering everyone back to work. On 15 March three members of the strike committee and 15 resistance members were executed.

People slowly went back to work, morale temporarily boosted by the fact that Amsterdammers had dared to resist tyranny. But the euphoria did not last long. There were no more posters urging the Dutch to trust their German friends. The kid glove was revealed to be covering a steel fist.

The nightmare begins

Jews watched in horror as the stories they had heard of Nazi brutality in the German ghettos became reality on their own streets. The sight of pathetic groups of people being hustled along by the military or plain-clothes police became an everyday reality that Amsterdam people were powerless to prevent. Jews were being forced to wear the yellow Star of David, six-pointed, black-bordered and bearing the word *Jood* (Jew). Even more restrictions were being introduced: Jews could not use public parks, could not own telephones or use public ones, and a nightly curfew was introduced.

More and more Jews were being transported to Westerbork camp, close to the German border, a transit camp for Auschwitz. From there the long journey east was made in locked cattle trucks; the railway line ended in front of the gates of the camp where the real horror began. As it started to dawn on the Jews that they were only being cooped up in the city for identification and processing in preparation for the cattle trains to the slaughterhouse, some lucky ones were able to disappear into hiding. To do this, they needed brave friends, because anyone caught harbouring Jews was shot without question.

Bravery and betrayal

Organisation of volunteers willing to take fugitives and provide their food – now only available with coupons – lay in the hands of an extraordinary group of people, with networks extending throughout the city and surrounding countryside. There were betrayals, too, with catastrophic results, as in the case of the now famous Frank family, who went into hiding in July 1942, after receiving a card calling up their 16-year-old daughter Margot for work in Westerbork. Their hideaway was a concealed apartment behind Mr Frank's Prinsengracht office (an *achterhuis* or "house at the back").

Anne Frank was then 13, already a clever and natural writer. But the unnatural ambience of eight people (four others joined the family) being incarcerated in a small room for two years, living in fear of discovery, brought out her true talents. She writes of the privations, and of the people who looked after the family, her father's partners, Koophuis and Kraler, and the office girls, Miep and Elli, who came to work each day to give an impression of normality; and of the greengrocer round the corner, one of 105 in the city who supplied people in hiding and did not ask any questions.

LEFT: the *razzia* (round-up) of Jewish youths and men by the Nazis, February 1941.
RIGHT: the famine of the Hunger Winter, 1944–45, which claimed over 20,000 lives.

At the beginning of August 1944, following a tip-off, the Germans led the family away. Only Mr Frank survived. Anne's last diary entry, written three days before her capture, reads: "I keep on trying to find a way of becoming what I would so like to be, and what I could be, if… there weren't any other people living in the world." Anne finally died of hunger and disease in Bergen-Belsen, as did her sister.

The Hunger Winter

The long-suffering Dutch were attacked by yet another enemy in the winter of 1944–45: starvation and extreme cold. The "Hunger

EYEWITNESS ACCOUNT

An Amsterdam man recalls watching a Jewish deportation: "On a beautiful autumn day... a group of prisoners passed by, mainly women and children, who had been hiding in a nearby house. They were Jews. I heard later the owner had been shot. One little girl, about three years old, stopped to pick up a leaf. I heard her mother sob as she called to the child. One of the guards butted her in the back with his rifle when she paused to wait for the infant. As they crossed a bridge I saw the child give the leaf to its mother… Then they were gone and silence returned. That was the moment I stopped believing in God."

Winter" claimed at least 20,000 lives, a large proportion of whom were Amsterdammers. The causes lay in Nazi reprisals, requisitioning, broken transport links, and the cold.

The Dutch government (exiled in London) called for a national rail strike in September 1944, thus reducing enemy troop movements in preparation for the ill-fated Allied "Operation Market Garden" in Arnhem. The Germans retaliated by banning all food transport to the west, which included Amsterdam. The ban was lifted on 8 November but was of little relief. Food transport had become virtually impossible: food depots in the harbours had been "requisitioned" by the Germans. The striking railwaymen, with financial aid from London, had gone into hiding. Barge skippers were afraid to take on any cargo. In November a small fleet was allowed to operate, with guarantees of immunity, but this too was of limited relief because on 23 December a big freeze began, making transport impossible.

Coal was also scarce. North and South Holland were cut off from liberated Limburg and the mines. Power stations were dependent on German coal, so domestic gas and electricity supplies were cut off in October. Apart from German interests the only institutions to receive fuel were some power stations, bakers, soup kitchens and hospitals. By 11 April

1945 the last power station ceased operating.

Amsterdammers were involved in terrible situations. To get a few potatoes people would cycle miles on bikes with wooden tyres (the Nazis confiscated all rubber) and barter goods or services with farmers at extortionate rates. On the way home, the food was often taken by German soldiers. Combustible material was looted, trees were chopped down and empty houses ransacked. Wood became so scarce that the dead were buried in paper coffins.

With the Canadians approaching from the west, the Germans blew up the sluices at IJmuiden, from where the North Sea Canal runs into Amsterdam. Suddenly water was

ROYALS IN EXILE

Prince Bernhard was ordered by his mother-in-law, Queen Wilhelmina, to accompany his wife and two daughters to Canada, via Britain. He was reluctant to do so but Wilhelmina was adamant: the royal bloodline must be protected. The prince, a fervent anti-Nazi, agreed to go on the condition that he be allowed to return to Britain, where he was made head of the Dutch free forces. The shy, lonely Princess Juliana, meanwhile, began coping alone in Canada, looking after the two young princesses. The elder, Beatrix, became queen of the Netherlands when Queen Juliana abdicated in favour of her daughter in 1980.

rising around the city, the sewage system broke down and a plague of rats ensued.

Then at last came salvation. Allied planes dropped food parcels, Hitler was dead, the Germans were on the run and the Canadians were in the city. The war was over – almost. Two days after the German surrender, Nazis opened fire on celebrating crowds at the Dam, killing 19 and injuring 117. For Amsterdam, a long period of reconstruction lay ahead, but war wounds, physical and emotional, took years to heal.

Freedom in Amsterdam

Over the centuries Amsterdam has become home to various political and religious others with fine artworks. This is the charm of Amsterdam: a place where visitors may admire 17th-century facades while strolling along a street with postmodern litter bins and New Age benches. Nothing is surprising.

Provos and protests

Since the mid-1960s, Amsterdam has acquired a reputation for seeing how far individual liberties can go before society in general is harmed. These experiments have produced memorable newsreel footage, such as the demonstrations of the late 1960s against autocratic university administrations, or the two-day battle in August 1970 when

refugees and witnessed all kinds of social paradoxes. This manifests itself in a freedom of expression that is seldom encountered elsewhere. Choices abound everywhere, whether it's a question of food, sexual orientation, cultural activities, drugs, alcohol or politics.

Any society that can maintain so much freedom of choice has to be fairly organised and therein lies the paradox, because on the street there is little to indicate a sense of order. Some public buildings, which would otherwise remain drab affairs, are adorned with graffiti,

LEFT: Seyss-Inquart, Nazi ruler in the Netherlands.
ABOVE: posters advertising a transvestite club.

police fought with hippies who had been living on the Dam and scaring the tourists away.

An anarchist-leftist movement that the press dubbed Provos, short for *provocateurs,* was active during the 1960s. Fully committed Provos probably never numbered more than a few dozen, but they had many spontaneous sympathisers who readily joined in the usually good-natured street "happenings". They protested against all manner of local and national government policies as well as other institutions and cultures, from art to marriage, that they considered to be part of the "Establishment" and in need of reform or removal.

The Provos did achieve some notable

political successes. Several members of the group, together with members of a splinter group called the Kabouters (Gnomes), were elected to the municipal council, where they smoked cannabis during meetings and put forward endless zany proposals, such as the planting of rooftop gardens on all city buses.

One Provo proposal that sounded wonderful in theory but failed in practice was the White Bike programme, whereby the city was to provide thousands of white bicycles and distribute them around Amsterdam. The idea was that the bikes belonged to no one and could be used by anyone. If you needed a ride, you simply grabbed the nearest white bike,

rode to your destination and left it there. Unfortunately, the experiment lasted only a few days – the time it took less community-minded people to steal the bikes, paint them a different colour and sell them.

Perhaps the most serious of the Provos' actions were the protests they organised against the wedding of Princess Beatrix and Claus von Amsberg in March 1966, which included throwing smoke bombs at the wedding carriage. The protest received a lot of support because, only two decades after the end of the war, many people in Holland were outraged that the princess was marrying a German who had served in the Wehrmacht

NETHERLANDS GOVERNMENT

The Netherlands is a constitutional monarchy with a parliamentary system of government and a constitution set up in 1814. The head of state is the hereditary monarch (currently Queen Beatrix). The political head of state is the prime minister, who is appointed by the queen. The prime minister presides over a cabinet that is responsible to parliament.

Due to the mixed political climate the cabinet is virtually always a coalition of several parties. The parliament, the States General, consists of two chambers. The upper chamber has 75 members who serve for a period of four years and are elected from the

provincial legislature. The lower chamber has 150 members who also serve a term of four years but are elected from a system of proportional representation. The lower chamber is responsible for passing new laws and acts. The upper chamber has a limited power of veto that is rarely used and acts more in an advisory capacity. The monarch has the right to dissolve either or both chambers on condition that new elections take place within 40 days.

Amsterdam city council is headed by a powerful mayor who invariably sets his stamp on the city's social and economic affairs.

(although the prince consort later won the respect and affection of the Dutch people).

Developments in the 1970s

In the 1970s, most protests were organised by the squatters' movement in response to severe housing shortages and heavy-handed council planning decisions – particularly the plan to demolish entire areas and relocate residents in order to build a Metro line through the city. Protests came to a head on the day Queen Beatrix was inaugurated as head of state in 1980, when the costly ostentation of the ceremony was contrasted with the lack of adequate housing. The 1970s was also the time when

soft drugs became rampant and effectively legal for personal use, and the Red Light District expanded as a centre for sex and tourism. Feminists, the *Dolle Minas* (Mad Minnies), marched against anti-abortion laws under the slogan *Baas in eigen buik* (Boss of your own belly). Policemen and soldiers were allowed to grow beards and long hair.

Prostitution is not strictly legal in Amsterdam; streetwalkers and hookers soliciting in

bars can still be arrested, although brothels were legalised in 1990. Prostitutes who perch in the windows of their "sitting rooms" can do so because of Amsterdam's long-held belief that what people do in their own homes is their own business.

The concept of a legalised Red Light District is nothing new in Amsterdam. In the mid-17th century, the English consul complained about the Amsterdam music-houses patronised by "lewd people of both sexes", and there was a sex exchange, modelled on the stock exchange. Prostitutes lived and worked without harassment, in an area just south of today's Red Light District. If one strayed out of the area the local bailiff sent his drum-and-flute guard to bring her back, by playing loudly outside the house where she was ensconced until she returned to the designated area.

The drug debate

Amsterdam and drugs seem to be synonymous in many people's minds. International reports have focused on clinics where registered addicts get their daily fixes and the marijuana "coffee shops" with menus listing the different types of grass and hash available that day. Those who don't want to smoke it can try "space cookies" or laced chocolate cake with their coffee.

LEFT: Provos launch the White Bike programme.
ABOVE: by the 1970s Amsterdam was established as the hippy centre of Europe.
RIGHT: the city police use bikes like everyone else.

Contrary to popular belief, all drugs are illegal, be they soft or hard, but in reality the police would never pursue anyone with less than 30 g (1 oz) of soft drugs unless they thought the person was dealing. The authorities sanctioned the use of cannabis in the 1960s, but since 1988 pressure from other European countries has led them to impose tougher penalties on traffickers, and ecstasy has been upgraded to a class "A" drug. During 1991–92 a major operation was launched, which reduced registered coffee shops from 750 to 250. A coffee shop now has to display a green-and-white licence plate in the window, may not hold more than 500 g (1 lb) of

soft drugs in stock, may not sell more than 5g (0.1 oz) per deal, and the lower age limit is 18.

Many citizens have mixed feelings about the merits of legalising drugs, but nonetheless defend registration and medical support for heroin addicts. Amsterdammers reluctantly concede their city's status as a world drugs capital, but blame drug-related crimes – they have one of the highest rates in Europe – on non-registered addicts from other countries. They also argue that things would be worse without the controls that registration imposes on perhaps a quarter of the city's estimated 8,000 addicts – a number that hasn't changed in years, according to officials.

Amsterdam's reputation for sex, drugs and rock 'n' roll has changed somewhat in recent years, due to efforts to clean up aspects of the city and improve its overall image. Official crime statistics for much of central Amsterdam have dropped since the early 1990s. The area around Centraal Station is now cleaner and safer than it was. A police station set up in 1999 appears to have displaced criminals on the main square to the rear of the railway.

New concerns

For many of Amsterdam's upright young citizens, however, the days of free drugs and free love have faded as they face new concerns over career, home and family. But even as they redecorate their canal houses or search out the newest and best in Mexican food or sushi, the new middle class of Amsterdam still carries a burden of civic and social concern. Nowhere in Europe, maybe in the world, is public sentiment stronger on issues such as the environment or nuclear weapons, and the Green Party has a significant following. Such is the depth of commitment on environmental issues that the centre-right coalition government, led by the Christian Democrats, was brought down in 1989 for proposing vehicle pollution rules that were not considered tough enough.

An example of the way the Dutch deal with current problems is the attitude towards euthanasia. In 2002, the Netherlands became the first country in the world to legalise regulated euthanasia. Doctors can now follow specified procedures for assisting terminally ill patients in ending their lives – sometimes with a lethal injection but more often by a potion of fast-acting poison. Patients undergo extensive counselling, including sessions with physicians brought in to advise on each case. The doctor directly involved, typically the family physician, often helps the patient and surviving relatives to plan a brief, simple ceremony for administering the poison. Studies estimate that doctors now assist in as many as one in eight deaths in Amsterdam.

Another example of liberal experimentation is the programme for dealing with child sex abuse. Under the Confidential Doctor Service teachers, relatives, friends and social workers can refer cases to government-financed centres staffed by doctors who sweep the entire family straight into intensive counselling. Experts believe the system helps prevent abuse and aids the child's recovery without necessarily breaking up the family.

However, the Dutch sometimes admit that they have let things go too far. One example is the child pornography that began to circulate in the 1960s and boomed after Sweden and Denmark outlawed it in the early 1980s. Soon after the US Customs Service branded Amsterdam "the 1984 version of Sodom and Gomorrah" and the British media made similar accusations, legislation was passed to outlaw the production and circulation of child pornography. But those who break the law

modern dance, whether home-grown or imported by the best of the world's troupes.

But the avant-garde in the Netherlands is best seen in the work of popular artists. The Van Gogh-inspired Expressionism of the first half of the 20th century gave way to a more questioning, witty, sometimes cynical style. Instead of expressing something, some artists avoided expressing anything at all; others suggested that everything and anything could be art. Others again created an updated version of the realistic style of the old Dutch School, combined with the distinct modern influences.

There are galleries all over the city where you can see contemporary works, and a high

receive only a three-month jail sentence, and only pictures of children performing sexual acts were outlawed, not all child nudity.

The cutting edge

Amsterdam still prides itself on being at the cutting edge of the arts, a centre for the avant-garde. The music that is played in late-night clubs, and even the way that Amsterdam clubbers dance, is pretty innovative. In terms of choreography, Amsterdam has become the place to go for developments in jazz and

percentage of Amsterdammers seem to have an interest in art, and take pride in the city's imaginative flair. They may complain about public money spent on spurious art-school projects, but would probably complain louder if such funding were withdrawn, for Amsterdam is a city of all kinds for all kinds.

This is a busy time for the city's major art centres. In 1999 the Van Gogh Museum was given a facelift and a new wing. In 2004, as part of a number of initiatives to upgrade the city's old cultural stock and add new elements, it was the turn of the Rijksmuseum and the Stedelijk Museum. Also in 2004, St Petersburg's fabled Hermitage opened an Amsterdam satellite. ❑

LEFT: Amsterdam's relaxed attitude to cannabis is well known. **ABOVE:** ...as is its nightlife.

Decisive Dates

Early History: AD 1200–1500

*c.*1200 The first communities of herring fishermen settle on the banks of the Amstel. The first dam, or sluice, is built to hold back the tidal waters of the Zuiderzee.

1275 Floris V, Count of Holland, grants the people of "Amestelledamme" freedom from tolls on their goods.

1300 The Bishop of Utrecht grants Amsterdam official city status.

1334 Work begins on the Oude Kerk, Amsterdam's oldest church.

1350 Amsterdam becomes the export centre for local beers and an entrepôt for Baltic grain.

1395 The first city hall is built on the Dam.

1452 Fire destroys many of Amsterdam's timber-and-thatch buildings. Laws ordain that new buildings shall be built of brick and tile.

1480 Walls are built to defend the city.

Religious Wars: 1500–1595

1519 As a result of war, treaties and marriage alliances, Amsterdam is part of the Spanish empire and nominally Catholic, but tolerant of Protestants (persecuted throughout Europe).

1535 Anabaptists invade the Town Hall to proclaim the Second Coming. The occupiers are arrested and executed. Catholicism is reimposed.

1566 The Iconoclastic Fury (Beeldenstorm). Calvinists protesting at the lack of religious freedom storm many of Amsterdam's churches.

1567 Philip II of Spain sends the Duke of Alva to restore Catholic control of Amsterdam. Many Protestants are executed or flee to England.

1572 The Dutch Revolt against Spanish rule begins in earnest, led by William of Orange.

1576 The city is besieged by Prince William's troops.

1578 Amsterdam capitulates to Prince William. Protestant exiles return to the city. Calvinists take over the churches and the reins of government in the peaceful Alteration (Alteratie) revolution.

1579 The seven northern provinces of the Netherlands sign the Treaty of Utrecht providing for mutual assistance in the event of attack. Protestant refugees from Antwerp, Amsterdam's trade rival, seek asylum in the city and help to lay the foundations for the Golden Age.

The Golden Age: 1595–1700

1595–97 Ships from Amsterdam sail east via the Cape of Good Hope to "discover" Indonesia.

1602 The United Dutch East India Company is established to co-ordinate trade with the lands east of the Cape, financed by a public share flotation.

1609 The Bank of Amsterdam is formed, placing the city at the forefront of European finance. Hendrik Staets draws up the plan for the Grachtengordel, the three concentric canals ringing the city.

1621 The West India Company is founded with a monopoly on American and West African trade.

1626 Peter Minuit "buys" the island of Manhattan and founds the colony of Nieuw Amsterdam (taken by the English and renamed New York in 1664).

1632 The Athenaeum Illustre, the forerunner of Amsterdam University, is founded.

1642 Rembrandt paints *The Night Watch*.

1648 The Treaty of Münster recognises the northern provinces as an independent republic.

1650 Amsterdam now has a population of around 220,000, the largest city of the new republic.

1652–54 The struggle for maritime supremacy results in wars with the English .

1685 Huguenot refugees flood into Amsterdam after the Revocation of the Edict of Nantes, reversing their rights to freedom of worship.

1688 William III of Holland is crowned as King of England, having married Mary Stuart. William's wars against the French strain the Dutch economy and the republic's trade begins to decline.

Slow Decline: 1700–1900

1702 William III dies without an heir. Amsterdam and the northern provinces suffer further inroads to their trade when the Austrian Emperor Charles VI sets up a rival East India Company in Ostend.

1744 France invades the southern provinces.

1747 William IV is elected hereditary head of state of the seven northern provinces, now unified under one leader and called the United Provinces.

1751–88 The United Provinces are torn between conservative supporters of the House of Orange and liberal reformers, called Patriots.

1795 France invades Amsterdam and, in alliance with the Patriots, forms a National Assembly. The United Provinces are named the Batavian Republic.

1806 Napoleon reverses the constitutional reforms and establishes his brother, Louis, as King of Holland, with Amsterdam as its capital.

1813 After the defeat of Napoleon, William VI is welcomed back to Amsterdam from exile.

1814 William VI is crowned King William I of the Netherlands.

1848 The new Dutch constitution comes into force, providing for a directly elected parliament.

1870–76 Socialist principles of government rapidly develop; improvements are made in education and public health, and the North Sea Canal revives Amsterdam's position as a port and shipbuilding centre.

The 20th century

1914–20 The Netherlands remains neutral during World War I, but food shortages lead to strikes, riots and support for the Dutch Communist Party.

1928 Amsterdam hosts the Olympic Games.

1930s During the Great Depression, the city's unemployed work on job creation schemes, including the construction of the Amsterdamse Bos park.

1940 Germany ignores the neutrality of the Netherlands and invades on 10 May.

1941 over 400 Jews are rounded up in Amsterdam on 22 and 23 February. Dockworkers lead a two-day strike in protest at anti-Jewish measures.

1942 Anne Frank and family go into hiding.

1945 After a bitter winter Amsterdam is liberated.

1963 Amsterdam's population reaches 868,000 and housing shortages lead to organised squats – occupations of empty buildings.

1965 The Provos, a movement dedicated to shaking Dutch complacency, win representation on the city council.

1966 Protesters disrupt the wedding of Princess Beatrix and Claus von Amsberg with smoke bombs.

1975 Police battle with demonstrators over plans to demolish areas of Nieuwmarkt.

1986 Despite strong opposition, the "Stopera" – Stadhuis and Opera – complex is completed.

1989 The government is defeated as its anti-vehicle laws are considered too soft.

1994 400th anniversary of the first tulip to be grown in Holland.

1998 The first Gay Games attract thousands of visitors; the pedestrianised Museumplein opens.

Amsterdam in the New Millennium

2000 The Passenger Terminal Amsterdam opens for cruise liners.

2002 Crown Prince Willem Alexander weds Argentinian Máxima Zorreguieta at the city's Nieuwe Kerk; and the world's first same-sex marriage with an identical legal status to heterosexual marriage takes place in Amsterdam.

2003 Most of the Rijksmuseum closes for major renovation work. It is not expected to reopen fully until 2008.

2004 The modern art Stedelijk Museum closes for renovation until 2006; a temporary branch opens near Centraal Station. The first phase of the Amsterdam Hermitage opens.   ❏

LEFT: late 19th-century painting by Hugo Vogel of Luther nailing his 95 points on the chapel of Wittenburg Castle. **RIGHT:** the Royal Wedding of 2002.

LIVING IN AMSTERDAM

Numerous changes have taken place in the environments in which Amsterdam's citizens live and work, but it remains a vibrant city, with a relaxed atmosphere, a rich cultural life and a sound economic structure

Providing residents with housing is a vital issue in any city, but in Amsterdam housing policy is not just about the construction or conservation of buildings – it is one of the most visible social-engineering tools. The city has abandoned the unpopular 1970s practice of clearing whole neighbourhoods in order to redevelop certain areas. The approach now is to restore decaying streets house by house, thereby preserving the social fabric.

By creating more and better urban housing, the municipal government hopes to keep Amsterdam as a living, residential city, with the well-heeled cheek by jowl with the less well-off. Since 1950, 143,400 new apartment units have been built for low- and middle-income tenants. Before 1970, 90 percent of this was on annexed suburban land. Today, 25 percent is directed towards the city centre.

Regeneration and renewal

The goal has been to boost the inner-city population to 725,000, in line with what is called the "compact city" plan, to prevent the city becoming the "Venice of the North" – the most dreadful epithet you could attach to Amsterdam, whose planners and residents see the Italian city as a slough of stagnant canals whose residents and businesses have abandoned the city to the tourists. This goal has been more or less realised, but new developments on the old shipping harbours (Java

and KNSM islands) are shifting the emphasis.

The redevelopment of these and other islands in the old harbour, from which the shipping installations have long since moved away, is re-focusing the city's centre of gravity towards the waterfront, a process encouraged by new transport links. The brand-new IJburg development, fast expanding on an archipelago of artificial islands out east in the direction of Muiden, will ensure that this trend continues.

Municipal government can exert such social influence because it owns about 70 percent of the city's land. Amsterdam is unusual in that only a small percentage of homes are owner-occupied, although since the early

PRECEDING PAGES: street musicians in the Dam.
LEFT: in the midst of the morning rush hour.
RIGHT: dressed up for the Queen's Day festival.

1990s there has been a growing number of home-owners. In 2002, home-ownership had increased by nearly 10 percent in five years. The rest, about 350,000 units, is rental property, of which the city owns about 40 percent outright. Much of the residential area beyond the inner canal ring is held in leasing arrangements, under which the city sells long-term rights to land developers, who in turn build or restore the housing and rent out the units.

Allocating accommodation

In both cases, units are set aside for a variety of income levels. Rents, compared with New York, London or Paris, are surprisingly afford-

sub-letting or re-renting city apartments from middle-men, or from tenants willing to move out in return for some financial incentive. Demands for "key money" – the fee paid to the resident or broker for a technically illegal sub-let – are not unusual. Key money remains illegal but it's difficult to avoid if you are desperate to find a place to live.

About half of the city's housing and most of the inner canal-side property is owned privately or by quasi-private housing corporations, many of which have benefited from city finance. Many stately canal-side homes and old warehouses have been converted into offices and studios to meet demand from pro-

able – but bound to continue rising as developers cannot renovate upmarket apartments fast enough for the moneyed professionals craving to move back into the city. Amsterdam is probably unique in Europe for having an upper-class housing shortage.

Housing is allocated by means of waiting lists. You could get into one of the suburban housing projects tomorrow if you are not fussy about where you live, but if you want to live in the centre, you could wait at least six years.

If you prefer to rent in the private sector, competition is ruthless. You will never find a good property except by word of mouth. Those without contacts are often reduced to

fessional and artistic people. Once renovated, the spacious, 17th-century buildings, often with their original brick and beams decorating the interior, will sell for between €750,000 and upwards of €3 million.

Squatters

Some of the well-to-do residents of these newly restored buildings formerly occupied them as squatters. In the early 1970s squatting was popular with young people, many of whom were willing to work hard to renovate dilapidated buildings. The exodus of many businesses from the city centre at that time had left scores of buildings unoccupied and the city without funds to renovate them. Squatting was also a protest against what were seen as insensitive and destructive local government housing policies. It was easy enough to establish a squat: change the locks and take the boards off the windows and it would take a legal crowbar to dislodge you.

The squatters, often students from one of Amsterdam's two universities, were instrumental in transforming neighbourhoods from forgotten ghost towns into lively areas with their own subculture of cafés, shops and cinemas. Huge banners usually announced the presence of a squat, and a few can still be seen around the city today.

legal, rent-paying ones. While these houses were being renovated, squatters were supposed to be relocated at the city's expense – often easier said than done. Violent protests often broke out at eviction time.

Despite all of this, the policy has proved largely effective. Squatters and city officials estimate that only a dozen or so large buildings are still occupied by squatters, and maybe another 50 smaller houses, and most of these are privately owned. Few city-owned buildings are still used as squats today and it is unlikely to be a long time before the last wave of controversial eviction proceedings is implemented.

Today it is hard to find anyone in Amsterdam over the age of 30 who does not claim to have squatted during that heady period of counter-culture and people power. There were well-organised squatters' advisory offices, which offered lists of vacant houses and city development plans, as well as expertise in carrying out title searches. By the early 1980s this situation more or less came to an end. City authorities began to erode public support for the squatters by building more inner-city housing and converting "illegal" squats into

LEFT: desirable properties on the Grachtengordel.
ABOVE: houseboat living.

Houseboat life

Many visitors to Amsterdam, seduced by the beautiful canals, dream of sailing back and mooring alongside Prinsengracht. Forget it. Amsterdam's generous public housing policy ends at the shore. The number of canal-side moorings is fixed at 2,600. About 5,000 people live on floating concrete slabs, converted barges and the occasional sea-going vessel.

Moorings are fixed and sold like building plots. A quiet spot behind Westerkerk can cost €20,000, and that does not include the boat. When expenses are totalled, houseboat living is no cheaper than a conventional apartment.

The attractions of canal-boat living are even

greater now that the conditions of the water-ways have improved. Ducks, swans and fish have returned as sea water is pumped in nightly through the city locks.

The Jordaan

Fashionable among bohemian artists and artisans, the Jordaan district is a warren of streets that has its origins in a zig-zag series of polders and ditches dug in the mid-1600s, and used to be home to thousands of working-class families. During the early 1970s, private developers acted faster and bid higher than the city authorities for many of the area's 700 historic listed buildings and converted them into

attractive apartments and studios. As a result, city housing initiatives, designed to accommodate long-time residents and senior citizens, have scarcely gained a toehold here.

Traditionally, the Jordaan was home to clothing factories, breweries, distilleries and other small industries. These activities have been relocated and the industrial buildings converted into flats, shops, studios and cosy brown cafés. Despite this trend towards renovation, many old buildings are considered beyond salvation and are now being rebuilt completely, a piecemeal process that has been clogging up the narrow streets for more than a decade, but at least means the neighbourhood is being carefully preserved.

Bijlmermeer

At the other end of the scale, modern Bijlmermeer appears, at least when viewed from the elevated Metro platform, to be a jewel made up of new, clean, high-tech business parks. But behind the ultra-modern, corporate facades and plazas, an open-air shopping centre snakes its way back to the honeycomb of concrete high-rises for which Bijlmermeer is infamous. The atmosphere may be futuristic, but it is alienating and impersonal. This 1960s experiment in social planning, designed to provide housing for some 50,000 people, was an expensive mistake. Today it has one of the highest crime rates and concentration of drug-related problems in the Netherlands.

On 4 October 1992, cargo flight El Al 1862 crashed into a corner of a Bijlmermeer high-rise. The 747 jet claimed an official death toll of 43 and sparked off a series of enquiries that compromised government ministers and state security. The jet had been carrying depleted uranium, although initially it was strenuously denied that there were any dangerous chemicals or toxins on board.

Perhaps it took such a catastrophe to re-highlight the social problems of Bijlmermeer, which has enjoyed more positive attention in recent years, with initiatives undertaken to make it a more liveable place. The council and large companies are involved with a new development that will include residential, industrial and recreational sites. The railway station is being expanded and is undergoing a major facelift to include a boulevard linking residential and work areas. Apart from the Amsterdam ArenA (home to Ajax football club) and Amsterdam Poort (a modern shopping centre), Bijlmermeer will be enjoying substantial additional investment, including a cinema complex and several theatres.

Working in the city

The working face of Amsterdam has changed in recent decades. As industry retooled in the late 1970s, the limitations of a 17th-century city surrounded by water became painfully obvious. Narrow canal-side streets were frequently blocked by delivery lorries. Beautiful historic buildings could not safely be expanded or legally demolished to create much-needed new office space. As a consequence, the big concerns moved out of the city centre. Shipbuilding was the first to go; in the early 1980s KNSM, the last remaining shipping company, moved to Rotterdam. The Mobil oil refinery and Ford assembly plant left Amsterdam about the same time.

By 1985 some 75,000 people, nearly a quarter of the workforce, were unemployed. Most of them were semi-skilled machinists and labourers, unprepared and untrained to participate in the technical revolution that was taking place. Unemployment in the city is down since then and still declining, but many of the former shipyard, refinery and assembly plant workers remain on the dole.

One of Amsterdam's oldest established businesses, Heineken Brewery, moved out to Zoeterwoude in 1986, deciding that transporting its famous nectar would be much easier from there. The old brewery building remains open for tours *(see page 189).*

A curious twist is the lack of skilled hands for the local building trades. Most people working on scaffolding are likely to be from the rural province of Friesland, or from Britain or Ireland. Employers can opt out of responsibility for paying social premiums for foreign workers by designing contracts in such a way that employees can never get a permanent position. There is legislation to prevent this sort of exploitation, but employees are seldom aware of their rights.

Foreign input and greenfield sites

The municipal government of Amsterdam, faced with loss of revenue from big businesses, has aggressively courted American, Swiss and Japanese multinational companies eager to establish EU headquarters and participate in the single European market. The city is pushing its multi-port advantage, combined with the Dutch facility for languages and the high productivity of the workforce.

Many companies have already answered the call. Some have taken up space in the new docklands regeneration scheme. The whole of the 15-km (10-mile) stretch of waterway that runs behind Centraal Station and northwest to

the North Sea is the site of a €500-million project that will eventually include conference centres, 20,000 housing units, and leisure facilities. Space for a smaller harbour, plus rail- and airport-related businesses will also be included. A new terminal has opened with a capacity for 2,500 cruise-ship passengers.

Shrewdly, the city also began creating new residential and commercial space in the southeast, an area well served by public transport. Farmland was annexed and marshes drained and filled. The big banks, such as ABN, AMRO and ING, were among the first to move and their computer support services were quick to follow. The country's major teaching hospital,

LEFT: apartment blocks on Bijlmermeer.
RIGHT: 1950s advertising for the Dutch firm, Philips.

Amsterdam University's Academic Medical Centre, also moved to the area, taking with it a host of medical research companies.

The only representatives here of the industrial sector are the large printers, and they, probably more than anyone, have taken advantage of the technological revolution. Some of the city's daily newspapers and major publishers have left the centre to relocate here, or gone to Wibautstraat to the east of the city.

The contemporary workforce

The largest single employer is the government. When staff from two universities and the large social service programmes are

included, civil servants total more than 120,000 people, or 30 percent of the workforce. Another constant is tourism. Around 1.6 million annual visitors contribute about €750 million to the local economy.

The liberal and tolerant reputation of the city has also made it a mecca for the country's intellectuals and artists. The influx of highly educated people has created a positive boom in what economists call "informal economic activity" and self-employment. Astonishingly, 12,000 Amsterdammers are freelance. One labour economist estimates that as much as one third of all business and economic activity in the city comes from the self-employed.

As a result, every canal-side house seems to contain the basement or studio of an architect or graphic artist. They obviously enjoy their high profile, and their curtains and blinds are never drawn because the brightly lit studios are advertisements for the values and affinities of the occupants.

Actors, writers and musicians also regard Amsterdam as their natural habitat. The city has more than 50 theatres and 175 stages; it is home to two symphony orchestras, in addition to the national ballet. There are 150 art galleries in Amsterdam and this does not include the craftsmen whose studios clutter the Jordaan, or the 170 antiques shops. For these artists, artisans and dealers, there simply is nowhere else to live and work. Their influence on the character and spirit of the city is clearly visible, their value immeasurable.

The increased demand from newly affluent residents and tourists has fuelled an explosion of shops, and a walk through the city gives an impression that the official figure of 10,000 retail outlets is a conservative estimate. In addition there are 26 markets selling everything from marijuana pipes to fruit and vegetables.

This, however, has given some small-shop-owners cause for concern over the future character of city. When the rents go up, it forces out the marginal businesses such as antiquarian bookshops, traditional grocers and specialist retailers trading on slim margins. Those same shops give Amsterdam's side streets their enviable charm. The city's small, specialist shops contribute to the quality of life that Amsterdammers adore.

Local pride

Residents shrug off the economic and work-based upheaval of the past two decades, pointing out that their city – unlike Rotterdam – has always had a commercial base, not an industrial one. Amsterdammers, especially inner-city residents, have a deep affection for their town. They may have political disagreements with the city government, but very few of them would ever want to live anywhere else. To them, quality of life is important and this is the best place to enjoy it. ❏

LEFT: affluent residents and tourists have led to profitable times for the city's shopkeepers.

The Ethnic City

Amsterdam is a genuine melting pot, with immigrants from many countries. The city has a history of receiving political or religious refugees with open arms over the centuries. The fact that you may choose from at least 40 different national cuisines is a good indication of the city's cosmopolitan lifestyle.

Postwar industrial development, economic growth and a housing shortage contributed to a substantial deficit in skilled and non-skilled workforces. To overcome this shortage people were drafted in from other countries as "guest workers". Many of them, particularly the Turkish and Moroccan guest workers who came in the 1960s, enjoyed living conditions previously unknown to them and instead of returning home opted to bring their families to the Netherlands. This phenomenon was not always well received by the indigenous population, but the more liberal are quick to point out that guest workers undertook work the Dutch didn't want to do.

In the run-up to Surinamese independence in 1975, many immigrants moved to Amsterdam and were steered towards the vacant housing units of Bijlmermeer. Now the area's 35,000 Dutch-speaking Surinamese residents make up the second-largest Surinamese community in the world. They also make up the largest proportion of the city's immigrants – 5 percent – and, coming from a former Dutch colony, have the same rights as Dutch-born citizens. Connections with their South American home are still strong, however.

Other concentrations of immigrant communities are found all round the fringes of the old city, and they make up an increasingly visible and fast-growing part of Amsterdam's population – nearly 25 percent in total. Many Turkish and Moroccan families live in the housing projects on the eastern and western fringes. First-generation immigrants,

especially those from Muslim countries, remain very close knit and have not integrated well. Language is the biggest barrier, but so is modern culture. The liberal, often agnostic or atheistic Dutch are seen as godless. As is usually the case, children have generally integrated better than their parents.

De Pijp, a highly compact housing area south of Frederiksplein, is a neighbourhood where Turks, Moroccans, Surinamese, Indians and Dutch mix better than they do in other areas of the city. The area's shops and restaurants cater to all tastes and act as the glue that holds the

area together. Dapperplein, just east of Artis Zoo, is similar in ethnic make-up.

Despite occasional racial conflicts, Amsterdam remains a harmonious mix of cultures. The liberal Dutch attitude results in thousands of requests for asylum in the Netherlands every year – requests that, at least until now, have been met with more sympathy than they have elsewhere. The expansion of the EU in May 2004 has challenged this openness to some degree, as the Netherlands introduced curbs to prevent a large-scale influx of arrivals from the new member states of Eastern Europe. ❑

RIGHT: Amsterdam has the world's second-largest Surinamese community.

Performance Arts

Amsterdam calls itself the "Capital of Inspiration", and it is, indeed, a destination that will stimulate all the senses. No other city in Europe hosts so many international festivals during the summer months – when music, dance and theatre performances are held in parks, squares and historic concert halls, as well as on the water. There are hundreds to choose from, language is no barrier and some even offer free admission.

The Vondelpark, for example, hosts an open-air concert series from the end of May to the end of August. This popular series presents performances in a large, half-moon shaped bandstand from Wednesday through to Sunday. A wide selection of jazz, classical, pop and world music is presented, along with the occasional comedy, cabaret or dance performance. The highlight of the season is the special concert featuring the Royal Concertgebouw Orchestra.

Throughout the year, Amsterdam's various cultural institutions present a variety of performances. The Royal Concertgebouw Orchestra is renowned for its varied repertoire. During the summer months, a popular festival takes place in the large and small halls of the Concertgebouw, featuring the music of the great composers performed by some of today's finest musicians. Free "surprise" lunchtime concerts are offered on Wednesday from 12.30–1pm.

The Beurs van Berlage in Damrak, Amsterdam's former stock exchange, is the home of the Netherlands Philharmonic and the Dutch Chamber Orchestras. The red-brick classical building, dating from 1903, is considered one of the most important Dutch architectural monuments. Concerts are held in two different halls with excellent acoustics, one made completely of glass.

The Muziektheater – also known as the "Stopera", because the grandiose building houses both the Amsterdam City Hall (Stadhuis) and Netherlands Opera – presents numerous international events, including those of its resident companies, the Netherlands Opera and Netherlands Dance Theatre.

The Carré Theatre along the Amstel River is more than 100 years old. It once hosted the famous Circus of Oscar Carré and these days is the venue for many musical theatre productions (some in English) as well as staging concerts by international pop and rock bands.

The elegant Stadsschouwburg (Municipal Theatre), a porticoed red- brick building dating from 1894, has theatre, music and dance performances throughout the year, and during June is the main venue of the Holland Festival, featuring a wide range of productions including opera, theatre and dance.

Just across the street on Leidseplein is the spot where street musicians, mime artists and fire-eaters have performed for decades. The traditional form of busking is still prevalent throughout the city, but many café owners are no longer receptive to having their terraces

LEFT: Peruvian street musician.

given over to entertainment – perhaps because some of the less talented performers began to harass more than entertain. The joy remains in encountering traditional buskers, sincere and dedicated to sharing their talents. One of the best places to do this is in the passage under the Rijksmuseum where one can encounter a spirited violinist, several steel-drum players or a traditionally costumed Tibetan horn player. The square in front of Centraal Station remains a prime spot for buskers, from Russian jazz musicians and gypsy violinists to magicians, puppeteers, *a cappella* choirs and chamber-music quartets.

The most traditional form of busking – one that deserves support – takes the form of ornately decorated barrel-organs, found in strategic points all over the city. Their carnival-style music, from classical pieces to popular songs, creates a nostalgic soundtrack. Small, brass collection tins are shaken vigorously, literally under one's nose, for donations.

Amsterdam is also the kind of place where performance artists perform in the streets, often to the bemusement of passers-by. Fabiola, who refers to himself as a "living artwork of no gender" has done this for many years with creative costumes that give an other-worldly impression of a fashion diva from outer space.

Besides the traditional arts and the street happenings, the city has a variety of venues where less expensive, or free, performances take place. The Amsterdam Music Conservatory on Van Baerlestraat, opposite the (temporarily closed) Stedelijk Museum, offers free concerts given by its students most evenings from 7.30pm. One can hear a variety of instruments from a range of periods. The IJsbreker, along the Amstel, is a café/concert hall that specialises in performances of new music by local and international guests (the music part of the operation is set to move to the new Muziekgebouw on the waterfront in 2005; *see page 180*).

There are also many music venues that feature jazz and blues, comedy, world music and alternative cinema. The Bimhuis (also due to move to the Muziekgebouw in 2005) is a jazz club which hosts local musicians as well as those of international repute. There are many Irish pubs in the city that have live music on certain days of the week. Winston Kingdom in Warmoesstraat began as an alternative space with poetry readings and music performances. The hotel/café now has an art gallery in addition to its performance space, and attracts a mixed public.

The Westergasfabriek (the former Gas Company at the Westerpark) is now a cinema that shows Dutch films, and there's a theatre, gallery and concert hall. They host many cultural happenings throughout the year. The West Pacific is a café/restaurant with reasonable prices and a disco at weekends.

The Uitbureau (26 Leidseplein) has an information centre and booking office, and publishes *Uitkrant*, a free monthly magazine listing events throughout the city. Although it is in Dutch, it is fairly easy to understand in terms of events, dates and venues ❑

RIGHT: live performance in a jazz bar.

FESTIVALS

Amsterdammers love to celebrate, whether it is New Year's
Eve or the Queen's birthday, and they don't do it quietly.
And on the rare occasions when the canals feeze over, an
impromptu festival takes over the entire city

Amsterdam is a festive city with a number of popular festivals throughout the year. The Dutch like to celebrate at the drop of a hat, whether it's the appearance of the sun or during those rare winter days when the canals freeze over and they take to the ice on skates.

Winter celebrations

Celebrations begin on **Oudejaarsavond** – New Year's Eve. On the preceding days the city becomes crowded with visitors from all over Europe, who come for the Amsterdam experience. Many come from warmer, southern European countries and roam the streets forlornly wrapped in layers of clothing trying to find reasonably priced lodgings.

Amsterdam's New Year is ushered in by the consumption of large quantities of currant-filled doughnuts (*oliebollen* or oil balls) and the launching of fireworks to chase away the evil spirits of the old year. The Chinese quarter (*see page 96*) in the heart of the Red Light District is the centre of attraction for colourful, noisy firework displays. Huge strings of firecrackers are suspended from the upper floors of buildings and ignited from the bottom, causing thunderous crescendos followed by wild applause. In recent years, the public has participated more directly, setting off fireworks in neighbourhoods throughout the city. So when the clock strikes twelve, there is an unrelenting hour of noise and brightly lit skies. After 1am, which the police have designated

as the end of festivities, the streets are covered with red debris and the air is thick with smoke.

Even during the mildest of winters there is a great deal of talk about whether or not the canals will freeze. When they do, the nation mobilises, delving into cupboards to dust off seldom-used skates, and certain city canals become a network of silver thoroughfares packed with woolly-hatted skaters, hot-chocolate vendors and enthusiastic spectators. The most recent severe freezes occurred in 1997, for two years in a row in 1985 and 1986, and before that in 1963. During the big freeze the main event is the **Elfstedentocht**, a gruelling race on skates between 11 towns in

---

LEFT: the exuberant Gay Pride festival takes place each August. **RIGHT:** celebrating Queen's Day.

the province of Friesland. The entire Amsterdam population, if not competing or spectating by the canal sides, is glued to the television set with hot cocoa permanently ready on the stove. Those who prefer to be active are skating in the Amsterdamse Bos or in Vondelpark.

Koninginnedag

Koninginnedag (Queen's Day) is on 30 April. Although events commemorating the former queen's birthday (the current queen's birthday is seasonally unfavourable) take place throughout the Netherlands, they take on a particularly chaotic form in Amsterdam with more than 500,000 in attendance. The

day is one of unbridled commercial fever, the result of a decree stating that anyone can sell anything, within the bounds of legality.

The initial idea was to create a day on which children could sell their handicrafts and play instruments on the streets, but the spirit of enterprise now pervades both old and young. The city becomes a cross between a jumble sale and a carnival, as sellers set up pitches on the prime sites. Thousands of stalls selling old ships' tackle, bric-a-brac and handmade items, along with people challenging all-comers at chess, egg-throwing contests at people dressed in costume, and various food vendors selling everything from kebabs to Vietnamese *loempia* (spring rolls) – form aisles along the pavements. During the day, the Dam, Vondelpark, the Jordaan and Leidseplein become prime spots to soak up the atmosphere.

As the day progresses a giant street party develops in the city centre. A solid jam of beer-drinking humans provides the audience for live bands which play outside the bars. By 7pm, the late shift of merry-makers witnesses convoys of water-jetting lorries which clear the streets of rubbish ready for the next day. Trams and buses start operating again and the streets return to normal. By the next day, the only memory is a collective hangover.

Summer celebrations

Founded in 1947, the **Holland Festival** runs throughout June and is the biggest dance, drama and music festival in the Netherlands. This carnival of the arts is an international crowd-puller and encompasses performances at numerous venues, but mainly at the Stadsschouwburg in Leidseplein.

The **Uitmarkt**, at the end of August in Museumplein, is a three-day fair in preparation for Holland's new cultural season. Groups of theatre, music and dance artists from across the country flock to the city.

Around the second week of September the Jordaan begins 10 days of merriment. Accordion groups and vocalists perform traditional folk music. Food stalls and stages are set up around the cafés. Less raucous is the flower parade, on the first Saturday in September, when decorated floats and costumed attendants go from Aalsmeer to the heart of the city.

Sint-Nicolaas

On the second or third Saturday of November, **Sint-Nicolaas** (also known as Sinterklaas) arrives "from Spain", proceeding up Prins Hendrikkade to the city centre. Looking rather like Father Christmas, but wearing a bishop's mitre, the saint greets the crowds of children.

A parade through the streets heralds the build up to Sint-Nicolaas's Eve; children put out their shoes for the saint and wake up to find them filled with marzipan cakes in a variety of fanciful shapes. On 5 December the children receive more substantial presents. ❑

LEFT: the festival of Sint-Nicolaas.

Gay Amsterdam

Amsterdam affords a freedom to gay people that is almost unparalleled in other European cities. Small wonder that the city is often called the "gay capital of Europe". With at least 35 gay bars (including two lesbian cafés), 14 gay or gay-friendly hotels and at least three gay discos, it is easy to speak of the "gay city quarters". There are three main areas where gays of all ages congregate. In the heart of the city in the Warmoesstraat area there are six bars, a cinema, several gay sex shops and gay hotels. Behind Rembrandtplein, on and around the Amstel, there are 10 bars, a disco and a gay "escort club". This is by far the most popular quarter for visiting and local gays. Lastly, there are four bars, a disco and three gay-friendly shops in Reguliersdwarsstraat.

Most shops are "gay-friendly", but some shop-owners pride themselves on their gay roots and are annotated in the Amsterdam Columbia Fun Map, a free map made by and for gay people, widely available at all gay outlets and a must for all gay visitors *(see page 231)*. In Kerkstraat and around Leidseplein there are also numerous gay bars, restaurants and hotels that are frequented by slightly older clients and offer a quieter and more relaxed atmosphere. Surprisingly, the demand for lesbian-orientated bars seems minimal, although they do exist.

The gay community didn't always have the freedom it now enjoys. In the 1970s it was forbidden to place wreaths for homosexual victims at the war memorial on the Dam on Remembrance Day. During World War II the Nazis forced gays to sew pink stars on their clothes, and many suffered the same fate in concentration camps as other victims of the Nazis. In 1988, in response to the fact that many gay soldiers were omitted from official rolls of honour, the Homomonument –

made of pink granite – was erected to the side of the Westerkerk. Initially founded to commemorate gay war victims, it now also functions as a memorial to Aids victims and gay people the world over who are discriminated against because of their sexual orientation. The ban on wreaths at the Dam on Remembrance Day has also been lifted.

The greatest annual gay event in Amsterdam is the Gay Pride celebration on the first weekend in August. On Friday bands play in the streets of the gay quarters, but Saturday is the highlight, with a colourful carnival parade on the water.

There are boats of all kinds, their crews in costumes ranging from mildly avant-garde to bizarre and blatant. This visual orgy of colour is enjoyed by all, gay or straight, young or old.

Any gay visitor to Amsterdam would be well advised to visit the national gay and lesbian organisation, the COC. Founded in 1946, this non-profit-making outfit serves a dual role in the gay community – to provide a meeting place for kindred spirits and to stand up for the rights, privileges and interests of homosexuals, bisexuals and transgenders *(see page 231)*. ❏

RIGHT: Amsterdam is known as the gay capital of Europe.

FOOD AND DRINK

Eating out in Amsterdam is a gastronomic delight, with
wholesome local specialities complemented by a variety of
ethnic dishes from around the world

When it comes to dining out in Amsterdam, it is possible to do so in almost any language, and find menus to suit all tastes. Just as the Dutch explorers once brought back spices from around the world, innovative restaurateurs are seeking inspiration in fusion cuisine, combining East with West. Thanks to the proliferation of ethnic restaurants, one can experience the delights of such varied, and often exotic, cuisines as Vietnamese, Ethiopian, Thai, Turkish, Spanish, Greek, Portuguese, Tibetan and Polish. Of course, there are also traditional French, Italian, Japanese and Chinese restaurants, from the fanciest with two Michelin stars down to the most humble pizzeria.

The basic Dutch *eetcafé* is usually favoured by local people, who come for the *dagschotel*, the daily special, which offers a choice of a meat, fish or vegetarian main course, served with vegetables and french fries – an excellent way to eat cheaply and well.

Otherwise, the sky's the limit. There are sushi bars with revolving belts bearing food, and authentic tapas or dim sum in the heart of the Red Light District. There are restaurants that specialise in fish, those that offer only vegetarian fare and some that are strictly kosher. And, of course, there's the local pancake house. Large pancakes are popular, whether sweet or savoury, and offer a variety of fillings, from apple and Grand Marnier to a creamy mushroom and beef ragout. At the

other end of the scale, *Poffertjes* are mini-pancakes, usually eaten with large quantities of sugar and butter.

Dutch favourites

For many years the Dutch kitchen was synonymous with potatoes, cabbage, bread, cheese, potatoes, herring, endive and more potatoes, with some sausage thrown in for good measure. Because the Dutch prefer to eat their national dishes at home, there are few restaurants in the Netherlands that exclusively offer Dutch specialities. However, Amsterdam favourites such as Dorrius, Haesje Claes, De Blonde Hollander and De Poort all take pride

LEFT: herring consumption the traditional way.
RIGHT: an *eetcafé* provides straightforward cuisine.

in serving most of the traditional dishes such as *hutspot met klapstuk* (hotch potch with meat, carrots and potatoes), *stamppot van zuurkool en worst* (sauerkraut mashed with potatoes and sausage), *erwten* (pea) soup and *bruine bonen* (brown bean). At the renowned d' Vijff Vlieghen (Five Flies) restaurant, the diverse menu is based on the "new Dutch cuisine", which features fresh local produce, prepared from traditional recipes, with a lighter touch than of old.

The most traditional winter dish, still popular among the older generation, is *boerenkool-stamppot met worst* (cabbage mashed with potatoes and served with smoked

sausage). Other specialities of the Dutch kitchen include white asparagus served with ham and chopped egg (in May and June), smoked eel, special puddings *(vla)* with whipped cream, pancakes and herring, known as "the poor man's oyster".

The price of your hotel room will most likely include breakfast. This comprises a plate of cheese and cold meats, boiled eggs and a bread basket, which holds a variety of breads, from pre-cut white to heavy, black rye and perhaps wholewheat, raisin and seed bread. A spiced cake, *ontbijtkoek* or *peperkoek*, often eaten with butter, is usually included as well. The *koffietafel* (coffee-table)

lunch which is served in private homes and in office canteens includes a variety of breads, cheeses and cold meats. The most popular accompanying drink is milk or *karnemelk* (buttermilk).

Colonial cuisine

When in Amsterdam, you must experience Indonesian food. Usually it is the unsophisticated, plainly furnished restaurants that serve the most interesting and authentic dishes. Restaurants such as these are often family-run, with mother or grandmother presiding over the kitchens and preparing dishes that are unique to a particular village or island in Indonesia. The menu is often extremely simple: some offer smaller variations of the more tourist-oriented *rijsttafel* and nothing else, which gives you a plate of rice with two or three small samplings of vegetables and meat. Some *rijsttafels* come with 15, 25, 30 or more side dishes of meat, vegetables, refreshing fruits and garnishes. When the *rijsttafel* is served, a hotplate is placed on the table to keep the separate bowls of food warm. You are then served from a large bowl of rice, which can be replenished.

The *rijsttafel* is eaten by arranging the rice on your plate, then placing a small portion of each dish around the edge, lastly filling in the centre. Typical dishes include vegetables in coconut milk, chicken, lamb or goat skewers served with satay, fried bananas, and fish and meat prepared in various ways. The dishes themselves are usually spicy rather than hot, but beware of the small saucers of fiery red *sambal*, likely to destroy your tastebuds for the rest of the meal. Beer or tea are the ideal drinks to have with *rijsttafel*.

Another popular cuisine is that of Suriname (a former Dutch colony in South America), which offers a spicy mixture of Creole and Indian. This includes hearty curries and typical dishes such as peanut soup and *pom*, a kind of sweet potato, served with *roti* bread.

Eating on the run

If you fancy something quick to eat on the run, there is a wide variety of options, from *broodje* (filled bread rolls) to Vietnamese *loempia* (spring rolls), pizza slices, or Middle Eastern falafels or *shoarma* (roasted pork or lamb in a pitta bread) from takeaway stands.

Broodjes, filled with a variety of cheeses, meats and salads, can be bought in most bakeries or in special *Broodjeszaken*. A *kroket* is spiced minced beef or veal, coated in breadcrumbs; it's best with mustard or eaten in a roll. A lengthy sausage, with very questionable stuffing, is a *frikandel kroket*. A *nasibal* is ball-shaped and stuffed with spiced fried rice.

You should definitely try the most popular snack: the Belgian-style *patat* (chips or *frites)* dipped in mayonnaise. The next most popular snack is herring, eaten raw or salted, with plenty of chopped onion. Herring stalls are a feature of Dutch life, especially in May when

smoked salmon, smoked eel and two varieties of succulent Dutch shrimp, the *Noordse* or *Hollands garnalen*, the North Sea's finest.

What to drink

Many people drink beer, especially *pils*, a light lager, though the favoured drink is *jenever* or Dutch gin, made from distilled malt with juniper berries. At about 5pm people drop into their local café for a *borrel*: a small glass of the colourless *jonge* (young) *jenever*, or the creamier *oude* (old), which has a pale yellow colour and a noticeably heavier, muskier flavour. The Dutch are also famous for liqueurs and fruit brandies.

everyone wants to try the mild *nieuwe groene haring* – the first green herring of the season. Some clients eat the herrings the traditional way, holding them aloft by the tail between the thumb and forefinger of the right hand and swallowing them whole. More often, however, they are eaten with a fork from a small plate. Others may prefer a *broodje haring*, slices of herring in a soft roll or just herring slices on their own. Whichever way you choose, chopped onions are de rigueur. If you prefer another sort of fish, the stalls also sell

Beer, mineral water or wine are drunk with meals. *Spa Rood* is sparkling mineral water, while *Spa Blauw* is the still variety. Most wines in bars are drinkable, but not excellent, although the quality is steadily improving.

Coffee is the Dutch national drink and *koffiedrinken* is the national pastime. A cup of strong coffee, a *bakkie*, is usually served black. Espresso is a popular alternative and *koffie verkeerd*, or "wrong coffee", with a lot of steamed milk and a little coffee for flavouring, is ubiquitous. Hot chocolate is mostly a winter drink, of course, and when people go skating, private stands are set up on the ice, with large urns steaming on stoves. ❑

LEFT: satay at an Indonesian restaurant.
ABOVE: sampling *jenever* at a taster bar.

AMSTERDAM CAFES

Amsterdam is big on cafés, and half the fun for visitors lies in wandering in and discovering for themselves their unique personalities

Amsterdam has a long café tradition. Some claim that the first bar, euphemistically called café, opened its doors in the 13th century, when two men and a dog in a boat drifted ashore on the marshy banks of the (then) river IJ. By the 17th century, there were countless taverns in Amsterdam, which slowly and surely would extend to other cities. Dutch cafés have as much cultural value as museums, and a visit to one is essential for the true flavour of the city.

Traditional brown cafés (so-called because walls and ceilings have turned brown from age and smoke) are identified by dark, cosy, wooden interiors. The only audible sound is the buzz of lively conversation and the tinkle of glasses being rinsed. Coffee is generally brewed, not machine-made, and if you fancy a snack to go with your beer or spirit, there is usually a plate of olives or cheese. These cafés define the Dutch word *gezelligheid*, which means a state of cosiness or conviviality. This is where locals come for a few beers after work, to play cards, engage in political debates and tell tall tales.

The more elegant and stylish grand cafés serve lunch and desserts, and tend to have high ceilings, more light, reading tables and a variety of music. There are also cafés where you can play chess, throw darts, or play pool or billiards. There are men's cafés, women's cafés and even night cafés, which close around 5am.

ABOVE: warm weather offers the perfect excuse to sit on a bar or café terrace and sip a beer in the sunshine. The hectic, lively Leidseplein remains a popular haunt for locals as well as tourists, particularly in the summer months.

ABOVE: in a densely populated city such as Amsterdam, the café is often regarded as a solitary retreat where one can read in peace. Brown cafés such as this remain a strong tradition – serving as a type of living room, for some they offer a home away from home.

RIGHT: a beaming grin and a fat spliff beckons customers to one of Amsterdam's many alternative cafés, which sell small quantities of marijuana in weed or hashish form.

ABOVE, RIGHT AND TOP RIGHT: hash cafés attract their own mellow public, and most tourists who fancy a walk on the wild side place a visit to a hash "coffee shop" at the top of their itinerary. You won't have to look too far to find one in the city centre. Green and white placards displayed in the window have replaced many of the marijuana leaf logos and Bob Marley imagery.

THE COFFEE SHOP SCENE

In Amsterdam, so-called "coffee shops" have sold cannabis under a quasi-legal status for more than 30 years. Their presence is tolerated largely because they segregate the users of soft drugs from the dealers who peddle harder substances. This way, the illegal drug trade is denied a sizeable portion of the market, while your average cannabis smoker is not exposed to harder drugs at every transaction.

There are currently around 300 establishments in the city where customers are able to sit back and indulge without suffering the paranoia of the wrong-doer. There are coffee shops to suit most tastes, from unassuming neighbourhood joints to multi-level coffee shops with internet access, pool tables and TV screens. They all have two other things in common: comfortable seating and a means of quelling the inevitable hunger pangs, from cakes and pastries to *tostis* and smoothies. Some even provide full-blown menus of edible goodies, including "space cakes". The quality of the grass and hash on offer varies widely from place to place, with the cheapest and best-quality goods available in the unassuming neighbourhood coffee shops – the ones favoured by locals.

Coffee shop etiquette, as you might imagine, is a fairly relaxed affair. One thing to avoid, however, is heavy drinking; rowdiness is not a word the Dutch like to associate with their coffee shops. In fact, drinking alcohol in coffee shops is currently being outlawed. Thanks to new legislation, coffee shops which currently sell both cannabis and alcoholic drinks will have to choose between the two when their licenses come up for renewal.

ARCHITECTURE

Domestic and civic architecture in Amsterdam is fascinating,
from the 17th-century gabled canal homes to the stylish,
early 20th-century innovations of the Amsterdam School

Amsterdam is undeniably a beautiful city, and the architectural splendours that local people may take for granted are a delight for visitors discovering the city.

The gable tradition

Nearly all the houses that line the canals are graced with a gable. Their basic shape defines them – there are clock, step, spout, bell, neck, raised neck and frame gables. No two are alike, and their ornamentation often reveals the profession of the original owner. Much pride and effort was invested in the construction of the gables, which decorated the homes of some of the wealthiest people in the world. This is particularly noticeable along the "Gouden Bocht" or "Golden Bend", a small stretch of the Herengracht, now home to international banks and prestigious offices.

Fine examples of bell gables are to be seen on Brouwersgracht, and two of special interest are on Leliegracht – one at No. 60 in the French style, with rococo ornamentation, and the other at No. 36 surmounted by a cat. Neck gables are by far the most common and can be seen everywhere, even though it became fashionable in the 19th century to replace them with frame gables (common in the De Pijp area). During the Golden Age, Italian and French influences made their mark, and Tympana triangular gable tops started to appear on larger buildings. These classical

forms can be seen on the West India Company building in Haarlemmerstraat and Felix Meritis Theatre *(see pages 113 and 128)*.

One of the most famous step gables is on the corner of Brouwersgracht and Prinsengracht. It is unique in that it is a twinned gable; one twin looks out over Brouwersgracht, the other over Prinsengracht. Protruding from all the gables are hoisting beams, which were originally used to hoist up goods delivered from barges to the attic and, in warehouses, to different storage floors. The older warehouses are easily distinguished from residences, as they tend to have a central column of wider windows with hatches (to receive merchants' cargoes).

LEFT: gabled 17th-century canal house.
RIGHT: hoisting beams were used to haul cargo from canal barges to attic storage space.

The hoisting beams are just as functional today. Since most houses still have their original, extremely steep, narrow staircases, it's impossible to move furniture up or down, but with the aid of a block and tackle the hoisting beam continues to be indispensable.

For many centuries, the houses and warehouses were not numbered, but instead had names. Many of the names have survived and are to be seen in gable stones, the mini-sculptural wonders embedded into the house facades. The house names are as diverse and humorous as the gable stones themselves, often reflecting an event in the owner's life, or an amusing anecdote.

By far the best way to see the gables is to take a round trip *(rondvaart)* on a canal boat, with an informative guide.

Almshouses

The wealthier residents of Amsterdam took their religion seriously, and nowhere is there better evidence of this than in the construction of the almshouses. The most famous one is at the Begijnhof just off the Spui *(see page 89)*. It dates back to the Middle Ages and is still home to widows and elderly women. The small courtyard contains a tiny former Catholic church, later given to Scottish Presbyterians (although it's called the "English Church").

Next to the church entrance is a plaque dedicated to the Pilgrim Fathers. The courtyard is an oasis of quiet in the middle of the city, and the residents' homes are adorned with gable stones dedicated to faith and devotion, with the occasional Latin banner from the Catholic period. In the centre of the courtyard is a small, well-kept garden. Entry to the *hofje* (courtyard) is free and it is well worth a visit, but remember that quiet is appreciated.

The Amsterdam School

At the turn of the 20th century, just as today, there was a housing shortage. However, there was still land available near the inner city to build on. With the introduction of a new Housing Act and a group of brilliant architects and artists, the Amsterdam School came into being. They set themselves strict rules in terms of design and form, and every construction connected with this movement is a listed building. Characteristic of Amsterdam School architecture are the expressive facades with projecting balconies, bay windows and sweeping curves. Lines, vertical and horizontal, were accentuated, thus making chimneys works of art. Other window shapes, such as trapezoid and parabolic, are also hallmarks, as was the use of different-coloured bricks as a sculptural medium, integrating organic shapes

Centraal (Carlton) by Rutgers in Vijzelstraat; the former head office of the municipal transport company by Marnette, in Stadhouderskade; and the old *Telegraaf* building in Nieuwezijds Voorburgwal, by Staal.

There were 37 members of the Amsterdam School, and their genius lay not only in architecture but a whole range of related disciplines, from interior design and furniture to masonry. Perhaps surprisingly, the radical, early 20th-century approach has integrated well with the rest of the city's buildings.

For a greater insight into the movement's achievements, a small, comprehensive pamphlet is available from the VVV tourist office

and forms. The Amsterdam School even created their own typeface, which can be admired in the carvings and house numbers.

The architects did not confine themselves to housing, as the Beurs van Berlage (Berlage Stock Exchange) clearly demonstrates *(see page 83)*. Other public buildings that should be included in the list are the Scheepvaarthuis in Prins Hendrikkade by Van der Mey *(see page 181)*, a monumental building with a series of figureheads; the Grand Hotel

(see page 234), outlining a walk that encompasses classic examples from the School.

Amsterdam Architectural Centre

The Amsterdam Architectural Centre (ARCAM; *see page 183)* at 600 Prins Hendrikkade (tel: 620 4878) is an excellent reference point. Entry is free and there is always an exhibition on contemporary architectural themes, and a wide range of relevant literature in English. They also sell detailed architectural maps of Amsterdam to help you explore the city. The centre focuses on current issues involving architecture in Amsterdam, and the staff all have architectural backgrounds and great commitment. ❑

LEFT: typical architecture in the Jordaan district.
ABOVE AND RIGHT: creative examples of Amsterdam School architecture.

PLACES

A detailed guide to the city, with the principal sites
clearly cross-referenced by number to the maps

Go to a café on Keizersgracht on a wet Sunday afternoon in spring. A blonde woman, dressed in black, carefully tops two glasses of *warme chocolademelk* with generous dollops of whipped cream. This is Amsterdam. Go to Brouwersgracht and stand on the bridge facing the Westerkerk in the glow of an autumn sunset. With the trees stripped bare, the view of magnificent houses bordering Herengracht is like a painting of the city's Golden Age. This, too, is Amsterdam. Walk through the passage under the Rijksmuseum: there is a man sitting on the ground cross-legged, dressed in an embroidered Tibetan suit and singing. Return the next day and there may be someone else "in residence" playing the didgeridoo or exotic drums. These are other Amsterdam moments.

The city is composed of many memorable scenes, but there is also a list of "must sees". The Rijksmuseum and neighbouring Van Gogh Museum; the Royal Palace and the Nieuwe Kerk at the Dam; the Rembrandthuis and the Jewish Historical Museum near Waterlooplein – every visitor should find time to visit these. But after that, Amsterdam is what you want it to be, whether you sunbathe in Vondelpark, enjoy the outdoor pavilion of the NEMO science museum or do a pub crawl from one brown café to the next.

Amsterdam has more than 1,000 bridges crossing more than 100 canals with a combined length in excess of 100 km (65 miles). Despite these statistics, the historic centre is very compact and lends itself to easy exploration. Take a canal boat to see the 17th- and 18th-century houses of the Grachtengordel, the half-moon pattern of canals which stretches from the Amstel River to Brouwersgracht. Do plenty of walking: along the canals in the Jordaan; across the side streets between Leidsestraat and Raadhuisstraat; even to the warehouses of the east and the Maritime Quarter. Later, hire a bicycle and venture further afield.

Above all, talk to the people. Language is rarely a barrier here. Amsterdammers will share, with frankness and generosity, their views on the city and the world in general. There are few places in Europe where human contact is so easy, and you will end up loving the city as much for its people as for its scenery. ❏

PRECEDING PAGES: on the Grachtengordel at dusk; an aerial view of the Jordaan district.
LEFT: looking down at the Dam from the roof of Koninklijk Palace.

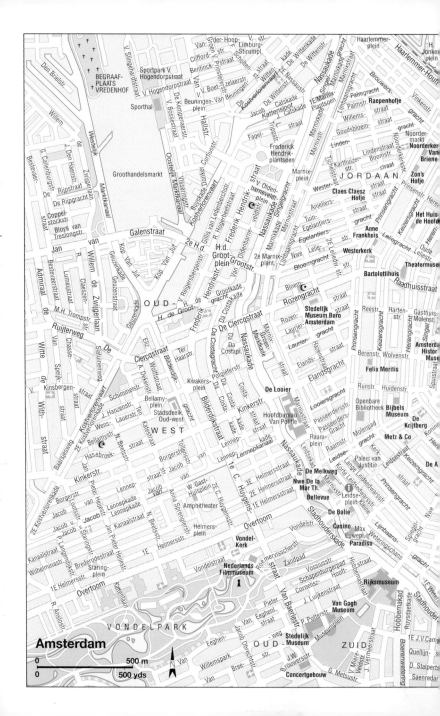

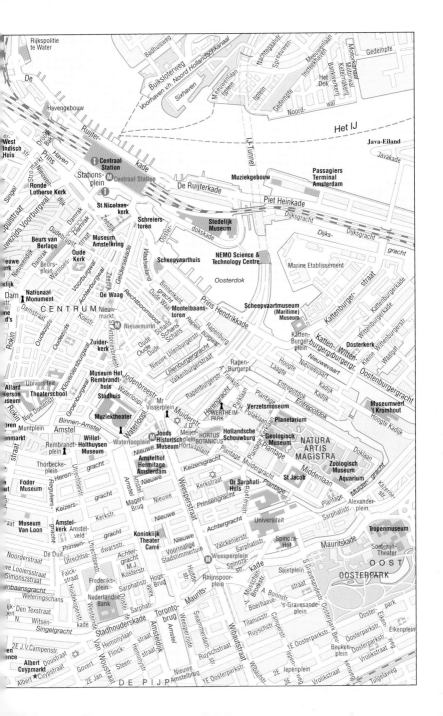

THE DAM AND CENTRAL AMSTERDAM

The heart of the city offers the best and the worst of Amsterdam, but feasting your eyes on its historical treasures, it's easy to imagine yourself back in the Golden Age

Standing in the square called the Dam today, it is tempting to try and block out the trams, cars, pedestrians, buskers and tourists feeding the pigeons for a moment and conjure up instead a romantic image of a medieval settlement built around a dam set back from the shoreline of the Zuiderzee (now the IJsselmeer). That ancient dam lives on in name only. But the very idea of it begs a few moments of mental reconstruction.

Historic centre

The dam of yore was built across the River Amstel around the year 1200, or a little earlier, and proved to be the catalyst for rapid growth; by the middle of the 16th century Amsterdam was a town of 14,000 people. At this time, the Amstel flowed freely through the heart of the city, emerging beyond the Dam as the Damrak.

Almost all of that central waterway was built over in the following centuries, and the Dam is now landlocked. All that is left on the harbour side of the square today is a small cul-de-sac of water opposite Centraal Station. In the other direction, beyond the Dam to the south, the Amstel comes to a halt opposite the eastern end of Spui.

The **Dam ❶** has always been the heart of Amsterdam, its status assured after the construction of the Nieuwe Kerk and Royal Palace, and at different times much of the city's public life took place here. Because navigation by small boats was possible from the seaward side as far as the Dam, this area was also a busy trading centre. Merchants came from all over the world to do business. Contemporary pictures show scenes of busy activity, with porters pushing wheelbarrows across the square, wealthy merchants with their entourages, and an assortment

Map on page 78

LEFT: Dam Square is the hub of the city.
BELOW: looking north to Centraal Station along Damrak.

City Centre
and Nieuwmarkt

0 ————————— 200 m
0 ————————— 200 yds

Ronde
Lutherse
Koepelkerk **8**

Renaissance
Amsterdam
Hotel

Smakst.
Nieuwendijk
Kattengat
Teerketelst.
Hekelveld
Martelaarsgracht
Prins Hendrikkade

Centraal Station
Stationsplein

Centraal Station 6

Noord-Zuid Hollands
Koffiehuis

Koggestr.
Klump-
weg
Spuistraat
Nieuwezijds Armst. Braak
Oude
Nwe-
zijds Kolk
St Jacobsstr.
Karne-
melkst.
Kolk-
st.
Nieuwendijk
Sexmuseum
Amsterdam

St Nicolaaskerk 7

Olofspoort
Oudezijds Kolk
Schreierstoren

Herenstr.
Langest.
Blauwburgwal
Krt. Korsjespoortst.
Krt.
Kolkst.
D.v. Hasseltsst.
Nieuwezijds Voorburgwal
Singel
Herengracht
Oude Nieuwst.
Lijnbaansst.
Mandemakersst.
Oudebrugst.
D'Leeuwenburg
Huis
H. Hoekst.
Vredenbur-
gersst.
Spook-
st.

**Museum
Amstelkring 23**

Nieuwe Brugsteeg
Nieuwe Zeedijk

Herengracht
Bergstr.
Singel
Mosterd-
potst.
St Nicolaasstr.
Zwarte Handst.
Gravenstr.
Zoutst.
Eggertstr.
Nieuwendijk
Beursst.
Warmoesstr.
Lange Niezel
Paternosterst.
Oudezijds Voorburgwal

**Koffie- en
Theemuseum
(Geels & Co.) 22**

**Beurs van
Berlage 5**

Damrak
Damrak
Oudezijds Voorburgwal
Zeedijk
Storm-
st.
Gelderskade
Waalst.

**Nieuwe
Kerk 3**

Torensluis
Faculteit
der
Letteren
Magna
Plaza
Mozes en Aaronstr.
Molst.
Beurspl.
Beursstr.
Effectenbeurs
St Annenstr.
Oudekerkspl.

Oude Kerk 22

St Antoniesbr.st.
Oudezijds Achterburgwal

**Fo Guang Shan
He Hua Temple 24**

Gelderskade
Amsterdams
Marionetten-
theater
Nwe Riddersst.
Rechtboomsloot

Raadhuisstraat
Koninklijk
Paleis **2**
Paleisstr.
Dam 1
Madame
Tussaud's
**Nationaal
Monument 4**
De Bijenkorf
Warmoesstr.
St Jansstr.
St Annenstr.
Voorburgwal
Oudezijds
Molenst.

**Erotic
Museum**

Monnikenstr.
Koningsst.
Koningsst.

De Waag

Paleis-
str.
Singel
Spuistraat
Jonge Roelenst.
Papen-
broekst.
Spaarpot-
st.
Kalverstr.
Rokin
Nes
Damstr.
Pijlst.
Servetst.
Oudezijds Voorburgwal
Gaperst.
St. Pietershalst.
P. Jacobszstr.
Stoofst.
Oude
Doelenst.

**Grand Hotel
Krasnopolsky**

**Tattoo
Museum**

**Hash Marihuana
Hemp Museum**
Steen-
houwersst.

**Brouwhuis
Maximiliaan**

Barndest.
Bloedst.
Koestr.
Bethaniënstr.

**Nieuw-
markt 15**

Keizerrijk
Wijdest.

Betty
Asfaltcomplex

Rosmarijnst.
Voorburgwal

**Amsterdams
Historisch
Museum 9**

10

St Lucienst.
Duifjesst.
Wijde Kapelst.
Enge Kapelst.
Gedempte Begijnensloot

De Brakke Grond
Enge Lombardst.
Bank van
Lening

Frascati

St Agnieten
str.
Oudezijds Achterburgwal
Kloveniersburgwal
Spinhuisst.
Rusland

Oude Hoogst.
**Oost
Indisch
Huis 19**

Walen-
pl.

**Waatse
Kerk**

Onkelboe-
renst.
Zand-
str.
Zandst.

18

**Ak. v.
Wetenschap**

Trippenhuis
Nwe Hoogst.

Zuiderkerk 17
Zuider-
kerkhof

**De Pinto
Huis 16**

Snoekjesst.
Oude Schans

M
Nieuwmarkt
Kleine
Krommboomssloot
Dijkst.
Krt.
Oude
Schans

**Begijn-
hof 10**

**Engelse
Kerk 11**
Maagdenhuis
Nieuwezijds Voorburgwal

**Huis aan de
Drie Grachten**
Grimburgwal
Universiteit

Nes
Waterst.
Takst.
Spui
Gedempte Begijnensloot

**Agnieten-
kapel 21**

De Engelenbak
Kuipersst.

**Allard
Pierson
Museum 12**
Turfdraagsterpad
Oudezijds
Voorburgwal
Oudemanhuispoort

20

Binnengasthuisstr.
Kloveniersburgwal
Groenburgwal
Verversst.
Zwanenburgwal

Doelenzaal

Raamgracht
Raamgracht
Moddermolenst.
Pattagon
Jodenbreestr.

**Museum Het
Rembrandthuis**

Holland Experience

Waterloopl.

**Oude
Lutherse
Kerk**
Universiteits-
bibliotheek

Spui
Handboogstr.
Voetboogstr.
Olieslag-
gersst.
Heiligeweg

Theaterschool
Vendelstr.
Doelenstr.
's
Gravelandse-
veer

Staalstr.
Staalkade

Stadhuis

★
**Vlooienmarkt
(Flea Market)**

**Muziek-
theater**

Koningspl.
Koningspl.

Munttoren 13

Bloemenmarkt 14

Singel

Kloveniersstr.
Munt-
plein

**Universiteits-
theater**

Reguliersdwarsstr.
Herengracht
Reguliersbreestr.
Vijzelstraat

Nwe
Reguliersbr.
Reguliersbreestr.

**Tuschinski
Theatre
Cinema**

Binnen Amstel

**De Kleine
Komedie**

Amstelstr.
Bakkerstr.
Balk in 't Oogst.
Halvemaan-
st.
Paardenst.
Amstelstr.
Reguliersbreestr.

Amstel

**Rembrandt-
plein**

**Willet-Holthuysen
Museum**

Blauwbrug
Nwe Amstelstr.
Amstel

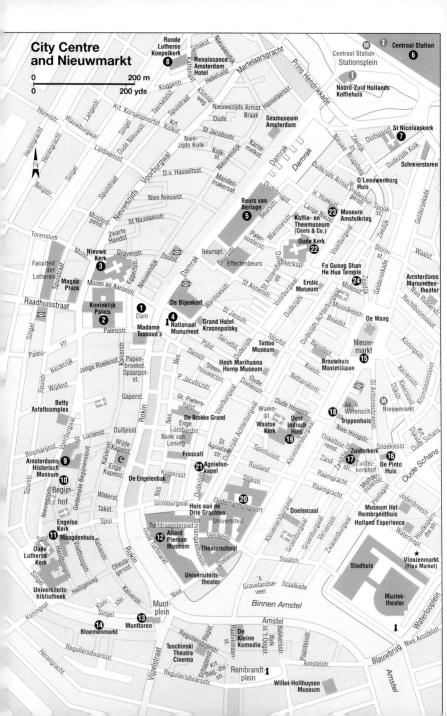

of traders and entrepreneurs – both local and foreign – doing business and cutting deals.

Although now sliced by shuttling trams, the Dam has kept some of its public character and is still a hive of activity. Most days, and especially at weekends, it provides a stage for various outlandish street performers. Throughout the years, it has been the scene of parades, executions, political demonstrations, war remembrances, celebrations and noisy and colourful funfairs with larger-than-life Ferris wheels and other gravity-defying attractions.

Royal Palace

The 17th-century construction of the new Town Hall, the great building flanking the west side of the Dam, which has since come to serve as the **Koninklijk Paleis** (Royal Palace) ❷, changed the scene at the Dam. (open Easter holidays and June–Aug daily 11am–5pm; Sept–mid-Dec and mid-Feb–May, except Easter holidays, Tues–Thurs 12.30–5pm; open days and hours may vary; entrance fee). Large and stately, the classical-style building was designed by architect Jacob van Campen and completed by Daniël Stalpaert. Work began on this new edifice at the height of the Golden Age in 1648. A total of 13,659 wooden piles – a figure all Dutch schoolchildren learn – were driven into the soft, sandy soil to provide foundations. When it was completed in 1655, it provided an expression of the confidence of what was one of the world's wealthiest and most powerful cities. While under construction in 1652, the old medieval Town Hall it was replacing burnt down. Rembrandt provided a record of the scene when, curiously, he drew the old building in ruins, rather than the new one rising beside it.

At its inception, the new Town Hall was a celebration of newly won Dutch independence and renewed peace. The poet Constantijn Huygens praised it as the "Eighth Wonder of the World", which was a tad overstated but captured the exuberant popular mood in Amsterdam at the time. Its symbolic importance to the city is emphasised by the innumerable paintings of the building that hang on the walls of the Amsterdam Historical Museum.

Sombre and somewhat heavy-handed, the exterior is embellished with pilasters and pedimented windows. Sea gods and unicorns representing the oceans pay homage to the Maid of Amsterdam, while bronze figures symbolising Prudence, Peace and Justice look on approvingly. At the rear, an allegorical figure of Amsterdam struggles against the IJ and Amstel rivers. The sandstone dome houses a carillon of bells from the 1660s by François Hemony, and is tipped by a weathervane in the shape of a sailing ship.

In compensation for the exterior, the light and elegant interior brims with white marble and a wealth of reliefs, ornamentation and sculptures

Map on page 78

Queen Beatrix succeeded her mother, Juliana, in 1980. The Dutch royal family receives foreign heads of state at the Koninklijk Palace.

BELOW: street theatre outside Koninklijk Palace.

ORIENTATION
This chapter covers the historic centre of the city: from Damrak and Rokin in the east to Nieuwezijds Voorburgwal in the west, and from Centraal Station in the north to the Singel and Amstel in the south.

BELOW: Koninklijk Palace dates from the Golden Age.

by the Flemish artists Artus Quellin the Elder and Rombout Verhulst, perfectly reflecting the wealth and good taste Amsterdam enjoyed during its Golden Age. Among the sumptuous state rooms are the Burgerzaal (Citizens Chamber), in which a sculpture shows Atlas shouldering the globe. Amsterdam is represented with all due modesty as the centre of the world in a map carved on the floor. In the Schepenzaal (Council Chamber) are paintings by Ferdinand Bol, Govert Flinck, Jan van Bronkhorst and Jacob de Wit. Judges pronounced on guilt and innocence in the Vierschaar (Hall of Justice), while images of Justice, Wisdom and Mercy kept a watchful eye on proceedings.

When King Louis Napoleon, the short-reigned King of Holland, came to Amsterdam in 1808, he transformed the building from a town hall into a royal palace, furnishing it with a rich collection of empire furniture, clocks and chandeliers.

Although the Royal Palace is one of Amsterdam's top attractions, during parts of the year it is off limits to

visitors due to the royal calendar. At such times, Queen Beatrix receives heads of state and other special guests here.

Behind the palace, across Nieuwezijds Voorburgwal from the Dam, is **Magna Plaza**, a shopping gallery housed in the magnificent setting of the city's former head Post Office, which dates from 1908. This neo-Gothic pile, replete with columns, arches and ornamental cast-iron, has been dubbed "De Perenberg" (Pear Mountain) by locals, for the pear-shaped spires on its roof.

New Church

Looming large next to the Royal Palace on Dam Square, the **Nieuwe Kerk ③** (New Church; tel: 638 6909; open daily 10am–6pm, Thurs to 10pm during exhibitions; free when there's no exhibition on) is sometimes described as the cathedral of the Netherlands, and is new in name only – the late-Gothic edifice goes all the way back to 1400. It was enlarged to its present size around 1500, when it was decorated

with paintings, sacred images and altars. After the Great Fire of 1645 the Nieuwe Kerk, by then in Protestant hands, was refurnished with elegant pews for the gentry, a copper gate in front of the choir and a highly decorative pulpit. Jacob van Campen, the architect of the Royal Palace, designed the housing for the enormous organ. It was, however, forbidden from having a tower, because the city fathers feared competition with the Town Hall.

Through its many tombs and monuments to maritime heroes and poets, the church acquired national importance. Among the numerous famous Amsterdammers buried here are the naval hero Admiral Michiel Adriaensz de Ruyter (d. 1676), in a magnificent marble mausoleum by Rombout Verhulst, and the 17th-century poet Joost van den Vondel (d. 1679).

The investiture of Dutch monarchs has taken place here since 1814. As kings Willem I, II and III, Regentess Emma and queens Wilhelmina and Juliana did before her, Queen Beatrix took the constitu-

tional oath in 1980 in a grand ceremony leading from the Royal Palace to the church. The Nieuwe Kerk is also the venue for the annual national Remembrance Service, held on 4 May.

In the late 1970s, the Nieuwe Kerk re-opened its doors following a 20-year restoration. Since then, it has been operated by a foundation that has succeeded in transforming the grand building into an active and respected secular cultural centre. In addition to temporary exhibitions, there are also popular concerts, including organ recitals in the summer and on Christmas Day and New Year's Day.

Tacked on to the church are several minuscule shops and the fashionable Nieuwe Café. For a more traditional experience, visit De Drie Fleschjes, a 17th-century *proeflokaal* (tasting house), tucked behind the church in Gravenstraat. This kind of watering-hole originally allowed customers to sample *jenever* (Dutch gin), but now serves an extraordinary range of spirits and cocktails.

Map on page 78

Amsterdam's coat of arms adorns the wall of the Begijnhof.

LEFT AND BELOW: the grand interior of the Nieuwe Kerk.

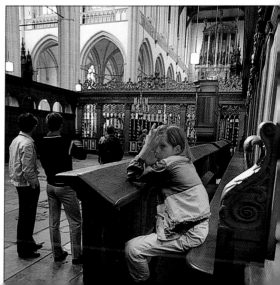

The Dutch version of London's famous Madame Tussaud's waxworks is very popular – be prepared to queue at weekends.

RIGHT: the Nationaal Monument commemorates the 1945 liberation.

Back across the Dam from the Nieuwe Kerk, you might well see queues formed outside **Madame Tussaud's** (tel: 552 1010; open July–Aug daily 9.30am–8.30pm; Sept–June daily 10am–6.30pm; entrance fee), an attraction that is looked down upon by many locals but is popular with visitors, both Dutch and foreign. This Dutch outpost of the famous London waxworks naturally focuses on local characters, so you'll find van Gogh, Rembrandt, Queen Beatrix, Mata Hari and many more, often portrayed in an "action" pose. International personalities from history, politics, stage, screen, sport and more are also featured.

Dam Square east

You need to cross over the tram lines to the east side of the square for a close-up look at the **Nationaal Monument ❹**. This obelisk, 22 m (72 ft) high, was erected after World War II to commemorate the nation's liberation from Nazi occupation. Embedded in the monument's base are 12 urns containing earth from the then 11 Dutch provinces (Flevoland, the 12th, was added in 1986 after being reclaimed from the waters of the IJsselmeer) and from Indonesia.

On this side of the Dam are the city's oldest department store and its oldest hotel – two institutions that are about as famous in their own way as the landmarks on the western side. The venerable **De Bijenkor** store boasts several floors filled with clothing, appliances and household furnishings, and features several fine restaurants and cafés. It is a good place to take a break in between tourist sights and busy Damrak. There are also branches in other Dutch cities such as The Hague, Rotterdam, Maastricht and Utrecht.

The once genteel 19th-century **Grand Hotel Krasnapolsky** – the "Kras" – may be the city's oldest, but for most people it is no longer its grandest. The grande dame of the Dam has seen many illustrious guests pass through her portals: composer Johannes Brahms, author Joseph Conrad, poet Paul Verlaine, numerous celebrities and countless

The Changing Face of the Dam

The Dam has changed a great deal over the years. Two prominent buildings – the old Town Hall and the Waag (Weigh House) – that once stood here and are depicted in many surviving old paintings as familiar elements in the historic townscape, have long since disappeared. The medieval Town Hall, with its squat tower, was a symbol of Amsterdam's municipal independence and a busy administrative centre. It burnt down in 1652, when construction on the new Town Hall (now the Koninklijk Palace) had already begun.

The Weigh House was built in 1565 as the city's first large Renaissance-style building. All goods weighing more than 23 kg (50 lb) had to be recorded here. It suffered an ignoble fate when in 1808 it was demolished at the order of King Louis Napoleon who, having made his palace in the new Town Hall, found that the building obstructed his royal view. Only the weather-vane and a wooden statue survived, and are on display in the Amsterdam Historical Museum.

The Dam continued to provide a busy focus for the city well into the 19th century, and countless paintings and engravings show how it looked at various times.

heads of state. It has come a long way from its early days as a modest yet colourful café, when it was said that "a traveller had not seen Amsterdam if he had not been to the Krasnapolsky". Opened in 1866 by Polish immigrant Adolph Wilhelm Krasnapolsky, the New Polish Coffee House quickly became popular – not only because of its selection of German beers, but for its good-value meals, high ceilings, reading table and billiards tables. Prior to the 1883 World Fair in the city, Krasnapolsky added a new building with 80 guest rooms. Today, the hotel, owned by the Spanish NH Hotels chain, has 468 rooms and still boasts the Winter Garden, known for its excellent breakfast and luncheon buffet, but otherwise lacks personality.

Damstraat, at the side of the Krasnapolsky, is a rather dingy street leading east into the Red Light District, while narrow Warmoesstraat runs north to the Oude Kerk *(see page 105)*. Just off Damstraat is narrow Pijlsteeg, where the restored **Wijnand distillery** can be visted *(see page 228)*.

Damrak

Walking north from the Dam along **Damrak**, you get a close-up look at what has become a tacky, downmarket – but nonetheless lively – street, awash with souvenir shops, amusement arcades, exchange bureaux, smoky cafés and cheap fast-food restaurants, and with fleets of canal tour boats moored in what's left of a waterway that once reached to the Dam.

This humdrum modern cityscape is interrupted by the presence of the monumental **Beurs van Berlage ❺** (Berlage Stock Exchange; 1 Beursplein; tel: 624 0141; open Tues–Sun 11am–5pm; entrance fee), formerly the Amsterdam Stock Exchange. Immediately catching the eye, this remarkable Dutch modernist building is now a cultural centre. One of the few large building projects undertaken in the last half of the 19th century, it was constructed between 1896 and 1903 from the designs of one of Holland's most famous architects, Hendrick Petrus Berlage. For many years the Beurs was considered the most important

Map on page 78

The Winter Garden at Grand Hotel Krasnapolsky offers faded gentility among potted palms.

BELOW: pavement cafés are everywhere.

TIP

At 62 Damrak is Allert de Lange, one of Amsterdam's finest bookshops. It was set up in the 1930s by a Jewish publisher to offer works of exiled German authors such as Bertholt Brecht.

BELOW: At the height of 'tulipomania' (see page 24), traders would gather in the arcaded courtyard of the old Exchange Building to speculate on the next harvest.

Dutch architectural *fin de siècle* monument. The stockbrokers have since moved away and these days the building is administered by a foundation, which puts on exhibitions on a variety of themes, concerts, cultural events, conferences and dinners.

Since 1988, the Beurs van Berlage has functioned as the permanent home of the Netherlands Philharmonic Orchestra (the "Ned-Pho") and the Netherlands Chamber Orchestra, and has one large concert hall and one small hall made of glass. Within its cavernous and echoing interior is an impressive mix of pastel-coloured decorative brickwork, wooden flooring, stone pillars, narrow arcades, Romanesque and neo-Renaissance motifs, and steel roof girders from which hang long pendular globe-shaped lights. Around the periphery of the hall, small wooden cubicles, where deals were made and fortunes won (and lost), are a reminder of the building's original function as an exchange. The new Stock Exchange, the Effectenbeurs, is a modern building in Beursstraat, along the edge of tree-shaded Beursplein, just next to the Berlage Exchange.

The origins of an Amsterdam stock exchange can be traced to informal dealings in neighbouring Warmoesstraat. These were given a formal home in the Exchange Building, built between 1608 and 1611 on Rokin at the Dam, and demolished in 1838. The Dutch have always been a nation of gamblers, and in the 17th century, when they would lay a wager on anything from the sex of a baby to the profits of a tulip harvest, much of this speculation centred on the Beurs. Joost van den Vondel, the great Dutch poet, railed against the Exchange as a "bringer of misery; sunlight never penetrates thy building." There was also an exchange building on the site of the present one, as can be seen on Bathasar Floriszoon's 1625 map – or bird's-eye view – of the city, in which a long-since demolished Coren Beurs (Corn Exchange) is tucked into the northern corner.

North of the Beurs, the tawdry nature of Damrak culminates in the

Sexmuseum Amsterdam (open daily 10am–11.30pm; entrance fee; under 16s not admitted), at No. 18. It's not quite the Temple of Venus suggested by the *faux*-marble columns and pediment at the entrance, but it does have some interesting and amusing exhibits, several of them veritable antiques, cataloguing people's fascination with the mysteries of the flesh.

Centraal Station

Centraal Station ❻ is many people's first point of contact with Amsterdam. Its construction at the end of the 19th century brought controversy, as the large structure blocked off the view over the harbour, seeming to sever the city from the sea that was its lifeblood and forcing it look inwards for its identity. However, the elegant red-brick neo-Renaissance building is hardly an eyesore. Designed in the so-called "national" style by Petrus Josephus Hubertus (better known as P.J.H.) Cuypers, who designed the similar-looking Rijksmuseum, it was built upon 26,000 wooden piles

on an artificial island in the IJ, the city's old inner harbour, and is adorned with monumental sculptures. The station gives little evidence of its watery origins until you cross over Prins Hendrikkade towards Damrak. Only then are you aware of the redundant stretch of water (if you exclude the tour boats and water taxis) that was once the western terminal of the Dutch empire, its quaysides and warehouses chock-full with goods on their way from the East Indies to Germany and the Baltic.

For people arriving by train, an encounter with Amsterdam begins among the organ-grinders, street musicians, jugglers, harried commuters, weary backpackers, never-weary pickpockets, tram stops, taxis and bicycles that daily crowd Stationsplein, in front of Centraal Station (*for Amsterdam's waterfront, which is centred on the rear of Centraal Station, see page 177*). This may be a disconcerting beginning, yet it's an appropriate one, in keeping with the city's voracious appetite for novelty, trade and travel.

Map on page 78

'Sex through the ages'. Delve back in time at the Sex Museum.

BELOW: Centraal Station and the tourist information office.

Let someone else plan your day for you at the central tourist office on Stationsplein.

BELOW: street performers welcome new arrivals at Stationsplein.

Stationsplein is nonetheless an untidy introduction to the historic heart of Amsterdam. Keep a tight grip on your luggage and other belongings at all times.

A good reason to come this way even if you're not arriving by train is to visit the **VVV Amsterdam tourist office** in Stationsplein *(see also page 234)*. This is just opposite the main entrance to the station, at the east side of the waterfront building that houses the **Smits Koffiehuis**, also known as the Noord-Zuid Hollands Koffiehuis, an ornate wooden café from 1911 with a terrace overlooking the water. The VVV shares this space with the city's public transport company, the Gemeentevervoerbedrijf Amsterdam (GVB), which has its Tickets & Info office here. There's another VVV office inside the station, on platform 1.

Just across from Stationsplein, to the east (left) as you emerge from the station, it is difficult to miss the imposing towers of the **Sint-Nicolaaskerk ❼**, the city's main Catholic church, on Prins Hendrikkade. St Nicholas is the patron saint of sailors, and the proximity of this church to the harbour easily explains the dedication. Built in 1887 in neo-baroque style, and extensively renovated in 1998, the church has an interior that's notable for a striking mix of black marble pillars and wooden barrel vaulting.

From here it's a short stroll to 85 Prins Hendrikkade, **Batavia Huis**, which for a time in the 17th century housed the offices of the Vereenigde Oostindische Compagnie (United East India Company), and has a facade adorned with terracotta heads of Indonesian women and elephants. Batavia, the Dutch name for present-day Jakarta, was the main Dutch colonial settlement in the East Indies.

The New Side

The area west of Damrak and Rokin is known as the Nieuwe Zijde (New Side), in distinction to the Oude Zijde (Old Side) to the east. **Nieuwendijk**, a snaking, pedestrianised shopping street one block west of Damrak, has a distinctly downmarket feel. The denim here is

more faded than in Kalverstraat (its southern continuation), the fast food is faster and sex has crept into the shopscape.

In the north, just beyond the point where Nieuwendijk crosses Nieuwezijds Voorburgwal, at 4–6 Kattengat, are a pair of attractive, crooked 17th-century gabled houses. Dating from 1614, they bear the fetching names of **De Gouden Spiegel** (The Golden Mirror) and **De Silveren Spiegel** (The Silver Mirror). During World War II Jewish families hid in their attics, and they are now occupied by the fine, if pricey, French/Dutch De Silveren Spiegel restaurant (*see page 93*).

A few doors along is the prominent baroque dome of the **Ronde Lutherse Koepelkerk ❽** (Round Domed Lutheran Church). Built between 1668 and 1671, the church was extensively restored in the early 19th century after a fire. Now deconsecrated and after another fire in 1993, it was restored again and serves as a conference centre operated by the adjacent Renaissance Amsterdam Hotel. It's not open to casual visitors – buttoned-down conference-goers are another story – but the handsome exterior alone is worth perusal.

Historical Museum

From the Dam you have a number of options. A good one is to go south for a short way on Kalverstraat, a busy commercial shopping street. On Saturdays in any month of the year this pedestrian-only street is impossibly crowded. Escape from the endless stream of shoppers and window-shoppers by turning in through a lopsided gateway adorned with the triple-cross arms of Amsterdam to a quiet courtyard. Beyond is the city's best history lesson, at the superb **Amsterdams Historisch Museum ❾** (Amsterdam Historical Museum, 92 Kalverstraat, 357 Nieuwezijds Voorburgwal, 27 Sint-Luciënsteeg; tel: 523 1822; open Mon–Fri 10am–5pm, Sat–Sun 11am–5pm; entrance fee), occupying 17th-century buildings that were once home to the Civic Orphanage – note the figures of chubby children dressed in black and red

Map on page 78

TIP

It's easier to find your way around Amsterdam if you remember the following suffixes:
-straat = street
-weg = road
-laan = avenue
-steeg = alley
-gracht = canal (refers to both the water and the street alongside)
-kade = waterside
-ijk = waterside dyke
-plein = square
-markt = market or a market square
(see also margin note on page 89)

BELOW: Amsterdam Historical Museum.

Gable stones surviving from the Golden Age are a feature of the Historical Museum.

BELOW: girls at the Civic Orphanage, which prior to 1960 occupied the buildings now used by the Historical Museum.

uniforms. Founded in 1578 on the site of St Lucy's, a former Franciscan convent, the orphanage was a tribute to Amsterdam's enlightened city government. The orphanage board had a seat on the city council because "the rich need the poor for the quiet of their souls."

Its orphanage days ended in 1960, and in 1975 the Historisch Museum relocated here from the Waag (Weigh House) in Nieuwmarkt (the museum was originally founded in 1926). In 1999, the exhibition space was expanded and updated, with many hands-on exhibits added focusing on life in Amsterdam, past and present. The renovation created a visitor-friendly environment, with informative captions written in both Dutch and English, and an efficient routing plan that gives a clear chronological and thematic insight into the city's rich history, making subsequent walks around town more informative and enjoyable. At the beginning of the route, one of the best displays is an illuminated plan of Amsterdam that shows clearly how the city

grew. Starting in the year 1050, a light picks out particular periods down through the centuries and simultaneously illuminates the relevant phase of the city's growth.

The museum affords an excellent overview of Amsterdam's history from the early 13th century to the present, but given that the richest archives have come from the 17th and 18th centuries, the collection naturally concentrates on those periods and includes Rembrandt's painting *The Anatomy Lesson of Dr Deyman*. It is particularly strong on the era of Dutch maritime exploration. A selection of paintings depicts all of the city's landmarks as they appeared in their contemporary cityscapes. It's possible to get a good picture of life in the city during its 17th-century Golden Age, at the turn of the 20th century, in the postwar years, and from other fascinating tableaux of times past. Numerous paintings trace the city's development, including two by Van Gogh dating from the brief time he spent in Amsterdam visiting fellow painter George Hendrik Breitner, who chronicled life in his beloved city until his death in 1927. Breitner's evocative paintings of Amsterdam are also on display, as are his palette and easel, and a half-completed painting of Rokin. Breitner's early work of ordinary moments in Dutch life has been described as "Amsterdam Impressionism" – though it has none of the colour of the French Impressionists, it excels in the emotional impact of Expressionism. Breitner (who was also a pioneer in photography) would later be considered a modernist, paving the way for Mondrian.

In the newest section, where the displays bring the history of Amsterdam up to date, paintings and photographs reveal the reasons why the city developed progressive welfare programmes from the mid-

19th century and how it coped with the problems of unemployment during the Great Depression of the 1930s. The presentation of Dutch anti-democratic movements deals frankly with the existence of Dutch fascist sympathisers and with the Jewish deportations during the German occupation.

The permanent exhibits are supplemented by temporary displays used to illustrate themes as diverse as personal collections of Amsterdam residents, the relationship between the Netherlands and Japan, fashion, Peter the Great's relationship with Amsterdam, and the diamond industry.

Be sure to leave time for a visit to the museum's **David & Goliath Café**, graced by giant wooden sculptures of those two worthies rescued from a fairground, and toast the original residents, the Sisters of St Lucy.

A covered passageway, the **Schuttersgalerij** (Civic Guards Gallery), leading from the Historical Museum to the neighbouring Begijnhof, is a modest history lesson in itself, and an unexpected art gallery as well. Hung along the walls is a series of oversized 16th- and 17th-century canvases depicting group portraits of the Amsterdam civic guard, posing in attitudes of grandiose self-importance.

The civic guard originated at the end of the 14th century, when Amsterdam marksmen began joining together for civic defence and to help maintain public order. They founded three guilds: St George's for the crossbowmen; St Sebastian's for the archers; and the Guild of Harquebusiers, armed with early firearms. Each had its own meeting place, with rooms for social and business gatherings and a shooting range in the garden. Around 1530, the civic guard companies began to commission group portraits to hang in their guildhouses. Their annual banquets were favourite occasions for such paintings. These portraits grew larger and livelier over the years, culminating in the enormous canvases of the 17th century and Rembrandt's masterpiece, *The Night Watch*, painted in 1642.

The guilds were merged in 1580 with other groups of militiamen drafted from Amsterdam's 11 municipal districts. In 1672, the old guilds were dissolved and the civic guard was reorganised. After 1650, no more group portraits were commissioned. Of all those painted in Amsterdam, some 50 have been preserved, forming the largest collection of paintings in this genre in existence.

The Begijnhof

Next door to the museum is the tranquil **Begijnhof** ❿ (access from Gedempte Begijnensloot; open daily during daylight hours; free), a magnificent diamond-shaped cobblestone courtyard of 17th-century buildings and among the most picturesque places you can visit in Amsterdam's centre. The freshly

Map on page 78

TIP

Amsterdam's side streets often take the name of the adjacent main street, with an added *dwars* to denote their "crossing" status. For example, Leidsedwarsstraat runs across the main Leidsestraat.

BELOW: a quiet spot at a brown café.

Stained glass in the chancel of the Begijn-hof's English Reformed Church – part of a sequence commemorating the Pilgrim Fathers' passage to America.

BELOW: the leafy courtyard at Begijnhof.

painted houses with their bright windowboxes, the cast-iron lampposts and an unexpected air of solitude and tranquillity make it difficult to believe the city's busiest shopping street, Kalverstraat, is just a minute away from this spiritual haven.

There are many *hofjes* (little courtyards) in Amsterdam, but the Begijnhof is the finest, the best-known and the easiest to reach. It was founded in 1346 as a cloister-like home for Catholic lay sisters – *beguines* – who chose to lead a partial form of convent life, including taking the vow of chastity and service to the community. The last *beguine* died in 1971, but the almshouse continues as a residential sanctuary, its quaint dwellings occupied by unmarried retired ladies "of good repute", who appreciate having their peaceful garden treated respectfully by visitors. In the 15th century, this religious quarter was literally an island, and although the once polluted Begijnensloot moats were filled in 1865, the Begijnhof remains a place apart from the rest of the city.

Most of the gabled houses date from the 17th century and are built of stone and brick. One of the last two wooden houses remaining in Amsterdam, **Het Houten Huys** (The Wooden House), dating from around 1470 (making it the oldest surviving dwelling in Amsterdam), has been moved to within the Begijnhof walls (the other is at 1 Zeedijk). These were erected before fire regulations prohibited such flammable building materials.

In 1578, with the Reformation sweeping through Holland, all the Catholic churches in Amsterdam became Protestant, including the beguines' own small, late-Gothic chapel standing within the Begijn-hof, and now known as the English Reformed Church – though it was originally granted to Scottish Presbyterian refugees in the city. It now hosts intimate concerts. This is not the only church here; the courtyard is also home to the concealed Begijnhof Catholic Church, which took over as the beguines' "secret" – it was an open secret – church. The dark, Italianate interior still smells

of candles and prayer books, and contains paintings and memorabilia relating to the Miracle of Amsterdam *(see page 20)*.

Amsterdammers are fondest of the Begijnhof in spring, when the lawn becomes a carpet of daffodils and crocuses. No. 26, one of the grandest houses, was the home of Sister Antoine, the last beguine, and has been preserved exactly as she left it.

Spui Square

You can also gain access to, and egress from, the Begijnhof at Spui. Directly across from the Begijnhof is the late-18th-century **Maagdenhuis**, formerly an orphanage for Catholic girls and now housing part of the University of Amsterdam. The irregularly shaped **Spui "Square" ⑪**, part of the University Quarter, is lively and home to several fine cafés. Café Hoppe, at No. 18, is one of the city's most celebrated brown cafés, frequented by artists and writers, and with a slightly louche atmosphere in tone with the nicotine-stained walls.

Opposite is Café Zwart (334 Spuistraat), outside which bankers and men in suits stand with their beers in warm weather. For elegance and great people-watching, stop by Café Luxembourg (22–24 Spui). To escape the crowds, there is Stoep (415 Singel).

On Fridays, an antiquarian book market in the square offers a good selection of English-language books at reasonable prices; and on Sundays from March to September, art marketeers set out their stalls. Just opposite is the Athenaeum, a book store and news centre that has a range of books, newspapers and magazines in English. Outside, in the square, is *'t Lieverdje (The Little Darling),* a bronze sculpture of a boy standing with hands on hips and grinning broadly at passers-by.

Leading off the south side of Spui, Voetboogstraat's houses have examples of just about every gable style possible: pointed, step, neck, bell and moulded *(for more on gables, see page 130).* This narrow alley runs into Heiligeweg, where at No. 19, you'll see the Rasphuis-

Map on page 78

LEFT: Het Houten Huys dates from around 1470.
BELOW: the *Little Darling* sculpture on Spui Square.

The "Mint Tower" is one of the city's many spires designed by Hendrick de Keyser.

BELOW: tulips at the Bloemenmarkt.

poortje (Grating-House Gate). This used to be the entrance to a prison, and got its name from the fact that the prisoners earned their keep, such as it was, by grating wood. A carved relief above the gate depicts a woman chastising two delinquents. Underneath is another relief telling the no-doubt highly symbolic, if slightly mystifying, tale of a pig, a lion, a fox and a puma cringing under the whip as they pull a cart laden with tree trunks.

Refined 16th-century traces remain in the unusual gable stones of the houses lining the canal end of the street. Note the traditional cigar-and-pipe shop **P.G.C. Hajenius**, at Nos. 92–96, whose humidors are world famous.

Rokin

When Amsterdam was beginning to come of age, the stretch of the Amstel which stood behind the Dam was named the **Rokin**. From here, barges departed with goods along the river to other towns in Holland. The commercial hub of the city in the 18th and 19th centuries, Rokin is today a busy thoroughfare between the Dam and Muntplein that has seen better days.

Across the water from the southern end of Rokin, past the canal boat dock, is the **Allard Pierson Museum** ⓬ (127 Oude Turfmarkt; tel: 525 2556; open Tues–Fri 10am– 5pm, Sat–Sun 1–5pm; entrance fee). This museum contains the not-very-extensive archaeological collection of the University of Amsterdam. Finds from Egypt, the Near East, Iran, Greece, Etruria and the Roman empire make for an academic but nevertheless interesting display of life in the ancient world occupying two floors. The changing exhibitions are often of greater interest, since they generally feature items from other international collections.

A short walk from here, busy **Muntplein** marks the junction of Rokin and Vijzelstraat, and the spot where the Singel canal comes to an end. The **Munttoren** ⓭ (Mint Tower) in the square was built in 1490 and is all that remains of the Regulierspoort gate in the since demolished city walls. For a short time in 1672 money was minted in the adjoining building, hence the tower's name. In 1620, Hendrick de Keyser added the ornate, lead-covered steeple. The tower's carillon bells ring out in concert on Friday from noon–1pm.

This area is always crowded. One of its premier attractions is the **Bloemenmarkt** ⓮ (Flower Market), which floats – kind of – on barges permanently moored in Singel. There has been a flower market here since at least the 17th century. Heaps of flowers change hands as fast as they can be wrapped. It's open from Monday to Saturday from 9am until 6pm, and locals shop here as well as tourists, since it's one of the best and most atmospheric places in town to buy cut flowers and bulbs. ❑

50 TULPEN 15.00

RESTAURANTS & CAFES

Restaurants

Dutch

De Silveren Spiegel
4–6 Kattengat
Tel: 624 6589
Open: D daily. €€€
You won't find a more typically Old Dutch-looking place than this, set in a pair of higgledy-piggledy houses dating from 1614. The menu is an updated interpretation of Dutch cuisine, with French added for respectability. The quality of service and cuisine is high, as are the prices.

D'Vijff Vlieghen
294–302 Spuistraat
Tel: 530 4060
Open: D daily. €€€
The "Five Flies" rambles through five old gabled houses and seven dining rooms, each with a different slant on Old Dutch style, complete with beams, tiles, candles and original Rembrandt etchings. The emphasis is on "New Dutch" cuisine in this pricey, picturesque setting.

Haesje Claes
273–275 Spuistraat
Tel: 624 9998
Open: L, D daily. €€
You don't get more down-home than this old-fashioned – and inevitably somewhat touristy – restaurant. It fully merits the description *gezellig* (meaning comfortable, cosy and welcoming). The traditional Dutch dishes and the steaks are pretty good, and the menu takes in some more adventurous options.

Dutch / International

Al's Plaice
10 Nieuwendijk
Tel: 427 4192
Open: L, D Wed–Sun; D Mon. €
If you want some good, straightforward British-style fish and chips, kidney pies, pickled onions and pickled eggs, this is the place to go. Eat in or take away.

Brasserie De Poort
Hotel Die Port van Cleve, 176–180 Nieuwezijds Voorburgwal
Tel: 622 0240
Open: B, Br, L, D daily. €€
Hotel restaurants are often soulless. Not this one, in an old beer hall decorated with Delft blue tiles across from the Royal Palace. Diners pile in to sample its trademark steaks and Dutch and international dishes.

Café Luxembourg
22–24 Spuistraat
Tel: 620 6264
Open: B, Br, L, D daily. €–€€
Brasserie-style Luxembourg is less pretentious and more friendly than many of the city's "grand cafés". Serves soups, sandwiches, snacks and other dishes.

Excelsior
Hôtel de l'Europe, 2–8 Nieuwe Doelenstraat
Tel: 531 1705
Open: B, L, D Mon–Fri; B, D Sat–Sun. €€€€
A swish gastronomic experience, in an elegant chandeliered salon with big windows overlooking the Amstel. Respectable dress (a jacket and tie for men) is a requirement. The menu is Dutch and Continental.

Indonesian

Kantjil en de Tijger
291–293 Spuistraat
Tel: 620 0994
Open: D daily. €€
Most Indonesian restaurants wear their ethnic colours on their sleeve, but Kantjil is cool and modern. The decor, tables and setting are spare yet convivial. The food could be described as Indonesian nouvelle cuisine, though the portions served are generous.

"World"

The Supper Club
21 Jonge Roelensteeg
Tel: 344 6400
Open: D Mon–Sat, L Sun. €€€
A unique, trendy world cuisine establishment. Instead of dining at tables, you recline on extravagant mattresses and no evening is ever the same. Reserve weeks in advance for weekends.

French

Vermeer
NH Barbizon Palace Hotel, 59–72 Prins Hendrikkade
Tel: 556 4885
Open: L, D Mon–Fri; Sat D. €€€€
Close to the top end of Amsterdam's dining scale, Vermeer's French focus is modified by some Dutch and Continental offerings. Housed in a pair of 17th-century buildings, it has good looks and good food.

Cafés

1e Klas
Platform. 2b, Centraal Station
Tel: 625 0130
Open: B, Br, L, D daily. €–€€
Pronounced Eerste (Airstuh) Klas, this is the old first-class waiting room transformed into a smart café-bistro. Soups and sandwiches, or three-course meals.

Hoppe
18–20 Spui
Tel: 420 4420
Open: 11am–1am;
11am–3am Fri–Sat. €–€€
This friendly brown café dates from 1670 and is a favourite with locals.

PRICE CATEGORIES

Prices are for a three-course meal for one, with wine and coffee
€ = under €20
€€ = €20–40
€€€ = €40–60
€€€€ = over €60

NIEUWMARKT AND THE RED LIGHT DISTRICT

From books to brewing, nuns to prostitutes, east to west, Nieuwmarkt is like a microcosm of the entire city, a living museum of all Amsterdam

Sex and drugs, noise and neon, antiques and old books, tastes of China and Thailand, one of Amsterdam's largest medieval buildings, the once brave face of 1970s redevelopment, photogenic Staalstraat and the seedy alleys off Zeedijk – this part of old Amsterdam to the east of the Dam is nothing if not varied.

Nieuwmarkt (New Market), the market square after which the area is named, is, strangely enough, an old marketplace squeezed into the space between the Kloveniersburgwal and Geldersekade canals. But walk for just a few minutes in any direction and you'll see that Nieuwmarkt is much more than this. Head northwest for the Red Light District, whose world-famous legalised prostitution is as active and lucrative as ever. Make your way down Oudezijds Achterburgwal and you are in one of Amsterdam's centres of learning, full of books, boffins and bicycles. Go southeast for Sint-Antoniesbreestraat, a redeveloped street that leads to the city's old Jewish Quarter. Stroll northeast to the tree-lined canals of tongue-twisting Kromboomsloot and Rechtboomsloot and you will find a tranquil neighbourhood that seems a long way from the busy city centre.

Nieuwmarkt

The wide square at **Nieuwmarkt** ⓯ was once a fish market, supplied with herring by boats that tied up at the southern end of Geldersekade. On the west side of the square, a small group of stalls keep the market tradition alive. Among them are a fishmonger, a cheese seller, a florist and a poultry and game seller. At weekends there is an antiques, book and curios market. Some of the characters that hang out around here are curios all by themselves.

Map on page 78

LEFT: in the heart of the Red Light District.
BELOW: De Waag and Nieuwmarkt Square.

The Lovers' Statue, which stands in the square at Nieuwmarkt, marks the fringes of Amsterdam's infamous Red Light District.

BELOW: a typical Chinatown restaurant.

The neighbourhood around Nieuwmarkt suffered with the construction in the 1970s of Amsterdam's Metro system, which runs from Centraal Station out into the southeastern suburbs. In protest against the large number of houses that were slated for demolition, squatters and others who didn't care to ride Metro trains moved in. But the hard-hitting Dutch riot police did their civic duty and cleared a path for the bulldozers. In the Nieuwmarkt Metro station, these stormy events are recalled in depictions of the demolition work and the wider history of the area. Today, the square and its surroundings, full of trendy bars, restaurants and clubs, have a new vibrancy and streetwise cachet that represent a big change from the not-too-distant past when this was a virtual drugs ghetto.

The bulky form of the medieval **Waag** (Weigh House), which sits in the middle of the square, has experienced its own share of redevelopment. The Waag started life as a turreted gateway, the Sint-Antoniespoort (St Anthony's Gate),

built in 1488 as part of Amsterdam's defensive walls. By the end of the 16th century, the city was expanding rapidly and the gate was redundant, so it was rebuilt around 1617 as a weigh house for checking the weight of ships' anchors and ordnance. Later on it functioned as a guild house for the civic guards, the stonemasons and the surgeons.

The octagonal tower at the centre wasn't added until around 1690; it served as the dissecting room *(theatrum anatomicum)* where the Surgeons' Guild gave lessons in anatomy. The guild commissioned Rembrandt's famous painting *The Anatomy Lesson of Dr Nicolaas Tulp* (now in the Mauritshuis in The Hague) and other pictures on similar subjects. In modern times the Waag has housed the Amsterdam Historical Museum, and later the Jewish Historical Museum, before both moved out to roomier premises. It is now home to the restaurant **In de Waag**, where diners enjoy good food illuminated by candlelight. The pavement terrace is very popular in summer *(see page 109)*.

Amsterdam's Chinatown

Standing in Nieuwmarkt and looking south, you cannot miss the Chinese supermarket that stretches across an entire building front. Inside is an emporium of oriental goods, ranging from exotic groceries to cooking implements and Chinese medicines. To the west and northwest of the square and leading up Geldersekade you'll notice Chinese apothecaries, acupuncturists and restaurants. During the annual Chinatown festival there are demonstrations of ancient crafts, music and dance, and a Chinese market. The most spectacular event is the Lion Dance Championships; the colours and movements of the costumes are every bit as dazzling as the music.

Towards the Jewish Quarter

Many of the 1970s buildings on **Sint-Antoniesbreestraat**, one of the few modern streets of central Amsterdam, which leads southeast from Nieuwmarkt towards the Jodenbuurt (Jewish Quarter; *see page 163*), were designed by well-regarded modern Dutch architects Theo Bos and Aldo van Eyck, and have earned prizes for architectural excellence – along with grouses from residents that they're just about uninhabitable.

This area, too, has seen city planners do battle with conservationists. Plans to develop the street controversially placed the much-prized 17th-century **De Pinto Huis ⑯** at No. 69 under threat of demolition. Isaac de Pinto, a Portuguese Jew who fled first to Antwerp and then to Holland to escape the Inquisition's clutches, was one of Amsterdam's wealthiest merchants. He bought this building in 1651. Subsequent alterations nearly 30 years later added elaborate painted panels and ceilings, and an ornate Italian Renaissance-style exterior, with decorative scrollwork around the windows.

Public opinion against the initial redevelopment won the day. The house was saved and is now a branch of the public library (open Mon–Wed 2–8pm, Fri 2–5pm, Sat 11am–2pm; free). Fittingly, the De Pinto House repays its debt to posterity by being home to a special section dealing with the protection of ancient monuments and city-centre restoration.

Sint-Antoniesbreestraat, however, is but a shadow of its former colourful self. Even so, among the modern buildings you can still see several original gables, and there is even a Jewish bakery. Although this is still known as a blue-collar district, many new residents include an alternative crowd, who often congregate at temples of style like **Café Tisfris** at No. 142, and **Café Dantzig** at the Muziektheater on nearby Waterlooplein. Beside the street is a statue of a turtle, representing Time and its loss for the Jewish community.

Just a few steps from the De Pinto House is an often windswept bridge, **Sint-Antoniessluis**, beside a picturesque lock-keeper's house and a

 Map on page 78

ORIENTATION
The area covered in this chapter extends east from Dam Square, Damrak and Rokin to Oude Schans, and from D'Leeuwenburg Huis in the north to the Amstel in the south.

BELOW: Chinatown is full of small and unusual shops.

TIP

At No. 59 Kloveniersburgwal, Café De Engelbewaarder plays host to the literati with readings and jazz, while at No. 86 the Perdu Foundation stages poetry and prose readings among other literary activities – interesting addresses for the dedicated bookworm. A further cultural recommendation: try to attend one of the excellent organ recitals at the Oude Kerk.

BELOW: looking north along Oude Schans from the old lock-keeper's house. The Montelsbaanstoren is in the distance.

cluster of gabled houses. From here you have a clear view north along Oude Schans all the way to the Montelbaanstoren and the NEMO science museum (*see page 182*). Sint-Antoniessluis was once a marketplace with a healthy proportion of street traders from the flourishing Jewish community east of Oude Schans and south of Jodenbreestraat.

From the lower end of Sint-Antoniesbreestraat, Zandstraat leads to the **Zuiderkerk** ⑰ (Southern Church; open Mon–Wed and Fri noon–5pm; Thurs noon–8pm; free), the first purpose-built Calvinist church in Amsterdam. Designed by architect Hendrick de Keyser – who lies buried within, along with three of Rembrandt's children – the rectangular, basilica-type, triple-nave church was begun in 1603 and completed in 1614, as the date inscription above the tower clock points out. It is reached via a gateway surmounted by a skull and crossbones in what used to be the church's graveyard. You can climb the Zuiderkerk's graceful tower

(Jun–Sept Wed–Sat 2–4pm; free) for great views over the surrounding *nieuwbouw* (new buildings), and the Nieuwmarkt area and Jewish Quarter in general. No longer consecrated, the church is now a "centre for urban renewal", and an exhibition space for the city's invariably inventive architects; the current focus is on the new residential districts along the waterfront. A permanent exhibition shows how the city has expanded over the centuries.

Kloveniersburgwal

This stately, picturesque canal south of Nieuwmarkt features five notable buildings from the city's Golden Age, and many more that are only a smidgen less notable. At 10–12 Koestraat, just off Kloveniersburgwal, the **Wijnkopersgildehuis** (Wine Merchants' Guildhouse) is actually three 17th-century buildings converted into one residence. Across the street, note the carvings of Faith, Hope and Charity on the facades of Nos. 7–11. Koestraat and neighbouring Bethaniënstraat run

anno 1695

de Sluyswacht

through the grounds of a former convent, the Bethaniënklooster. Centuries ago the nuns had water delivered by boat and hand-pumped into the convent for washing and brewing; probably more brewing than washing. Beer, however weak, was a safer option than drinking water in those days.

Today, at 6–8 Kloveniersburgwal, within the grounds of the former convent, is Amsterdam's smallest brewery, **Brouwhuis Maximiliaan** *(see also page 109)*. Apart from the guided tours (tel: 624 2778; upon request; closed Mon; entrance fee, includes one beer), a visit to the brewery allows you the chance to consume some of their finished product in the brewing hall, where you can admire a fresco outlining the brewing process and view the last surviving part of the Bethaniënklooster.

A few doors along, at No. 12, **Jacob Hooy & Co.** has been in business since 1743 selling medicinal and culinary herbs, each one stored in a small wooden barrel or a drawer with the contents labelled

with an enamel plate. Bulbous sweet jars contain a vast selection of all kinds of liquorice, sweet or salty, honey- or lavender-flavoured.

A more substantial landmark, at No. 29 on the eastern side of Kloveniersburgwal, is the grand **Trippenhuis** ⑱, designed in 1660 by architect Justus Vingboons for the brothers Louis and Hendrick Trip, who owned iron and copper mines and cannon foundries in Sweden. The Trips were powerful members of the "Magnificat", the clique of wealthy families that ran the city during the Golden Age. In acknowledgement of the owners' gunnery business, the chimneys on the roof were made to resemble mortars, and military insignia pepper the facade. Even though the Trippenhuis has a single facade, this once concealed two separate dwellings, one for each of the Trip brothers. The effect to the outside world was of a single household, but two main doorways at street level provided separate access. The house was converted into one unit in 1815–17 to accommodate the forerunner to the

The soaring spire of Zuiderkerk, said to have inspired Sir Christopher Wren, contrasts with contemporary Sint-Antoniesbreestraat.

BELOW: the Brouwhuis Maximiliaan.

TIP

When walking these streets pay attention to your valuables, and be extra careful in – or avoid entirely – deserted side alleys, particularly at night.

Rijksmuseum. These days it is used by the Academy of Science.

On the other side of the canal, at No. 26, is the **Klein Trippenhuis** (Small Trippenhuis), also known as the "House of Mr Trip's Coachman". The story that the coachman said he would be content with a home no wider than the front door of the Trippenhuis is probably apocryphal. Another version says the house was built with stone left over from the construction of the main building. In any event, at just 2.5 metres (8¼ ft) across, the Klein Trippenhuis is modesty itself.

If you go a little further south along Kloveniersburgwal and turn right into Oude Hoogstraat, you enter the courtyard of the **Oost Indisch Huis** ⑲ (East Indies House). The imposing red-brick building dates from the 16th century and was rented by the Vereenigde Oostindische Compagnie (United East India Company) in 1603 for its headquarters. It frequently received deliveries of precious commodities, such as spices, coffee, ebony and mahogany. Today it is used by the

BELOW: Oost Indisch Huis (East Indies House) on Oude Hoogstraat.

University of Amsterdam, and you can enter via a courtyard for a snoop around. On the same street, **Boekhandel Kok** is a large antiquarian bookshop spread over two floors, selling a wide selection of old prints and maps.

University Quarter

At the southern end of Kloveniersburgwal, turn left into **Staalstraat**. A photogenic view of the Zuiderkerk is to be had from the bridge that links the two sides of this street across Groenburgwal. Staalstraat itself is one of Amsterdam's many picturesque "film-set" streets, in olde worlde contrast to the modern architecture that looms into view at the Zwanenburgwal end. A smart Thai restaurant, a cosy bookshop and a chic coffee shop make Staalstraat even more attractive. The linen trade once flourished here, and at No. 7b sergeworkers met in the 17th-century **Saaihal** (Serge Hall). The stained-glass windows decorated with laboratory motifs here date from the 19th century, when the Saaihal was occupied by the

chemical laboratory of the Athenaeum Illustre, a forerunner to the University of Amsterdam.

From here you can sidestep a short way along Nieuwe Doelenstraat, to the modern "grand café" **De Jaren** *(see also page 109)*, set in a retired bank premises, and compete for seats at two of the finest outdoor terraces in town, beside the waters of the Binnen Amstel.

Back on Kloveniersburgwal, a covered passageway leads off to the left onto Oudezijds Achterburgwal. This is **Oudemanhuispoort** ⓴ (Old Men's Home Gate), an arcade lined with stalls selling secondhand and antiquarian books – some of them in English. You'll find some stalls open every day except Sunday, from 10.30am to 6pm, but Saturday is the busiest day. On the gablestone is a pair of spectacles – a symbol of old age. Halfway along is a courtyard of late 18th-century buildings, originally used as almshouses for accommodating elderly men (almshouses had hitherto been exclusively for women).

The **University of Amsterdam** has occupied these buildings since 1877, the year in which the institution was founded, and the surrounding streets form the main hub of the city's university life. On weekdays there is always a tangle of bicycles, left by students attending lectures, attached to the railings along Grimburgwal, the narrow lane which cuts across the southern end of Oudezijds Voorburgwal and Oudezijds Achterburgwal. In the midst of this handsome area of houses and offices in old gabled canal-side buildings is the photogenic but somewhat overrestored, red-brick **Huis aan de Drie Grachten** (House on the Three Canals). Built in 1609, it takes its name from its scenic location at the junction of Oudezijds Achterburgwal, Oudezijds Voorburgwal and Grimburgwal. Today it is a bookshop specialising in art and literature.

There are more university buildings around Grimburgwal, behind a former hospital, the Binnengasthuis (converted to private houses), with a small white tower bearing the date 1875 and a relief above the entrance depicting two sick men, and around Gasthuisstraat and Vendelstraat.

The university has its roots in the Athenaeum Illustre, founded in 1632 in the **Agnietenkapel** ㉑ (Agnieten Chapel) at 231 Oudezijds Voorburgwal. Originally a chapel attached to the Convent of St Agnes, dating from 1470, today it houses the notably underwhelming Historical Collection of the University of Amsterdam. The Athenaeum originally existed to prepare students for higher schooling elsewhere but, ever since the Napoleonic-era French occupation of the Netherlands, it has provided full tertiary education.

On the far bank of Oudezijds Voorburgwal stands a complex that includes a former meat market, municipal bank and pawnshop, and the **Bank van Lening** (Lending

Map on page 78

Oudemanhuispoort is not all students and musty hardbacks: postcards fly off the shelves too, thanks to the steady trickle of tourists who pass through this quarter.

BELOW: searching for secondhand books.

Dutch bakers were stuffing bread with beef and butter long before the Earl of Sandwich gave his name to the world's favourite snack food. For a taste of the real thing, ask for belegde broodjes.

BELOW: 17th-century view of the university district.

Bank). The oldest part of the building is in adjacent Enge Lombardsteeg and served as a peat store for the residents of neighbouring houses. The pawnshop was built in 1614, and the long facade that extends to Oudezijds Voorburgwal in 1669. The entrance to the Bank van Lening bears the hallmarks of the ubiquitous master-architect, Hendrick de Keyser.

The names of the two main canals here, Voorburgwal and Achterburgwal ("before" and "behind" the city wall), refer to the city's early defensive walls that once ran through this area. The "Oudezijds" that precedes them refers to the Oude Zijde (Old Side) of the city, also known as "Mokum", the Yiddish word for "place". The vanished walls give the district another of its several names, "De Wallen" (The Walls), or, as is often used to refer to the Red Light District section alone, "De Walletjes" (The Little Walls). This southern tip of Oudezijds Voorburgwal was dubbed the "Velvet Canal", in reference to the wealthy merchants who came to live in this neighbourhood.

Heading back north on the east bank of Oudezijds Voorburgwal takes you past a former **Stadhuis** (Town Hall), at No. 197. In the 16th century, a Catholic monastery was established on this spot, but after the city's 1578 Protestant Alteratie, it was taken over by the Admiralty, and later became the Prinsenhof, a royal inn for housing assorted blue bloods, among them Prince William of Orange and the Earl of Leicester. When, in 1808, King Louis Bonaparte claimed for his palace the "new" Town Hall on the Dam, which is now the Koninklijk Paleis *(see page 79)*, the city's aldermen upped sticks and decamped to this location, something they had done once before, in 1652, while the then new Town Hall was under construction and after the old Town Hall burned to the ground. In 1927, the entire building was renovated and extended so that all that remained of the original structure was the pillared façade, believed to be the work of architect Daniël Stalpaert.

Since 1992 the building has housed The Grand Sofitel Demeure,

one of Amsterdam's swankiest hotels. Its smart **Café Roux**, a popular meeting spot for the city's movers and shakers, in what was once the Town Hall cafeteria, sports a Karel Appel mural, *Inquisitive Children* (1949). The city's administrators found it so repulsive they demanded it be covered up. Today, this work by the Cobra artist – restored to the light of day – is a place of pilgrimage for lovers of modern art. And in the meantime, the municipal authorities moved once again, in 1986, to the *new* new Stadhuis on Waterlooplein *(see page 165)*.

Red Light District

At the southern end of Oudezijds Achterburgwal everybody is busy pursuing academic knowledge – or at any rate giving a good impression thereof. But follow this canal north a little way, past Oude Doelenstraat and Oude Hoogstraat, and the pursuit of carnal knowledge becomes the name of the game.

Amsterdam's celebrated **Rosse Buurt** (Red Light District) is concentrated in Oudezijds Achterburgwal but also occupies parts of Oudezijds Voorburgwal and the alleys connecting and branching off from them. There are sex shops, porn shops, live sex (or "life sex", as it's sometimes named), performances involving bananas, video porn and video cabins everywhere, specialised appliance shops and bookshops filled with illustrated works by experts in diverse areas of human relationships. A museum offering "erotic art and specialities" is another way of delivering the same lubricious product.

All of these venues are lit pink, purple, magenta, violet – and the canals themselves are occasionally hung with a canopy of red fairy lights reflected in the dark water below. Prostitutes in lacy underwear tempt from within their neon-lit glass-fronted cubicles. Some of the girls stand smiling and give a sharp beckoning tap on the window if you stop for just a second. Others look shell-shocked, expressionless, and stultified – often as a result of indiscreet groups of tourists ogling at

Map on page 78

TIP

While ogling the prostitutes is acceptable, within limits – such is the decidedly un-PC nature of the trade – if you linger too long, you may receive a graphic indicator that it's time to move on. The strongest prohibition, though, is on taking pictures – try that openly and you could wind up in the nearest canal.

LEFT AND BELOW: images of the Red Light District.

The Bulldog is where it all began – though it's now the haunt of toking tourists rather than cannabis connoisseurs.

BELOW: gay kitsch in the Red Light District.

them like some fairground attraction.

Lots of visitors tour this zone out of curiosity or just for fun. You don't need to worry overmuch about crime as long as you stick to the busier streets. If you're up for a closer experience of the district's often suffocating atmosphere, stroll down the short Trompetersteeg into Sint-Annendwarsstraat, off Oude-zijds Voorburgwal close to the Oude Kerk. You have literally to squeeze past the women in the doorways of this constricted alley, affording them an ideal opportunity for a form of in-your-face marketing.

Although this part of the Oude Zijds has been blighted by the sex industry, the district's dilapidated condition should not blind you entirely to the wealth of architectural treasures hidden behind uninviting facades. And you should note that many ordinary people live here, and go about their everyday business seemingly unaware of the sleazy activity going on all around them. There are even some great second-hand and antiquarian bookshops.

With so much to catch your eye on these streets you could be excused for missing a couple of incongruities. Above the main entrance to the **Erotic Museum** at 54 Oudezijds Achterburgwal (open Sun–Thurs 11am–1am, Fri–Sat 11am–2am; entrance fee), is a historic stone decorated with maritime motifs; it proclaims boldly *God is myn burgh* (God is my stronghold). The museum itself includes a bunch of 19th-century photographs showing Victorians being far from prim and proper. In Oudezijds Voorburgwal, on the other side of the canal to the Oude Kerk, is the Amsterdam Chinese Church, situated right next to a coffee shop with a brightly lit sex cinema below. A figure of Christ peers through the window on one side, a scantily clad prostitute touts for business on the other.

The **Hash Marihuana Hemp Museum** (130 Oudezijds Achter-burgwal; open daily 11am–10pm; entrance fee) is an educational experience on the many and varied uses of the hemp plant, not all of which involve drawing its smoke down into your lungs, though you are

given the lowdown on the high too.

In this district, perhaps more than elsewhere in the city, the smell of marijuana is accompanied by the sure knowledge that harder drugs are there for the asking.

The Old Church

Going north along Oudezijds Voorburgwal, you come to another incongruous sight. Set like an island of virtue in a sea of iniquity, the venerable **Oude Kerk** ㉒ (Old Church; Oudekerksplein; tel: 625 8284; open Mon–Sat 11am–5pm; Sun 1–5pm; entrance fee), is all but surrounded by red-fringed prostitutes' parlours and sex clubs. Aptly named, this is the city's oldest church, begun in 1200 when it was the original, wooden church of Amstelledame's fishing community, though the present late-Gothic, triple-nave structure dates back to a rebuilding begun around 1300. Pilgrims flocked here to celebrate the Miracle of the Host *(see page 20)*.

Before the city's 1578 "Alteration", the changeover from a Catholic to a Protestant city council during which the Oude Kerk also became Protestant, many stained-glass windows and paintings were destroyed by Protestant iconoclasts. Yet enough treasures remain to make this the best-preserved of Amsterdam's churches – beautiful works of art survive on the wooden roof vaults, including pictures of ships, reminding us that the church is dedicated to St Nicholas, patron saint of sailors. The Great Organ, built by Christian Vater in 1724–26 and substantially rebuilt by Caspar Müller in 1738, is mounted on a square-columned marble base that spans the west door. It was played by the composer Jan Pieterszoon Sweelinck (1562–1621) and is still used in excellent organ recitals, often given by music students from the city's Sweelinck Conservatorium.

Inside this often cold church, the dusty carved medieval misericords, heavy grey flagstones, half-erased family crests and faded murals give the interior a forsaken feel. This contrasts with many other Dutch churches, which tend to be over-

Map on page 78

Amsterdammers have transformed smoking a 'fat one' into a civilised pastime, thanks in no small part to the spread of unassuming 'coffee shops'.

BELOW: Dutch houses turned into fridge magnets.

After Calvinist fathers stripped the Oude Kerk of its original dedication to St Nicholas, it became a refuge for travellers, tramps and pedlars, who would set up stall along the aisles.

BELOW: Geel's & Co. tea and coffee merchants.

restored and clinical. There is much to admire, from the ornate organ to the wooden vaulted ceiling and cherubic statues. The gravestone of Rembrandt's wife Saskia van Uylenburgh is also here. Some stained-glass windows, a kaleidoscope of reds, blues and purples depicting scenes from the life of the Virgin, date from 1555. A good time to appreciate these is when low-angle sunlight shines through the coloured glass. The church hosts exhibitions, organ recitals and performances featuring soloists and ensembles, and author's readings.

Its graceful tower, the **Oudekerkstoren** (open June–Sept, Wed–Sun 2–4pm; Sept–Apr Sun–Fri 1–5pm, Sat 11–5pm; entrance fee), was completed in 1565. In the summer you can climb to the top for panoramic views across the city. On Saturdays, listen out for the beautiful 17th-century carillon of Hemony bells, which is played in concert from 4–5pm.

Opposite the Oude Kerk, at No. 57 Oudezijds Voorburgwal, is **D'Leeuwenburg Huis**, a fine step-gabled house from 1605 by Hendrick de Keyser, with a basement projecting out onto the street and an accolade arch. The gable portrays the arms of Riga, which points to trade relations with this Baltic port.

Behind the Oude Kerk is cramped, dingy **Warmoesstraat**. In the 17th century, this narrow street was the centre of the fabric and furnishing trades. Its shops stocked Nuremberg porcelain, Lyons silk and Spanish taffeta, as well as Delftware and Haarlem linen. Fallen on harder times, the narrowest shopping street in town now relies on cafés and restaurants. Yet a smattering of traditional trades retains a presence here. For instance, **Geel's & Co.** at No. 67 is a long-established coffee and tea merchants, which offers more than 25 varieties of coffee and 150 varieties of tea. Its owner is a mine of local information, and there's a small but fascinating **Coffee and Tea Museum** on the premises.

Despite the presence of such pockets of respectability, Warmoesstraat glows, if not red hot, at least a

warmish pink, befitting its status as a kind of suburb of the Red Light District. At the Condomerie Het Gulden Vlies (Golden Fleece), a post-Aids boom means that the shop sells nothing but condoms – from run-of-the-mill to novelty ware – with sales assistance from helpful staff.

Hidden church

Evidence that the Red Light District is not merely a den of vice but a neighbourhood of contrasts can be found in the **Museum Amstelkring** ㉓ (40 Oudezijds Voorburgwal; tel: 624 6604; open Mon–Sat 10am– 5pm; Sun 1–5pm; entrance fee), one of Amsterdam's most rewarding, yet least visited, museums. A 17th-century house, originally named Het Hart (The Heart) after its Catholic merchant owner, Jan Hartman, conceals the church of Ons' Lieve Heer Op Solder (Our Lord in the Attic), the finest of the city's – indeed the country's – surviving clandestine churches. Don't let the sombre "Museum" sign outside deter you from investigating. The Museum Amstelkring is, appropriately, one of Amsterdam's best-kept secrets and offers many surprises, from the cellar all the way up to attic.

From the time of the 1578 Alteration, Catholics were compelled to hold their religious gatherings secretly, in domestic rooms, attics or barns *(see page 21)*. After the middle of the 17th century, Catholic worshippers began to build clandestine churches, which in time were enlarged and heightened by the addition of galleries resting on pillars. There used to be scores of such churches in Amsterdam. Wealthy merchants like Jacob van Loon and Aernout van der Mye, who in 1662 were immortalised in Rembrandt's painting *De Staalmeesters (The Syndics)*, were among the owners of these houses of worship hidden behind plain domestic exteriors.

In 1661 a certain Jan Hartman started building a residence in Oudezijds Voorburgwal, together with two adjoining houses in Heintje Hoekssteeg. He furnished the combined attics of these three houses as a church. The lower part of the house gives an accurate glimpse of its domestic past. Over the years Hartman's buildings underwent various alterations but the **Sael** (living room) is still preserved in all its 17th-century sobriety and beauty, and the combined coat of arms of Jan Hartman and his wife stands proudly above the imposing fireplace.

The church under the eaves was separate from the house proper, with an entrance in the side alley, and for more than two centuries was a parish church. In the beginning, when it was smaller, the officiating priest lived in a tiny room on the landing of the house. Around 1740 the church was enlarged and a new altar was built, while the priest moved into the house itself. Apart from the pretty Maria chapel, decorated with fresh flowers and

Map on page 78

BELOW: the Museum Amstelkring is one of the city's most interesting sights.

Map
on page
78

A road sign in China-town forbids access to bicycles – a rare thing in Amsterdam, where the majority of commuters roll to and from work on two wheels.

BELOW: wall frieze at Fo Guang Shan He Hua Temple.

18th-century paintings, the charm lies in odd details, like the revolving mahogany pulpit, ready to be hidden at a moment's notice. The clandestine situation continued until 1795, when the occupying French authorities restored Catholics' right to worship openly, and worship here continued until the Sint-Nicolaaskerk, near Centraal Station, was completed *(see page 86).*

It is difficult to imagine how the services here managed to remain clandestine. With 60 seats spreading back from the altar and additional seats in a further two storeys of galleries above, several hundred worshippers would have been squeezed into the creaky-floored space. Neither does the church organ compromise on size. A full congregation belting out the Lord's praises would have been about as discreet as a claustrophobic bull locked in a barn. The truth is the existence of these churches was often an open secret, though they had to be unobtrusive enough for the city authorities to be able to turn a blind eye.

Since 1888, the house has functioned as a museum. Fine statuary, ecclesiastical paintings, silver chalices and other sacred vessels and ornaments, a Roman Catholic liturgical collection and 17th- and 18th-century furniture make this church all the more worth visiting.

Zeedijk and Chinatown

The northern edge of Nieuwmarkt, around Zeedijk and Geldersekade, is the heart of Chinatown. **Zeedijk** itself traces the line of a sea dyke that once protected Amsterdam from the sea. This curving street, originally lined with tough sailors' bars, and later the haunt of pimps, pushers and addicts, has cleaned up its act and undergone a transformation. It now has a string of shops and restaurants representing not only China *(see box on page 96)* but other cultures too.

The new Buddhist **Fo Guang Shan He Hua Temple** ㉔ is a *trompe l'œil* apparition set in this quintessentially Dutch street (nos. 106–116). It was opened in 2000 by a member of the Dutch royal family, highlighting the beginning of the three-day annual "Chinatown Festival". Nieuwmarkt and De Waag form the epicentre of this extravaganza. During the festival you can expect demonstrations of ancient crafts, music and dance, a Chinese market and culinary delights. The most spectacular event is the Lion Dance Championships, with the blazing colours and movements of the costumes.

At Zeedijk's northern end are two of the city's architectural gems. The 15th-century **Sint-Olofskapel** (St Olaf's Chapel) is now a conference centre belonging to the NH Barbizon Palace Hotel. Across the street, at No. 1, is **'t Aepje** (The Ape), a well-restored gabled house from 1550. This is the second oldest of the city's two surviving wooden houses; the oldest is in the Begijnhof.

RESTAURANTS & CAFES

Restaurants

Continental

In de Waag
4 Nieuwmarkt
Tel: 422 7772
Open: Br, L, D daily. €€
In the atmospheric setting of the old city gate that later was used as a weigh house, diners tuck into good Continental food, illuminated by candlelight. The outdoor terrace is very popular in summer.

French

Brouwhuis Maximiliaan
6–8 Kloveniersburgwal
Tel: 626-6280
Open: daily 11am–2am. €€
You can do guided tours of this wood-floored, brown-café-style small independent brewery – one of just two in the city – housed in a former convent off Nieuwmarkt, and sample one or more of the ten different kinds of beer produced here, along with French-style dishes in the attached rustic restaurant.

Chinese

Golden Chopsticks
1 Oude Doelenstraat
Tel: 620 7040
Open: L, D daily. €
This hole-in-the-wall in the Red Light District offers delectable Chinese fare like steamed oysters in a black-bean sauce, Peking duck, and whole fish with vegetables and tofu. If you prefer a more upmarket ambience, go upstairs to the Oriental City restaurant. Both attract a loyal crowd of Chinese customers.

Nam Kee
111–113 Zeedijk
Tel: 624 3470
Open: L, D daily. €–€€
Chinese restaurants don't come much plainer than this one just off Nieuwmarkt, where the decor is so minimalist as to be non-existent. Nor do they come better, and there are often queues for a table. The food is authentic and the service is authentically rushed.

Japanese

Morita-Ya
18 Zeedijk
Tel: 638 0756
Open D Thurs–Tues. €€
A reasonably priced Japanese restaurant with good, simple fare, on the edge of the Red Light District. The sushi is excellent, or order the razor-thin beef, which you cook at your table. Try to get the sole table with a canal view.

Cafés

Café Roux
Grand Sofitel Demeure,
197 Oudezijds Voorburgwal
Tel: 555 3560
Open: L, D daily. €€–€€€
This superior brasserie-style eatery at the upscale Grand Hotel sports a modern, art deco-inspired interior (along with a 1949 mural by Cobra artist Karel Appel that was covered up for affronting the workers when it was the Town Hall staff restaurant), and a French slant to its cultured cuisine.

De Engelbewaarder
59 Kloveniersburgwal
Tel: 625 3772
Open: 11am–2am daily. €
This smoky, friendly place is essentially a brown café but it does sell some snacks, including highly regarded *frietjes* (french fries) with homemade mayonnaise.

De Jaren
20–22 Nieuwe Doelenstraat
Tel: 625 5771
Open: Br, L, D daily. €–€€
Spacious grand café in a former bank with a wonderful view over the Amstel from two waterside terraces – much in demand. A mixed clientele of students and prosperous locals dining on continental snacks and meals is convivial but not too crowded.

PRICE CATEGORIES

Prices are for a three-course meal for one, with wine and coffee
€ = under €20
€€ = €20–40
€€€ = €40–60
€€€€ = over €60

RIGHT: In de Waag restaurant.

CANAL CIRCLE NORTH AND THE JORDAAN

The concentric Grachtengordel (canal belt) of Amsterdam is the most distinctive feature of the city; along the banks of these canals are some of the most important historical and architectural landmarks

Amsterdam's horseshoe-shaped network of concentric canals is instantly recognisable. The long semicircle of three parallel canals – called the *Grachtengordel* (canal belt) – was part of an ambitious piece of town planning that reflected the city's wealth and aspirations. These three canals are probably among the first place names in Amsterdam that visitors learn. Moving outwards, they are: **Herengracht** (Gentlemen's Canal), **Keizersgracht** (Emperors' Canal) and **Prinsengracht** (Princes' Canal). West of Prinsengracht on the northern stretch of the canal is the Jordaan, a lively neighbourhood replete with second-hand shops, ethnic restaurants, boutiques and bookshops *(see below)*.

By 1600 the medieval town that had grown up around the Dam was spilling out beyond its tight boundary along the River Amstel and the Singel canal. In 1609 city planners decided to dig three canals beyond Singel that would enclose the existing nucleus and provide accommodation for a wealthier and expanding population.

Hendrick de Keyser was appointed city architect and by 1613 execution of the plan was under way. The first phase of digging took the new canals from near the port down to the bottom of the horse-

shoe, as far as Leidsegracht. The second phase began in 1665 and the canals were extended to the Amstel. Parks were built on the opposite bank of the Amstel (the Plantage) and the entire project was finally completed at the end of the 17th century. As grand houses sprang up along the canals, the merchant class gradually moved from the insalubrious Oude Zijde to the relative opulence of these new waterways. It was a mark of distinction to build a house on the new canals.

Map on page 112

LEFT: quintessential Amsterdam.
BELOW: maintaining the artisan tradition in the Jordaan.

ORIENTATION
This chapter is divided into two parts. The Canal Circle North section covers the area bounded by Haarlemmer Houttuinen in the north and Raadhuisstraat in the south, and by Prinsengracht in the west and the Singel canal in the east. The Jordaan section runs from Brouwersgracht (north) to Leidsegracht (south), and from Lijnbaansgracht (west) to Prinsengracht (east).

BELOW: cycling along Brouwersgracht.

The authorities imposed strict regulations to preserve the tone of the new neighbourhoods. They prohibited barrel-making because of the noise, brewing because of the smell, and sugar-refining because of the fire hazard. But trade was not excluded altogether. The houses were also used as warehouses, with storage space in attics and basements.

Walking along the three canals it is possible to notice significant differences in style. The innermost canal, Herengracht, was the most sought-after, with the most elegant and expensive mansions, followed in exclusiveness and cachet by Keizersgracht, the most approachable and varied waterway. Prinsengracht, the humblest of the three, has a greater number of converted warehouses.

Each of the three canals is about 3 km (2 miles) long, so it may not be an attractive proposition to walk the entire length of each one. Since the waterways are not far apart and are linked by side streets, it's easy to meander and switch between them.

The **Singel**, dug and developed earlier than the three Grachtengordel waterways, and lined with former warehouses and workshops, is not strictly one of them, but it may be considered so by proximity and association. This marks the boundary between the old city centre and the canal belt covered in this and the following two chapters.

In the summer, the Grachtengordel canals seem to form one long, leafy suburb, and you can pause to admire the view from a conveniently placed bench, a bridge, or a waterside café terrace. As you stroll along, be sure to look out for some of the delightful ornamentation: wood-panelled doors, wrought-iron grilles, cast-iron stair rails, carved gable stones, and houseboats moored to the banks.

The northern section of the canal belt covered in this chapter is the least visited by tourists. Yet the area

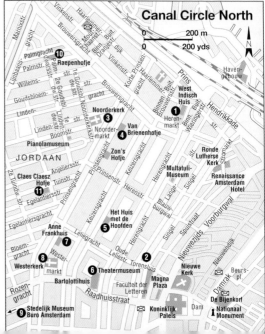

bounded by Brouwersgracht to the north and Raadhuisstraat to the south is both manageable and worthwhile.

Canal houses

From **Brouwersgracht** (Brewers' Canal) – where the handsome old brewery *pakhuizen* (warehouses) have been converted to chic apartments – you can enjoy picturesque vistas down each of the canals. The outlook is clearest in winter, when the trees bordering the waterways have been stripped of their leaves, allowing uninterrupted views to the point where the waterways bend.

These canals were made possible by the wealth of the new Dutch empire, and before setting out to walk along them, you can visit a centre of that empire. Backing on to Herenmarkt, a neat little square off Brouwersgracht, the **West Indisch Huis** ❶ (West Indies House) was constructed in 1617. It was rented to the Dutch West India Company from 1623 and became the headquarters of all western operations. When the naval hero Admiral Piet Hein captured a Spanish silver fleet

off Cuba in 1628, a prodigious booty of silver was stored here. Further north, in 1625, New York (then Nieuw Amsterdam), was born when a fort was built on the tip of Manhattan Island. A statue of Nieuw Amsterdam's governor Peter Stuyvesant, a restaurant named after Hein, and the offices of the US-Dutch John Adams Instituut are reminders of this past history.

Returning to the Grachtengordel, most of the canal-house facades date from the 17th and 18th centuries. Buildings of significant historical and aesthetic value – a definition that could have encompassed just about all of them – are classed as *Stadsmonumenten* (City Monuments), and their upkeep is the responsibility of a variety of institutions, which between them spend millions of euros annually on repair and restoration.

In the 17th century, taxes were levied on property owners according to the width of their house frontage – the maximum permissible width was 10 metres (33 ft) but the depth could extend to 60 metres (195 ft). As a result, many houses

Map on page 112

West Indisch Huis, 17th-century HQ of the Dutch West Indies Company. The empire's greatest riches may have come from the East Indies (Indonesia), but the Dutch also had interests in the Americas and the Caribbean.

LEFT: canal tour.

The Rondvaart (Round Trip)

Having arrived in the "Venice of Northern Europe", it would be bordering on the unforgivable not to go on a boat trip around the canals. There are several companies to choose from and the majority are located opposite Centraal Station, with a few opposite the old Heineken Brewery. After paying for your ticket you may buy a drink or snack to take on board. There is usually a photographer to take your picture as you step aboard; you can buy a print at the end of the trip.

Standing next to the skipper there will be a guide who will point out and explain the many features and buildings which seem more apparent from the water. Sitting in a *rondvaart* boat gives you a perspective rarely encountered – just above the water looking up at centuries of history unfolding before you. All the guides speak English and are happy to answer any questions. You can expect to see the narrowest house, the "Skinny Bridge" and the "Seven Sisters" bridge, among many other sights. The trip usually lasts about an hour. For wealthier tourists there are water taxis, and for true romantics there are candlelit dinner cruises – relevant information is available at any of the ticket kiosks or the tourist office.

Cheap clothes – new and secondhand – are easy to find at Amsterdam's many outdoor markets.

were built narrow but deep, "end-on" to the canals. The original owner of No. 7 Singel must have been determined to pay as little tax as possible, as he built the narrowest house front in Amsterdam, just 1 metre (3 ft) wide, and then allowed his property to bulge out to a more normal width behind.

On the opposite side of the canal is another curious household, the "cat boat", which provides board and lodging for "orphaned" cats. A short way south along Singel, the first bridge, the **Torensluis** ❷, housed a 17th-century prison in the stonework of the bridge itself. The unfortunate souls incarcerated here would frequently have found themselves up to their waists in foul water as the level of the canal changed with the incoming tides.

At the north end of Herengracht is **Het Huis met de Pilastergevel** (House with the Pilaster Gable) at Nos. 70–72. This house dates from 1642 and, unsurprisingly, has a gable ornamented with pilasters – slightly protruding flat stone columns.

BELOW: picturesque Prinsengracht.

Markets and almshouses

On Monday morning and Saturday afternoon, the square at **Noordermarkt**, a short way south on Prinsengracht, hosts a flea market and farmers' market respectively. The atmosphere here is more laid-back Jordaan than upmarket chic. From the flea market you can pick up everything from fabric and sewing items to books, toys, tools and ethnic snacks. The farmers' market sells organic produce, natural breads, whole-food grains and other health-oriented products; and there's a flea market section on this day, too, with secondhand clothes, vinyl records, books and ethnic jewellery. It attracts a lively crowd of shoppers, street musicians and tourists. On market days, a queue will doubtless have formed outside the neighbouring **Winkel Café**, famed for its luscious *appelgebak met slagroom* (homemade apple pie served warm with whipped cream).

In Noordermarkt stands the **Noorderkerk** ❸ (Northern Church; open erratically; free), Hendrick de Keyser's last great church, con-

structed between 1620 and 1623 in the shape of a Greek cross with its exterior angles filled in by the later addition of small houses. It is open for religious services and occasional concerts, and underwent an extensive renovation paid for by public donations that was completed in 1999. Still a functioning church with a congregation – something of a rarity in this nominally Calvinist city – the building is notable for its subdued interior.

On the exterior is a memorial to 400 local Jews deported in reprisal for the killing of a Dutch Nazi during a street battle. Another memorial, a stark sculpture on the square, is in keeping with the Jordaan's radical past. This statue of chained figures is a monument to the 1934 Jordaanoproer (Jordaan Uproar), unemployment riots during the Depression years. Jordaaners commemorate the uprising every year with poems, posters and floral tributes.

Noordermarkt is set amid the measured, bourgeois calm of Prinsengracht. The elegant clusters of typical facades range from grey to ice-cream pink. Guessing the meaning of the many illustrated gable stones provides an interesting game: Jesus and the loaves and fishes gives way to the Three Wise Men, two turtle doves, and finally to St Paul blowing a trumpet. Some gables overlooking Noordermarkt feature agricultural images – cows, chickens and the like – that recall the square's historical role as a market. Note the large hook placed just below the gable on each building. Purely functional, these serve for transporting furniture and other household goods by rope into and out of the house. Many front doors are painted a dark "Amsterdam green" – a colour chosen long ago (though not mandatory) for its compatibility with the colour of the canal water.

On the other side of Prinsengracht are two *hofjes* (courtyards surrounded by almshouses) that are worth a closer look. Stemming from the early Dutch republic's belief in the virtue of personal charity, such almshouses nowadays represent the institutionalised form, but manage to

Map on page 112

One of the six busts of Roman gods on the House with the Heads.

BELOW: catching up with the news.

retain a tangible spirituality. The **Van Brienenhofje ④** at Nos. 89–133 is an impressive cluster of restored almshouses overlooking a wide, peaceful courtyard. Wealthy merchant Jan van Brienen, who is said to have locked himself inside his own safe and been rescued from suffocating just in time, showed his gratitude by founding these almshouses for the poor. In the middle of the courtyard is an old water pump. The *hofje* is also known as De Star, named after a brewery foundation that ran the place for a time.

A little further along, at Nos. 159–71, is **Zon's Hofje**, reached via a passageway between two houses. The pacifist Frisian Mennonite community in Amsterdam bought a building here called De Kleine Zon (The Little Sun) in 1720. It was used as a church and renamed De Arke Noach (Noah's Ark). In 1765 the church was converted into almshouses for widows. Try not to disturb the residents if you come here, but do sit quietly on the bench and enjoy a taste of secluded, tranquil living.

If you turn left along Prinsenstraat, passing by its stylish cafés and shops, you come to Keizersgracht. Turn right on the eastern bank until you reach No. 123, **Het Huis met de Hoofden ⑤** (House with the Heads), built by Hendrick de Keyser for a wealthy merchant in 1622. The name refers to the six classical busts ranged on either side of the entrance, depicting the deities Apollo, Ceres, Mars, Athena, Bacchus and Diana.

Also at No. 123 are the offices of the main organisation involved with conserving Amsterdam's architectural heritage, the Bureau Monumentenzorg (Office for the Care of Historic Buildings), established in 1953. Amsterdam has some 7,000 officially recognised historic buildings which cannot be modified (or demolished) without a permit.

Theatre Museum

Amsterdam's greatest asset, the magnificent buildings lining Herengracht, Keizersgracht and Prinsengracht, are wonderful to admire from the outside, but most people's natural instinct is to want to stop and look inside. Unfortunately, of course, the vast majority are private and off-limits (if it's any consolation, they are also off-limits to most of the city's residents, commanding prices of millions of euros per storey).

Opportunities to see within are restricted to visiting the handful of museums that help preserve a sense of 17th-century opulence. A good place to start is at the **Theatermuseum ⑥** (tel: 551 3300; open Tues–Fri 11am–5pm; Sat–Sun 1–5pm; entrance fee), occupying two adjacent buildings – **Het Witte Huis** (The White House) at No. 168 Herengracht, which runs into the stately **Bartolottihuis** at Nos. 170–172. The former dates from 1638 and has a grey, neo-classical sandstone facade. It was built for a

certain Michiel Pauw, who in 1630 set up a trading settlement named Pavonia near the Dutch colony at Nieuw Amsterdam (New York). Pauw's house featured the first ever neck gable in the city. Subsequent owners excised some of the ornamental flourishes that emphasised Pauw's sense of his own importance, among them his coat of arms.

It is worth visiting to view the two ground-floor reception rooms. The grand murals and illuminated ceilings were part of an extensive redecoration from 1728 to 1733 in the Louis XIV style. Isaac de Moucheron and Jacob de Wit, two fashionable artists, were commissioned to paint the murals in oils on canvas. De Moucheron handled the landscape and De Wit was responsible for the figures and the ceiling. Other aspects of the dazzling interior include a spiral staircase and complex stuccowork.

The ornate red-brick Bartolottihuis next door dates from 1617, a Renaissance cascade of decoration designed by Hendrick de Keyser for Guglielmo Bartolotti, who made his fortune as a brewer and later in life became a rich and successful banker.

The Theatre Museum's permanent exhibition includes a variety of props, shoes, hats, hand puppets, masks and assorted paraphernalia from its theatrical collection. An adjacent room features period costumes in a range of materials, from heavy damask to featherlight tulle. The formal garden is laid out in baroque and Renaissance styles, and in the summer you can enjoy the "backstage" ambience of a canal house that affords a fine view of the Westerkerk tower.

Anne Frank's refuge

Visiting the **Anne Frankhuis ❼** (Anne Frank House; tel: 556 7100; open Apr–Aug daily 9am–9pm; Sept–Mar daily 9am–7pm; closed Yom Kippur; entrance fee), at 263 Prinsengracht, has become a tourist pilgrimage, something at the top of most visitors' lists. As a symbol of Jewish suffering during World War II, this building certainly deserves a strong measure of respect. But the sheer volume of visitors has its

Map on page 112

TIP

Located in Haarlemmerplein is a popular "art house" cinema called The Movies, with four screens offering a range of films, many in English (tel: 638 6016 for details).

BELOW: canal-side contemplation.

Just as London cockneys are born within earshot of Bow Bells, to be a true Amsterdammer one must be born within the sound of the Westerkerk's bells.

down side. What should be a sobering and contemplative tour of rooms made world-famous by a gifted Jewish adolescent diarist who spent two harsh years in hiding here with her family is, during the peak summer months at least, a crowded and sometimes frustrating procession through constricted passageways. Even so, the 1999 renovation and expansion has improved things to give a better impression of the surroundings and circumstances that shaped Anne's diary. The addition of an adjacent building has given extra space for temporary exhibitions relating to racism and prejudice, and for the Educational Department, a multimedia resource centre, a bookshop and a café.

From 1942 to 1944, the Frank family and some Jewish friends hid in a secret annexe here, sustained by helpers who provided them with food bought on the black market, until police raided the house and discovered their hideout. The refugees were deported, first to the transit camp at Westerbork, and then

to Auschwitz and Bergen-Belsen. Anne died of hunger and disease at Bergen-Belsen.

The rooms in which the Frank family hid are as sombre and bare as on the day their occupants were betrayed and taken to the death camps. Using your imagination and powers of empathy, you can try to put yourself in Anne's situation, awakening as a young woman, and telling her secret thoughts to her diary. Anne's life was extinguished; her spirit lives on.

The earlier you arrive the better; conversely, between April and August, when the museum stays open until 9pm, going late helps avoid the crowds and the queues.

Westerkerk

Passing by – or dropping into on the way – the Caribbean-style café-restaurant **Rum Runners** at No. 277 Prinsengracht, continue into Westermarkt with its bronze sculpture of Anne Frank. In this square stands the **Westerkerk ❽** (West Church; open Apr–June and Sept Mon–Fri 11am–3pm; July–Aug Mon–Sat

BELOW: Anne Frank.
RIGHT: the Frank house in the 1940s.

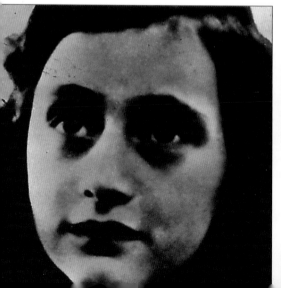

11am–3pm; free), built in 1630, and yet another Amsterdam landmark created by Hendrick de Keyser. Renovated in 1990, it is considered *the* masterpiece of the Dutch Renaissance style, and the city's finest church. Compared with the Oude Kerk *(see page 105)*, its interior is slightly disappointing, but its popularity is secured by the fact that Rembrandt was buried here, though his tomb has never been found (indeed his bones were probably removed to a charnel house 20 years after his interment). Classical music concerts are held on certain days.

The church's soaring tower, the **Westertoren** (open June–Sept Mon–Sat 10am–5pm; entrance fee), is the highest in the city at 85 metres (280 ft), and crowned by a glinting red, blue and gold imperial crown, a reminder of former Habsburg rule. If you are feeling energetic, the view from up here is memorable, stretching to the Rijksmuseum in the south and to the harbour in the north. Anne Frank, who heard and admired them from her Prinsengracht refuge, described the Westertoren's carillon chimes in her diary. Today you can still hear them toll on the hour, and there are occasional outbursts of a popular or classical refrain, depending on the occasion.

At the east side of Westermarkt is the **Homomonument**, a sculpture made up of pink marble triangles – a visual reference to the symbol the Nazis forced homosexuals to wear. The memorial commemorates homosexuals who died in the Nazi camps, or suffered persecution in the past, or do so today.

The canals and streets around Westermarkt are notably chic and occasionally over-restored. Even so, the neighbourhood remains eclectic, with its attractions ranging from the cool elegance of French restaurant **Christophe** at No. 46 Leliegracht to cosy lunch rooms, minimalist architects' studios and secondhand bookshops. If you want a simple snack, there are several stands on Westermarkt selling herring and *patat* (french fries).

The Jordaan

The area stretching west from Prinsengracht to Lijnbaansgracht comprises a tight east–west grid of narrow streets, canals and compact houses, bounded on the north by Brouwersgracht and on the south by Leidsegracht. With its bouquet of canals and streets named after trees, flowers and plants – Palmgracht, Bloemgracht, Rozengracht, Laurierstraat – the **Jordaan** probably takes its name from the French word *jardin* (garden). This French connection has been present since Protestant Huguenot refugees fleeing Catholic persecution in France settled here in 1685.

But the Jordaan's history goes back to the preceding century. At that time, the district lay beyond the city walls and was inhabited by immigrants and the lower classes. There is evidence that much of the land was

Map on page 112

Though Rembrandt's tomb can be found in the Westerkerk, his bones have since disappeared. They were probably destroyed during the construction of an underground car park.

BELOW: view along a frozen Prinsengracht to Westerkerk.

Anne Frank

On Monday 6 July 1942, during the Nazi occupation of Holland in World War II, the young Jewish girl Anne Frank accompanied her family into hiding in the *achterhuis* (rear annexe) of the house at 263 Prinsengracht. Born in Frankfurt in 1929, Anne was not escaping from Nazi persecution for the first time in her life. Her family had already fled their native town in the summer of 1933. Life in Amsterdam brought a respite that lasted just seven years. After the Germans had invaded Holland in 1940, the country was subjected to the same anti-Jewish measures as other occupied nations. In February 1941, the Nazis began their first round-up of Jews in Amsterdam. Though Anne's father Otto had been forced by the Germans to leave his prosperous business, he was able to prepare several rooms on the top floors of his company's office as a secret hiding place. The safety of his family and four other Jews was to hinge on a swinging cupboard concealing the stairs to the back of the building. Another family, Mr and Mrs Van Daan and their son Peter, joined them. In November another refugee, Albert Dussel, became the eighth member of this clandestine household.

Anne's record of life in their secret refuge is remarkable not just as a diary of a Jewish family in hiding; the fascination of her book comes from witnessing the intellectual growth of a young girl blessed with literary talents as she reaches adolescence. The second entry of her diary is as a naive 13-year-old: "I had my birthday on Sunday afternoon. We showed a film *The Lighthouse Keeper* with Rin-Tin-Tin, which my school friends thoroughly enjoyed. We had a lovely time." In July 1944, now 15, she wrote: "It is a great wonder that I have not given up all my expectations because they seem absurd and unfeasible. But I still cling to them, despite everything, because I still believe in the inner goodness of humanity. It's ... impossible for me to base everything on death, suffering and confusion."

Just 20 days later, on 4 August, following a tip-off thought to have been provided by a Dutch informer, the Gestapo discovered the hiding place. All eight were sent to Westerbork, the Dutch staging post to concentration camps further east. On 3 September, the day the Allies liberated Brussels, they were among the last shipment of around 1,000 Jews to leave the Netherlands. Of all the occupants of the "Secret Annexe", Anne's father alone returned after the war. Anne Frank died in Bergen-Belsen concentration camp in March 1945 at the age of 15, only three weeks before the British liberated it.

Anne's diary had been left behind among old books lying on the floor. The most famous quotes come from the final paragraphs of her entry for 15 July. Three months previously she had written: "I want to live on after my death." The house is more than the place in which the diary was penned or a voyeuristic opportunity to see the premises in which she and her co-refugees lived. It is a living monument to all victims of racism, fascism and anti-Semitism during World War II and since. ❏

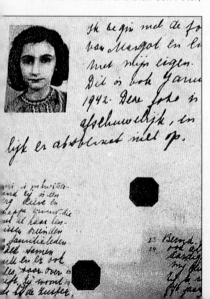

LEFT: excerpt from Anne Frank's diary.

occupied by vegetable growers, who sold their produce at a weekly market. As a mere suburb, the Jordaan was outside the city's jurisdiction and prey to property speculators, resulting in a motley array of architectural styles and standards. Its later development was linked to the construction of the Grachtengordel. While many of the district's workers were employed in digging these canals, architect and city planner Hendrick Staets was creating a self-contained community for artisans.

One famous resident was Rembrandt, forced by poverty to move out here towards the end of his life. In 1656 the artist had been declared insolvent and in 1658, along with his mistress Hendrickje and son Titus, he went to live in Rozengracht. He died nine years later. Another celebrity was Jan van Riebeek, the founder of Cape Town, who lived in Egelantiersgracht from 1649 to 1651.

By the 19th century, the Jordaan housed the main concentration of the city's industrial working class and was known as a hotbed of political activism. Protests and strikes were frequent. At the beginning of the 20th century, it was becoming a slum. One protest provoked Holland's first ever asphalt road programme, when the street cobbles were torn up and thrown at Queen Wilhelmina during an official visit in the 1930s.

In the years after World War II the district was gradually improved and refurbished, before undergoing a major facelift in the 1970s. It began to attract professionals and arty and "alternative" Amsterdammers. With property prices increasing, and rent controls decreasing, a good portion of the local population was forced to relocate to new zones outside the city. However, the Jordaan retains at least some of its former character,

and more than 800 buildings are listed as being of architectural or historical interest, among them a cluster of *hofjes* (courtyards).

The area still retains its shops and artisans, among around a thousand small businesses – bookshops, secondhand shops, trendy boutiques, art galleries, bakeries, brown cafés and bars – that give the neighbourhood a homely feel. Above all, the Jordaan offers an escape from the crowds of tourists that are an inevitable part of Leidseplein and Museumplein. Things can get livelier in the evening. In several cafés, such as **Café Nol** at 2 Westerstraat and **De Twee Zwaantjes** at 14 Prinsengracht, locals join together in singing popular Dutch songs.

Seven of the original 11 canals have been filled in. Rozengracht, for instance, no longer has a waterway; a tram line has taken its place. Bloemgracht, one of the most popular streets, has fared better. With its numerous gabled houses, this became known as the Jordaan's "Gentlemen's Canal" – a comparison

In the 1970s parts of the Jordaan were earmarked for demolition, but thanks to widespread protests, the narrow streets were preserved, complete with period features such as these antique street lamps.

BELOW: one of the area's many boutiques.

TIP

In the bohemian Jordaan, the thing to do is to have lunch at a popular *eetcafé* (café with food) like Café de Tuin at 13 Tweede Tuindwarsstraat, or Café de Prins at 124 Prinsengracht. For dinner, try a simple ethnic restaurant. You can choose from a variety of cuisines, including Spanish, Greek, Italian and Indian.

BELOW: video installation at the Stedelijk Museum Bureau.

with the Grachtengordel's stately Herengracht. The distinctive step gables at Nos. 87–91 belong to a building from 1642 owned by the Vereniging Hendrick de Keyser, a foundation established to preserve the prolific Golden Age architect's surviving works. Egelantiersgracht has also retained its handsome canal. At one end is **Café 't Smalle** *(see page 125)*, the site of a distillery established in the late 18th century by Peter Hoppe. He produced a Dutch gin called Hoppe Jenever that became famous around the country.

Around Rozengracht

Rozengracht, a hectic multi-ethnic street, marks a Jordaan dividing line. The section to the north of here, and more particularly above Westerstraat, is a maze of small alleys, quiet restaurants and thriving workshops, and retains many of its working-class roots. It has many true Jordaaners – traditionally, those who live close enough to the Westertoren to be able to hear the tinkling of its bells – independent-minded students, crafts and trades-

people born and bred in the quarter. The section below Rozengracht is more gentrified, with highly individualistic shops on delightful side streets adjacent to the larger canals, and a variety of renowned brown cafés.

A point of interest for fans of cutting-edge art is the **Stedelijk Museum Bureau Amsterdam** ➒ (open Tues–Sun 11am–5pm; free), at 59 Rozenstraat. This offshoot of the city's modern art museum is where the most promising, and occasionally the most weird, modern art being created in the city gets its 15 minutes – or days – of fame. With the Bureau's parent museum's Museumplein premises closed until mid-2006, and the permanent collection occupying temporary quarters near Centraal Station, there might be some more "mainstream" modern art on display for a while. At 109 Elandsgracht and 38 Looiersgracht are entrances to the vast **De Looier** indoor antiques market (open daily except Friday) that makes for excellent browsing *(see also page 134).*

Specific routes through the Jordaan are unnecessary, since there are no really major sights, and its appealing canals and geometric alleys entice strollers to abandon fixed plans and wander.

Jordaan *hofjes*

The Jordaan has more than its share of concealed *hofjes* (courtyards), including the pretty cobblestoned **Raepenhofje ⑩**, built by Pieter Adriaenszoon Raep in 1648, at 28–38 Palmgracht in the north of the district – note the sculpted turnip on the gable, a pun on the fact that *raep* means "turnip".

Funded by an inheritance from Pieter Janszoon Suyckerhoff, the 15 small houses from 1670 belonging to the **Suyckerhoff Hofje**, at 149–163 Lindengracht, were bequeathed as a refuge for Protestant widows and women of good moral standing and "tranquil character" who had been abandoned by their husbands. The *hofje's* narrow entrance corridor leads to a tranquil courtyard garden filled with flowers and plants.

Off Lindengracht, **Karthuizerplantsoen** is a square that preserves the memory of a now vanished Carthusian monastery. Adjacent **Karthuizersstraat** has a row of neck-gabled houses (Nos. 11–19), dating from 1737 and named for the four seasons: De Lente, De Zomer, De Herfst and De Winter. On the same street, the **Huyszitten-Weduwenhof** almshouse (Nos. 61–191) has a shady courtyard with a garden surrounded by small houses that were once homes for poor widows and are now student quarters.

On the way between Tuinstraat and Egelantiersstraat, a passage on the left leads to the **Claes Claesz Hofje ⑪**, dating from 1616, a cluster of attractive little courtyards surrounded by tiny apartments. In one of the courtyards is a magnificent lion fountain. One of the finest Amsterdam almshouses is the **Andrieshofje**, also dating from 1616, at 107–145 Egelantiersgracht, where a corridor lined with blue and white Delft tiles leads to a flower-bedecked courtyard garden – an "Oasis of Peace" as the sign says. ❏

Near Amsterdam's largest hofje on Karthuizerstraat is one of the city's best examples of a neck-gabled terrace.

BELOW: browse to your heart's content at De Looier antiques market.

RESTAURANTS & CAFES

Restaurants

Dutch

Pancake Bakery
191 Prinsengracht
Tel: 625 1333
Open: L, D daily. €
This cosy 17th-century canal-side converted warehouse is the place to try oversized Dutch pancakes, from a range of around 70 varieties, savoury or sweet, with ingredients from around the globe. It's touristy, for sure, but as many Dutch diners as visitors pile in, and it's especially good for families with children.

Spanjer & Van Twist
60 Leliegracht
Tel: 639 0109
Open: L, D daily. €€
This fine restaurant has raised the simple Dutch concept of an *eetcafé* to something of an art form, without losing the simplicity that gives it life. The menu isn't overly ambitious but the taste is there. A table beside the canal in summer is a most desirable location.

Continental

De Belhamel
60 Brouwersgracht
Tel: 622 1095
Open: D daily. €€–€€€
This romantic and congenial canal-side eatery looks a bit like a brown café from the outside but the art nouveau interior is far more elegant than most such places. You dine on continental cuisine that's mostly carefully considered, if not always professionally served, to a background of classical music.

French/Mediterranean

Christophe
46 Leliegracht
Tel: 625 0807
Open: D Wed–Sat.
€€€–€€€€
Owner-chef Jean-Christophe Royer shows how he earned his Michelin star, with imaginative cooking that merges southern French dishes and ingredients with influences from North Africa. His upscale canalside restaurant's tastefully chic style is appreciated by, among others, local foodies and discerning expense-account visitors.

Bordewijk
7 Noordermarkt
Tel: 624 3899
Open: D Tues–Sun. €€€
The cold, grey-and-black decor at this trendy eatery just off Prinsengracht is almost painfully chic, and you might wonder if you're allowed to enjoy the food or must be content with making a fashion statement. Fortunately, the superb Franco-Mediterranean cuisine saves the day.

Italian

Toscanini
75 Lindengracht
Tel: 623 2813
Open: D Mon–Sat. €€
This Jordaan Italian's reputation seems to rise and fall about as often as the tides on the IJ channel. But through all the ups and downs it continues to turn out good food, with an emphasis on South Italian, in a country-style setting with open kitchen.

Spanish

Duende
62 Lindengracht
Tel: 420 6692
Open: D daily. €
Tapas is the scene at this cool but convivial specialist. The single-euro price classification could easily jump by one step if you do as many do and keep ordering up more dishes.

Seafood

Albatros Seafoodhouse
264 Westerstraat
Tel: 627 9932
Open: D Thurs–Tues. €€€
You can almost smell the sea air at this Jordaan seafood specialist, thanks to a nautical decor and a non-smoking area. The fish is generally plainly cooked to let

its flavour shine through, but you can smother it in sauces if you prefer. In summer there's a sliver of terrace out on the street.

Vegetarian

Bolhoed
60–62 Prinsengracht
Tel: 626 1803
Open: L, D daily. €€
The "Bowler Hat" does its best to make vegetarian dining an enjoyable experience. It succeeds and is rightly popular for its soups, salads and inventive hot meals, and for its friendly service.

Filipino

Banana Rama
91 Westerstraat
Tel: 638 1039
Open: D daily. €€
A South Seas island mural helps you settle into tropical mode at this Jordaan restaurant. The food is Filipino, with an added mixture of South Pacific items, and is served in small portions so that you can mix and match.

Tex-Mex

Rose's Cantina
38 Reguliersdwarsstraat
Tel: 625 9797
Open: D daily. €€
This is a Tex-Mex temple of fun that is almost always busy, bustling and convivial. The food is hardly top-notch, however, and your meal may take a long time to

arrive, but you can while away the waiting time with a jug or two of margaritas.

Thai

Rakang
29–31 Elandsgracht
Tel: 620 9551
Open: D daily. €€
Thai restaurants rarely make it into the rarefied heights of Amsterdam's hot and trendy scene, but this Jordaan example has not only made it and stayed there, but has managed to retain a reputation for great, authentic food while doing so.

"World"

De Luwte
26–28 Leliegracht
Tel: 625 8548
Open: D daily. €€
For world cuisine served in an elegant setting that mixes style elements from around Europe, you can't do better than this. The food is consistently good, the service is friendly, and there's always a buzz of conviviality in the air.

Caribbean

Rum Runners
277 Prinsengracht
Tel: 627 4079
Open: D daily. €–€€
This Caribbean-style café-restaurant between the Anne Frankhuis and the Westerkerk scores by reason of its location, breezy decor – which includes parakeets in

bamboo cages – great cocktails, reggae music in the evening, and adequate Latin American and island food.

Cafés

Café Chris
42 Bloemstraat
Tel: 624 5942
Open: 11am–1 or 2am daily.
Located not far from Westermarkt (and reportedly where the church's builders received their wages), this Jordaan brown café is Amsterdam's oldest, dating from 1624.

Café 't Smalle
12 Egelantiersgracht
Tel: 623 9617
Open: 10am–1 or 2am daily.
Close to the Anne Frankhuis, but across the canal on the edge of the Jordaan, this brown café is housed in a former *jenever* (gin) ware-

house ddating from 1786. The interior can be busy enough but in good weather, the canal-side terrace on a tiny jetty over the water is very popular.

De Prins
124 Prinsengracht
Tel: 624 9382
Open: L, D daily. €–€€
There's no friendlier place in the city than this 18th-century canal-house brown café-cum-restaurant, and the stylish Dutch and Continental cuisine is good value for money.

Papeneiland
2 Prinsengracht
Tel: 624 1989
Open: 11am–1 or 2am daily.
An Amsterdam institution, with thick, low-hung beams, dark walls adorned with etchings and prints, and tables bedecked with tiny Persian rugs.

LEFT: traditional Dutch pancakes.
RIGHT: Papeneiland is an Amsterdam institution.

CANAL CIRCLE CENTRAL AND LEIDSEPLEIN

Perhaps Amsterdam's greatest glory is its canals and the 17th- and 18th-century gabled houses lining the banks. But it is also a city of culture and has an exhaustive variety of nightlife

Visually, the central stretch of the Grachtengordel between Raadhuisstraat and Vijzelstraat is the most rewarding. If you don't want to walk too far or you have limited time, restrict yourself to this area. The picturesque canal-side buildings cost a fortune to rent or buy, so many belong to banks and consulates or serve as the Dutch headquarters of multinational companies. Most of the time you can do little more than admire their ornate but faceless facades, though you should take a walk along the canals at dusk to catch fleeting glimpses of the lit-up interiors through uncurtained windows – few windows in Amsterdam are protected by curtains, and it is socially acceptable to gaze discreetly inside, though not to press your nose up against the glass and stare.

Nine Little Streets

As you make your way south on the initial stretch, from Raadhuisstraat down to Leidsestraat, be sure to dip into and out of some of the **Negen Straatjes** (Nine Little Streets) that connect the canals from Prinsengracht in the west to Singel in the east. Doing so is necessary in any case if you want to cut back and forth between the canals to peruse places of interest, rather than stick-

ing to the course of a single one. Ranged in rows of three from north to south, these nine little streets – tiny, in several cases – are: Reestraat, Hartenstraat and Gasthuismolensteeg; Berenstraat, Wolvenstraat and Oude Spiegelstraat; and Runstraat, Huidenstraat and Wijde Heisteeg. They hold a varied range of exclusive – or merely interesting – small shops specialising in candles, ceramics, leather, toothbrushes, chocolate, cookery books and more.

Map on page 128

LEFT: canal-side cycle lane.
BELOW: the city's canals occasionally freeze over in winter.

ORIENTATION

This chapter covers the area around the three famous canals of Herengracht, Keizersgracht and Prinsengracht bounded by the main roads Raadhuisstraat to the north and Vijzelgracht to the southeast.

Walking south from Raadhuisstraat along Herengracht, you initially pass a jumble of house styles, though there are several fine 18th-century gables on the west side of the canal. A good example is **De Witte Lelie** (The White Lily) at No. 274, which has a Louis XIV-style balustrade rising to a crested peak. Further south, on the stretch between Huidenstraat and Leidsestraat, is the greatest variety of gables, spanning Renaissance and neo-classical styles.

The equivalent section of Keizersgracht has a number of stylish exteriors. At No. 209 a statue of Hope holds a basket of fruit. A short way along, at No. 220, a Syrian Orthodox church breaks up the skyline.

Switching to Prinsengracht, head down to the **Woonbootmuseum ❶** (Houseboat Museum; open Mar–Oct Wed–Sun 11am–5pm; Nov–Dec and Feb Fri–Sun 11am–5pm; entrance fee), moored beside No. 296, at Elandsgracht. The *Hendrika Maria,* built in 1914, is one of the very few houseboats open to the public; step aboard to find out about life on the water in the spacious accommodations of this converted canal barge.

Felix Meritis

Close by on Keizersgracht is **Felix Meritis ❷**, at No. 324, instantly recognisable from its four thick neo-classical pillars. It was built in 1787–88 for the Felix Meritis (Latin for Deservedly Happy) Society, whose aim was to broaden knowledge of the arts and sciences. Haydn and Grieg both conducted music in the building's concert hall. From 1946, this was the headquarters of the Dutch Communist Party. In the 1960s, the Shaffy Theatre Company took rooms here and set up one of Amsterdam's first experimental theatres. The communists later moved out and the Shaffy subsequently took

BELOW: the Felix Meritis building hosts theatre, dance and music performances.

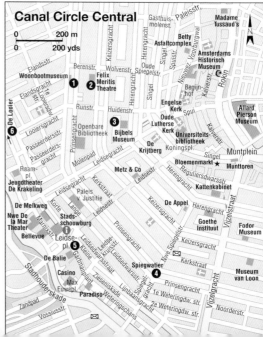

Canal Circle Central

over the whole building. Since 1989, Felix Meritis has hosted international theatre, dance and musical performances, as well as lectures and readings. Its popular café is open daily.

Look across to the other side of the canal to see a good example of a neck gable, at 319 Keizersgracht, designed by Philips Vingboons in 1639. Back on the western shore, you'll see a gateway at No. 384. This was the entrance to the former Stadsschouwburg (City Theatre), destroyed by fire in 1722, after which it was rebuilt and functioned as an almshouse. Renovated in 1999, it was transformed into the exclusive Blakes Hotel. The Stadsschouwburg is now in Leidseplein.

Look across the canal again to see the **Vergulde Ster** (Gilded Star) at No. 387, an excellent example of the elevated neck-gable style, from 1668. The building styles change so rapidly in this zone that it is difficult to take in all the detail. Just look at Nos. 440–54, near the junction with Leidsegracht. With its huge windows and a decorative mixture of sandstone and red brick, No. 440 is a stark contrast to No. 446, a Louis XIV-style dwelling from the 1720s, which was at one time the home of well-known art collector Adriaan van der Hoop. Both of these buildings back onto and form part of Amsterdam's **Centrale Bibliotheek** (Central Library; entrance on Prinsengracht). Another contrast is provided between the pillars and balconies of the bank occupying No. 452. And No. 454 is a stylish example of how Amsterdam's warehouses can be converted into comfortable apartments.

Golden Bend

When the city expanded during the 17th century, Herengracht was the most desirable of the three new canals. Where it turns southeast at Leidsegracht and east just before Vijzelstraat is where the most splendid houses were built, on double-fronted lots (twice the width of most canal-side plots), on a stretch dubbed the **Gouden Bocht** (Golden Bend).

Take in a fine view of this area from the bridge over Leidsegracht. There is much to enjoy here in quirky sculptural details, and gables

Map on page 128

You can get an idea of the long-running desirability of the properties along the Golden Bend by comparing prices. In 1820, for example, a house on Herengracht would have sold for 30,000 guilders while an equivalent house in the nearby Jordaan distict would have fetched only 3,000.

BELOW: this area is a highlight of a canal-boat tour.

Behind the Gables

One of the defining features of Amsterdam's elegant canal houses is their decorative gables. Take a *rondvaart* canal-boat tour – by far the best way to engage in a little gable-spotting – and your tour guide's main concern will be to point out the different styles of gable that grace the skyline. A typical "Dutch" gable is the ornate upper part of the facade used as an ornament to disguise the shape and appearance of the roof behind. Though this feature is not unique to Amsterdam, the range and ornamentation of gables here is unusual; the most common types are the step, spout, neck and bell gables. You don't have to be an architecture buff to spot these, but a little guidance will make a walk along the canals more enjoyable.

The early pointed or spout gable, an inverted V-shape reflecting the slope of the roof, characterises many of Amsterdam's warehouses. This old-fashioned style was gradually replaced by the simpler step gable, a Gothic style that ascends geometrically like a small stairway up to the pinnacle. Builders often

used pale sandstone to offset the darker red brickwork. This type of gable is very much associated with the architect Hendrick de Keyser. Step gables are a good indication that the building dates from the late 16th or early 17th centuries (though there are later versions).

In the 1630s, the gracious neck gable often attributed to Philips Vingboons became fashionable and remained so for two or three decades. It takes the form of an elevated centrepiece culminating in a triangular pediment, often in association with heraldic statuary. From about 1660, the flowing bell gable, recognisable by its round top with concave sides like a church bell, was popular, but was superseded. Facades were often decorated with heraldic motifs, or other religious or self-promotional devices, which, at a time when there were no house numbers, helped to identify the occupants. Typical designs feature coats of arms, trade signs, mythological animals, cherubs and Biblical scenes.

All gables feature hoist beams complete with iron hooks. These enabled goods to be winched to upper floors. The deliberate forward tilt of many canal houses helped prevent goods from crashing into windows on their way up.

Gables do not account for all of the canal-side facades. When the Golden Age had passed, Dutch architects imported much from France, especially the baroque Louis XIV style. The most ostentatious patrician houses had broad-pedimented neo-classical facades decorated with garlands or extravagant sculptures. During the late 17th century and the 18th century, gable-fronted houses gave way to squarer facades and Italianate straight or triangular cornices. You can, by and large, trace these developments as you go along the Grachtengordel from north to south then east, following the timeline from the earliest designs to the latest. ❑

LEFT: an ornate neck gable adorned in Classical style on Prinsengracht.

decorated with dolphins and mermaids. Great mansions compete with each other in size in a vain exercise in grandeur. Most of them now house opulent hotels, offices and banks, and No. 502 is the official residence of Amsterdam's *burgemeester* (mayor). The magnificent gardens at the back of these Herengracht mansions – few of which can be visited – are mostly laid out in the formal French style.

The grandest of Amsterdam's canal-side mansions were built with a warehouse in the basement, lavish reception rooms on the ground floor and, above, a dining room and banqueting room. Inventories from the time describe Persian silk furnishings, Turkish rugs, Japanese lacquerware, Venetian or ebony-framed mirrors, and oil paintings and alabaster statues in most rooms. The small room that projects from the front of some of the houses was called the "pan room". In order to keep the kitchen spotless, domestic staff were not allowed to clean the dirty pots and pans there, but were sent to the pan room instead. All in all, the greatest houses outshone even the *palazzi* of Venice – and this in a republic that claimed to place virtue before gold.

The **Cromhouthuizen** (Cromhout Houses) at Nos. 364–370 Herengracht, date from 1662, and feature four sandstone gables. Designed by Philips Vingboons, they derive their name from the crooked piece of wood that was the trademark of wood merchant Jacob Cromhout, who lived at Nos. 366–368. Today, these two adjacent canal houses are home to the **Bijbels Museum ❸** (Biblical Museum; tel: 524 2436; open Mon–Sat 10am–5pm; Sun 1–5pm; entrance fee). The elegant interior features an elaborate painted ceiling by Jacob de Wit and exudes the atmosphere of past centuries. Varied exhibits include a rare

Bible collection, archaeological finds from Egypt and the Middle East, religious objects from the Jewish and Christian traditions, models of the Temple in Jerusalem, and a world-famous model of the Tabernacle dating from 1851. The tranquil garden, an oasis in the summer, is one of the few canal-house gardens open to the public.

The goddess of vanity and the goddess of hunting adorn the crown gable at No. 376. So ornate is the decoration at Nos. 380–382 that it stands out even among its opulent neighbours. It was built in 1889–90 for tobacco merchant Jacobus Nienhuys, who wanted to emulate the chic mansions of New York's Fifth Avenue – in this case the US model had itself been built to emulate a sumptuous French chateau. Its gables and windows, embellished with reclining figures, cherubs and mythical characters, dwarfs the adjoining Renaissance gables.

Further along, No. 386, another Vingboons building, has a neoclassical pilastered facade, and an imposing gable incorporating Doric

Map on page 128

The Dutch love their tulips, whether real or woodcarved.

BELOW: in the Bijbels Museum.

The huge outdoor chessboard on Max Euweplein was the idea of an inspired five-year-old, who proposed his idea to the authorities back in the early 1990s.

and Ionic capitals. The gables of Nos. 390–392 are adorned with a carving of a man and a woman stretching a rope between them. They date from the mid-17th century, as do Nos. 396–398, known as the "Twin Brothers", matched by the "Twin Sisters" at Nos. 427–429 on the opposite bank. Note the monumental flight of steps at No. 402, by Justus and Philips Vingboons. Another highlight is No. 475, dating from the 1730s and built in an ornate Louis XIV style.

Shopping places

If all this street-level facade-gazing is proving tiring, head for **Metz & Co.**, an upmarket department store on the corner of Keizersgracht and Leidsestraat. A large clocktower, designed by De Stijl architect Gerrit Rietveld, makes it easy to spot; at night the roof of the building is illuminated. Go up to the top-floor café and enjoy rooftop views of Amsterdam. Unfortunately, the food is overpriced, unremarkable and served unenthusiastically. Settle for a cappuccino and some apple pie and

hope to get a table by the window.

The wonderful old shops of the **Spiegelkwartier** ❹ generate plenty of custom. Antiques dealers have been doing business here for more than a century, attracted by the proximity to the Rijksmuseum, which opened in 1885. The first dealers opened their shops in **Nieuwe Spiegelstraat**. Later they were joined by art dealers who opened galleries along **Spiegelgracht**, helping to create what has since become a centre for fine art and antiques. The area developed rapidly in the 1960s when antiques became more popular and some provincial dealers, who saw their trade disappearing, moved to Amsterdam out of necessity, swelling the number of shops here.

Although the branch of Sotheby's auction house moved out to larger premises in the southern suburbs in 1999, other prestigious dealers have moved to the Spiegelkwartier. In a street only 300 metres (330 yds) long, there are around 60 antique dealers and 15 galleries. Many shops have specialists who can advise buyers, though you should still ask for a

signed certificate of authenticity when making a purchase.

At 34 Nieuwe Spiegelstraat a number of dealers have gathered together under one roof to create the **Amsterdam Antiques Gallery**, which sells icons, dolls and 19th-century paintings. At No. 58, Frans Liedelmeijer specialises in the decorative arts and Dutch design, art nouveau and art deco pieces. At No. 65, Inez Stodel is known for her period jewellery. At 3 Spiegelgracht, Jaap Polak specialises in oriental art. Altogether the choice is wide and antiques available in the Spiegelkwartier include earthenware, furniture, porcelain, engraved glass, Asiatic art, Russian icons, art nouveau and art deco objects, sculpture, jewellery, clocks, medical and nautical instruments, drawings, books, pewter, old Dutch tiles, and engravings. Many of these *antiquairs* deal directly with the Rijksmuseum and have international reputations. Their shops are a bit like precious miniature museums – but don't be put off by the exclusive ambience. Feel free to browse. The proprietors are invariably friendly and helpful, and visitors – who might turn out to be customers, after all – are always welcome.

Also in this area is the **Stichting De Appel** (open Tues–Sun noon–5pm; entrance fee), at 34 Nieuwe Spiegelstraat, a foundation named after the Cobra artist Karel Appel, that provides an exhibition space for the latest art. With changing exhibitions in place for around two months at a time, the artists get the kind of exposure that might lead to greater things.

Leidseplein

At the end of the shopping thoroughfare of Leidsestraat is one of the main hubs of Amsterdam, **Leidseplein ❺**, a frenetically busy square beside what was once one of

Amsterdam's city gates, the Leidsepoort (Leiden Gate). This is a major centre for Amsterdam's nightlife – and daylife too, for that matter. There are cinemas, cafés with street terraces, dope cafés ("coffee shops"), restaurants and clubs aplenty. For jazz, drop by **Alto Jazz Café**, 115 Korte Leidsedwarsstraat; for blues, jazz, soul and more, visit **Bourbon Street**, 6–8 Leidsekruisstraat; while the **Maxim** piano bar, 35 Leidsekruisstraat, attracts a loyal crowd of music lovers who like to sing along. Street performers are invariably at the centre of attention (some of them even deserve to be); jugglers, mime artists, magicians and musicians take their turn at entertaining, and extracting money from, the crowds. In **Max Euweplein**, a satellite of Leidseplein named after a Dutch chess grand master, you're likely to find people playing street chess with large plastic pieces. Here too is **Holland Casino Amsterdam**.

Two notable buildings stand in Leidseplein. The **Stadsschouwburg** (City Theatre), a red-brick construc-

Map on page 128

BELOW: one of the many al fresco cafés in Leidseplein.

Map
on page
128

The American Hotel in Leidseplein, still a fashionable meeting place.

BELOW: Leidseplein is well known for its nightlife.

tion with a wide veranda and mini turrets, dates from 1894 and is still busily occupied serving up highbrow homegrown and international dance and theatre. Opposite the Stadsschouwburg is the **American Hotel**, an art nouveau extravaganza with more than a touch of Venetian Gothic designed by Willem Kromhout. It dates from 1902 and has sweeping arches, sumptuous decoration and an elegant clocktower, while its **Café Américain** overlooks Leidseplein and has long been a fashionable meeting place. For many locals and tourists, this is a popular place to see and be seen. Afternoon tea, dessert and coffee are recommended rather than main meals, which tend to be overpriced.

Leidseplein caters to all tastes in entertainment – the conservative and the progressive. A shrine to the latter is the renowned **Melkweg** (Milky Way) in Lijnbaansgracht. Rock, jazz, world, latin and reggae music, fringe theatre productions, art exhibitions and video performances all make for a lively "multimedia" arts centre that stays open into the small hours. De Melkweg first became the centre of alternative arts in Amsterdam when the former dairy building was converted in the 1960s, and it is still going strong.

A kindred spirit, across Leidseplein and along Weteringschans, is **Paradiso**, another nightspot which emerged in the 1960s and provides a lively venue for rock, hip hop and world music. Comedy clubs have become popular in the city in recent years, and of the three in town, **Boom Chicago**, housed in the old **Leidseplein theater,** is the best. Based on the US tradition of improvisational comedy, the troupe presents irreverent revues (in English) on current events and such topics as love and relationships.

If at the end of a day tramping around the canals you are in need of refreshment and entertainment, spend at least one evening in Leidseplein. But don't plan to make an early start the next day.

Antiques market

Starting from Leidseplein is a good way to explore the southernmost section of the Jordaan *(see page 122)*, where the district bumps into Leidsegracht and comes to an end. From Leidseplein, go along Lijnbaansgracht to **Looiersgracht**. At the first hint of sunshine, locals bring chairs out into the streets here, and those lucky enough sit sunning themselves on balconies. Just north of Looiersgracht, **Elandsgracht** is best known for its idiosyncratic indoor market, **De Looier ⑥**, a mass of stalls selling anything from 1950s memorabilia to handmade pottery, and old dolls and toys.

Lauriergracht, the next canal north, has some fine gabled houses at its eastern end. Along the way you can check out somewhat seedy **Lijnbaansgracht**, where African music blares out at night from a clutch of vibrant bars. ❑

RESTAURANTS & CAFES

Restaurants

Dutch

De Blonde Hollander
28 Leidsekruisstraat
Tel: 627 0521
Open: L, D daily. €€
Formerly De Blauwe Hollander, this inexpensive, cosy restaurant is a good place to come for straightforward Dutch food.

International

Café Américain
Crowne-Plaza Amsterdam-American Hotel,
97 Leidsekade
Tel: 556 3232
Open: L, D daily. €€–€€€
A superb art deco dining space inside Amsterdam's premier art nouveau hotel (both of them listed monuments) adds up to a visual treat. If the international cuisine isn't quite as memorable as the surroundings, that's not entirely surprising, considering the challenge. And it's still wonderful to see and be seen here.

Greek

Traîterie Grekas
311 Singel
Tel: 620 3590
Open: D Wed–Sun. €–€€
A no-frills Greek taverna and takeout with a few tables and authentic food, where you can

enjoy dinner in an unpretentious atmosphere. It's a vegetarian's delight, with a variety of mezes and salads, but also a place for those who love a good gyros pitta, a moussaka with bite, and hearty meat stews.

Indonesian

Bojo
51 Lange Leidsedwarsstraat
Tel: 622 7434
Open: L, D Fri–Sat; D Mon–Thurs. €
This plain eatery just off Leidseplein isn't the place to go for the full Indonesian dining experience, but for good-value, spicy food it's hard to beat. The kitchen is open until 2am so it attracts night owls who've discovered the need for some food to accompany the beers they've already drunk.

Seafood

Le Pêcheur
32 Reguliersdwarsstraat
Tel: 624 3121
Open: L, D Mon–Fri; D Sat. €€€
If seafood were art, then this upscale restaurant would be something of a meticulous masterpiece, with prices to match. There are few more romantic places in town to dine on a summer evening than in the man-

sion's flower-bedecked back garden, and at all other times the graceful, low-illumination interior salon takes some beating.

Cafés

Café Reijnders
6 Leidseplein
Tel: 623 4419
Open: 11am–1am daily. €
This authentic old café really deserves to be somewhere other than on the over-touristy Leidseplein. But there it is, doing its best to maintain traditional standards in a setting where easy come easy go is the general rule. It has a great glassed-in seating area looking out on the square.

Het Molenpad
653 Prinsengracht
Tel: 625 9680
Open: L, D daily. €
Behind the traditional brown-café look is a modern café artfully designed to look old – the illusion is a good one, and the place is convivial. You get bar food and a variable range of specials. The outdoor terrace by the canal is a huge draw in summer.

RIGHT: *maître d'* at the Café Américain.

CANAL CIRCLE EAST AND REMBRANDTPLEIN

From viewing historic houses preserved in their original glory to the pleasures of beer-drinking and shopping, the eastern canal region is well worth a day's exploration

The final short stretch of the Grachtengordel, completing the stage of canal construction that took place after 1665, runs from Vijzelstraat to the River Amstel. Commentaries on the canal-boat tours often dry up on this southeasternmost part of the waterways and, if your stay in Amsterdam is governed by priorities, an exploration of the canals between Vijzelstraat and the river can be put low on your list. But don't write off this neighbourhood altogether. Several of Amsterdam's best museums are tucked away here. And a stone's throw north of Herengracht is Rembrandtplein, a square that's always bright and busy at night.

Just before you get to Vijzelstraat, however, on the north bank of Herengracht, you might want to visit the **Kattenkabinet** (Cat Cabinet; open Mon–Fri 9am–2pm; Sat–Sun 1–5pm; entrance fee), at No. 497. In this museum dedicated to cats, sculptures, paintings and prints depict all things feline in art and culture down the centuries.

Museum Van Loon

Across Vijzelstraat, at 672 Keizersgracht, the **Museum Van Loon ❶** (tel: 624 5255; open Sept–June Fri–Mon 11am–5pm; July–Aug daily 11am–5pm; entrance fee)

provides a glimpse into old Amsterdam. The centrepiece is a sequence of portraits of the successive generations of the building's wealthy occupants spanning the period from the 17th to the 20th centuries.

Architect Adriaen Dortsman built this house in 1672, and its first tenant was the painter Ferdinand Bol, one of Rembrandt's pupils. Among subsequent owners were Abraham van Hagen and his wife Catharina Trip, who lived here in the mid-18th century (they left a discreet note to

Map on page 138

LEFT: Magere Brug ("Skinny Bridge") is illuminated at night. **BELOW:** Golden Age splendour at the Museum Van Loon.

A cherub in the formal rose gardens of the Museum Van Loon.

BELOW: cigar shop on Reguliersbreestraat.

posterity by initialling the staircase balustrade). The Van Loon family – who had helped create the United East India Company – arrived on the scene when the building was purchased by Hendrick van Loon in 1884, and the family lived here until after World War II.

In 1964, the Van Loon Foundation began restoration work, and their efforts have paid off handsomely. The period rooms are replete with richly decorated wood panelling, stucco work, mirrors, marble fireplaces, elegant furniture, porcelain, medallions, chandeliers, rugs, and more. The marble staircase with its intricately designed balustrade is itself a masterpiece. In contrast to the glitz of the Willet-Holthuysen house *(see page 140)*, the fixtures and furnishings have been worn by time. Uniquely among historic Amsterdam houses, there is also a well-preserved formal garden, with shrubs, flowers and statues.

Thorbeckeplein

Cobblestoned, shady **Thorbeckeplein** ❷, off Herengracht, is the southern extension of Rembrandtplein. Ringed by cafés, hotels and restaurants, the pavement terraces are usually packed in summer, and even in winter seldom lack custom. You can stagger from bar to bar here, but if you're passing on a Sunday afternoon between mid-March and October from 11am to 6pm, you'll encounter a sophisticated little art market that sits incongruously beside the topless bars.

In the middle of the square stands a statue of J.R. Thorbecke, a significant figure in the history of the Netherlands. In 1814, after a brief interlude under the rule of Napoleon, the former Dutch republic had become a monarchy. By 1848, the Netherlands had a new constitution, for which Thorbecke was largely responsible. It may seem ironic that the statue celebrat-

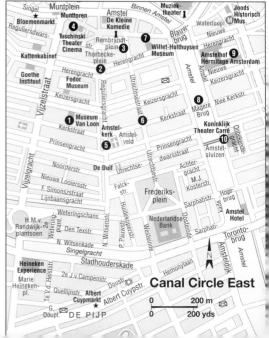

ing a serious man who played such an important role in the development of his country should stand amid all this carefree merriment, but Thorbecke was, above all, a liberal, part of a political tradition that ultimately accounts for much of this country's pragmatic outlook.

If you've already been on one of the canal-boat tours by the time you get to Thorbeckeplein, you'll probably recognise the six-arched bridges of **Reguliersgracht** just south of the square. The view down Reguliersgracht cuts across all three of the main canals almost as far as Singel, a perspective particularly favoured by photographers.

Rembrandtplein

If Leidseplein is Amsterdam's most popular haunt at night, **Rembrandtplein ❸** runs it a close second. The square was originally part of the 16th-century city ramparts; later it was the site of a butter market and a fairground. It took its name in 1876 from the statue of Rembrandt, facing towards the Jewish Quarter, at the centre of the square.

Topless bars, music bars, small bars, large bars – Rembrandtplein has them all. Unfailingly lively any night of the year, it has inevitably become very commercialised, a fact reflected in the over-inflated prices of drinks and the invariably indifferent service you're likely to encounter. One superior oasis, however, is **Café Schiller** at No. 26, a place that seems to have let time slip through its fingers: the pace is relaxed, the interior elegant and the service friendly. Trendy **Royal Café de Kroon** and glittery **Grand Café l'Opéra** across the square are also worthwhile.

Heading northwest out of Rembrandtplein, you enter crowded Reguliersbreestraat where, among the fast-food stalls, you will find the **Tuschinski Theater ❹** cinema. Go to see a film here just to enjoy the interior. The man behind this beautiful art deco building was a Polish Jew, Abraham Tuschinski, who came to Amsterdam after World War I with ambitions to build a unique theatre. He duly purchased a piece of land in Reguliersbreestraat occupied by slum buildings known as the Duivelshoek (Devil's Corner), and was then closely involved in the lavish design, perfectly in tune with the era of cinema's heyday.

The cinema opened in 1921. Tuschinski himself died at Auschwitz in 1942, though the cinema – one of the most beautiful interiors in Amsterdam – ensures that his name lives on. You can enter the foyer for free, where a plaque behind the bar commemorates Tuschinski and his two co-founders. In summer there are guided tours (Jul–Aug Sun–Mon 10.30am). Fortunately, the current owners have preserved and restored all the fixtures and fittings so that the original style is just about unblemished. Amsterdam has a rich collection of art deco buildings but the Tuschinski is the proudest of them all.

Map on page 138

Lamps outside the Tuschinski Theater hint at the extravagant art deco flourishes of the interior.

BELOW: the wonderfully ornate Tuschinski Theater cinema.

The wooden Amstelkerk divides its time between God and gastronomy: the once neo-Gothic nave is now home to a hip restaurant.

ORIENTATION
This chapter covers the area between Vijzelstraat in the west and the River Amstel in the east.

BELOW: boats take priority over road traffic.

Amstelkerk

On Prinsengracht, in the wide open space of the Amstelveld square between Reguliersgracht and Utrechtsestraat, stands the wooden **Amstelkerk ❺** (Amstel Church). Designed by Daniël Stalpaert, it was built in 1670 as a temporary place of worship for Protestants, but the plan to replace it with a more permanent brick structure never materialised. It is best seen on Mondays, when a plant market is held in the adjacent square. The church has been subject to alteration, most notably during the 19th century. By the late 1980s it had fallen into a state of disrepair and was in danger of collapse. Restoration began in 1988 and two years later it was reopened. Part of the premises is now occupied by the South Seas restaurant **Moko**, which has a terrace on the the square, but worshippers still attend services in the church on Sunday mornings and concerts are given during the week.

A walk along **Utrechtsestraat ❻** has much to offer. This street, once notorious for prostitution, has transformed itself into a rich row of shops and restaurants. A lot of the locals are academics, so it comes as no surprise that there are four bookshops in the street. There are many other shops of note, too: **Concerto** is a large CD shop spanning several buildings with every form of music; **Loekie** is a delicatessen of epicurean proportions; a shop towards the end of the street sells maps of everything (including the moon). Down Kerkstraat, if you're lucky you might hear the Russian Orthodox church choir rehearsing. There's also a wide selection of cafés. In **Café Krom**, apart from a lick of paint, nothing has changed in 50 years. **Oosterling**, a dark old brown café at the end of the street, was originally a distillery – to which the large vats inside bear witness.

Museum Willet-Holthuysen

To enjoy a lavish interior in a fine example of a 17th-century stately home, and gain an insight into the life of both patricians and servants in the grand canal houses from that century to the 19th, visit the **Museum Willet-Holthuysen ❼**, at 605 Herengracht (tel: 523 1822; open Mon–Fri 10am–5pm; Sat–Sun 11am–5pm; entrance fee). This three-storey building with a street-level basement was built in 1689 for prominent Amsterdam burgher Jacob Hop and his wife Isabella Hooft. The house changed hands many times and eventually, in 1855, came into the possession of Pieter Gerard Holthuysen. When he died three years later his daughter continued to live here. In 1861 she married Abraham Willet, and together they built up a valuable collection of glass, ceramics, silver and paintings. Willet, who had a keen interest in art, was a friend of many of the artists of his time. The couple had no children and so, when Mrs Willet died in 1895, the house and its contents were left to the city.

Map
on page
138

One condition of the legacy was that the premises were to be opened to the public as a museum. This was duly done on 1 May 1896. But the public showed no interest. A standing joke ridiculed the museum for being one of only two places in Amsterdam where a gentleman could meet his mistress unobserved (the other was Kalverstraat on a Sunday morning).

Extensive restoration has widened the scope of the museum so that it contains a number of period rooms, including an 18th-century kitchen and a late-19th-century bedroom. Oriental cabinets, antique clocks, carpets, chandeliers, a grand stairway with gilded cast-iron banisters, painted ceilings, wall tapestries, silver, porcelain, pottery and glass are part of a valuable collection in the stately interior. During the restoration many discoveries were made, notably the original wallpaper which has been faithfully reproduced. The attic houses temporary exhibitions.

Today the Museum Willet-Holthuysen is no longer ridiculed, nor does it lack visitors. Constructed three years after the final stage of the Grachtengordel was completed and almost the last building on this the most elegant of the three main canals, the Willet-Holthuysen is a grandiose endpiece to Herengracht.

River Amstel

The **Amstel** was at one time the city's main artery. Amsterdam was named after this river, which until the 16th century flowed freely to the IJ. Once you have adjusted to the scale of the city's canals, the breadth of the Amstel seems strangely out of place in the heart of the old city, but its banks are still pleasant for a stroll.

The river used to be an invisible border line that marked the beginnings of the Jewish Quarter *(see page 163)*. Nieuwe Keizersgracht and Nieuwe Prinsengracht, because of their position on the east side of the Amstel, were not popular among Amsterdam's wealthier citizens, and this allowed some of the richer members of the Jewish community to move in. The effect has survived, and there is still a strong contrast between the streets on either side of the river.

The wood panelling, subdued lighting and nicotine-stained walls of Amsterdam's brown cafés gave traditional Dutch pubs their name.

BELOW: the view across the Amstel.

Map on page 138

The Blauwbrug, a sturdier, greyer version of the original "blue bridge" which once served as the main entry point to the city.

BELOW: the Magere Brug.

Just north of the junction of Herengracht and the Amstel is the **Blauwbrug** (Blue Bridge), which leads to Waterlooplein. There was once a blue-painted wooden bridge here, but about the only trace of blue in this handsome 1884 replacement, based on the Pont Alexandre III in Paris, is on the ornamental lanterns.

One of the most prominent landmarks on this stretch of the river is the **Magere Brug** ❽ (Skinny Bridge), further south, which connects Kerkstraat with Nieuwe Kerkstraat on the far bank. This rebuilt wooden drawbridge, a 20th-century replacement for the 17th-century structure, gets its name from an even narrower bridge that once stood here. Though there are many theories as to the origin of the name, experts tend to agree on the story of the two wealthy Magere sisters who lived on opposite sides of the Amstel; tired of making detours to visit each other, they built a bridge. Today, it is one of the last hand-operated drawbridges in existence. Featured on canal-boat tours, postcards and tourist brochures, the bridge has become one of the clichés of scenic Amsterdam, and is beautifully illuminated at night.

A noteworthy landmark on the eastern bank is the neo-classical **Amstelhof** ❾, a nursing home dating from 1681, when it was built for aged Protestant women. It has undergone major alterations to accommodate the new **Hermitage Amsterdam** (tel: 530 8755; open daily 10am–5pm; entrance fee) art gallery, a 'branch' of the famous Hermitage in St Petersburg. The first section opened in 2004 in the Neerlandia Building, an annexe of the Amstelhof, with its entrance at 14 Nieuwe Herengracht. This joint project restores a connection between Amsterdam and St Petersburg that dates back to the reign of Tsar Peter the Great, who founded the Russian city and was a great admirer of Amsterdam, which he visited several times, and of Dutch maritime prowess. He based the design of the Russian flag on that of the Dutch.

Further upstream beside the Amstel's houseboat-lined shore, the 19th-century **Koninklijk Theater Carré** ❿ (Royal Carré Theatre) was built as a circus, and its stage is circular. Today it is used for local and international productions.

The stately **Amstel Hotel** on this side of the Amstel has been *the* address for cosmopolitan society since 1897, when it first opened as a spa. Back then, a *Baedeker Guide* listed it as one of Amsterdam's top hotels, its rooms priced at an astronomical three guilders a night. These days the prices are more amenable to captains of industry and the jet set. After an extensive facelift in the 1990s, the Amstel was restored to its former glory as the temporary address for guests such as the Queen of England. It remains a popular spot to enjoy Sunday brunch or afternoon tea, and its French restaurant **La Rive** has two Michelin stars. ❏

RESTAURANTS & CAFES

Restaurants

International

Brasserie Schiller
NH Hotel Schiller, Rembrandtplein 26–36
Tel: 554 0723
Open: B, Br, L, D daily.
€€–€€€
Since being restored to its art deco glory, this hotel restaurant has become something of an insider's tip. There are French seafood dishes, along with a variety of Dutch and international offerings.

Sluizer
41–43 Utrechtsestraat
Tel: 622 6376
Open: L, D Mon–Fri; D Sat–Sun. €–€€
A perennially popular, slightly old-fashioned brasserie that doesn't have overly great ambitions for its French and Dutch food. An associated seafood restaurant next door (at No. 45) is open only for dinner. Both are open late

Vegetarian

Golden Temple
126 Utrechtsestraat
Tel: 626 8560
Open: D daily. €–€€
Some people come here just for the great salad buffet at this small, alcohol-free, non-smoking vegetarian restaurant. Others come

for the main courses. feature creative ethnic dishes based on Indian, Middle Eastern and Mexican cuisine.

Indian

Memories of India
88 Reguliersdwarsstraat
Tel: 623 5710
Open: D daily. €€
This remains one of the best performers in a town that's patchy for Indian cuisine. The food is consistently good, and a certain amount of design flair inflects its decor – witness the brass palm trees.

Indonesian

Tempo Doeloe
75 Utrechtsestraat
Tel: 625 6718
Open: D daily. €€
With decades of perfecting its act behind it, this smooth performer has plenty of dedicated local fans, who appreciate the elegant table settings and love the fiery nature of its style of Indonesian cuisine.

Polynesian

Moko
12 Amstelveld
Tel: 626 1199
Open: L, D daily. €€–€€€
Many local foodies still regret the demise of the outstanding Kort in this location (in the Amstelkerk), but Moko comes

close to being a worthy successor, due mainly to its intriguing Polynesian food and its comfy, laid-back style.

Middle Eastern

De Falafel Koning
2 Regulierssteeg
Tel: 421 1423
Open: L, D daily. €
Tucked away down a narrow alley across from the Tuschinski cinema, their trademark falafel in pitta bread or served on a plate with salad is worth seeking out.

Cafés

Café Schiller
Rembrandtplein 26
Tel: 624 9846
Open: L, D daily. €–€€
Well established as one

of the city's most fashionable yet least pretentious cafés. Bar snacks and simple meals.

Royal Café de Kroon
17 Rembrandtplein
Tel: 625 2011
Open Br, L, D daily. €–€€
This well known grand café has a superb, glassed-in balcony area overlooking bustling Rembrandtplein from the first floor. The food ranges from snacks to Continental dishes.

PRICE CATEGORIES

Prices are for a three-course meal for one, with wine and coffee
€ = under €20
€€ = €20–40
€€€ = €40–60
€€€€ = over €60

RIGHT: Indonesian cuisine at Tempo Doeloe.

THE MUSEUM QUARTER AND VONDELPARK

Amsterdam's museums rate among the finest in the world, exhibiting priceless pieces from the Dutch Golden Age and highlighting two Dutch Masters: Rembrandt and Van Gogh

For art lovers, the real centre of Amsterdam is **Museumplein** ❶, just south of Singelgracht, a short stroll from Leidseplein in the Oud Zuid (Old South) district. Before 1999, Museumplein was a somewhat bedraggled, wide-open space. With the redevelopment of the square, designed by Swedish landscape architect Sven-Ingvar Andersson, the city acquired a public space that links its three major museums – the Rijksmuseum, the Van Gogh Museum and the modern art Stedelijk Museum – along with the Concertgebouw concert hall.

Grassy areas extend uninterrupted across Museumplein, creating a grand promenade and making its cultural citadels easily accessible. Colourful benches and stylish lanterns have been placed throughout the area. Skateboarders have their terrain on one side and *boules* and basketball players on the other. A grand café-restaurant paying homage to the Cobra Movement *(see page 194)* was constructed facing the Rijksmuseum; its outdoor terrace can seat nearly 200. Just beside it, a long pond sometimes freezes in winter to become an ice-skating rink. The Van Gogh Museum and Rijksmuseum have a joint gift-shop pavilion selling posters, cards and souvenirs relating to their collections, and there's a tourist-oriented branch of the Albert Heijn supermarket chain.

Underground garages have swallowed up the massed ranks of tour buses, cars and taxis that once disfigured the square, and traffic no longer passes through. Various public events continue to be held in the square, among them the annual Uitmarkt cultural festival in August.

The separate visions of the three museums and the presentation of their permanent collections enables

Map on page 148

PRECEDING PAGES: admiring the art at the Rijksmuseum. **LEFT:** images of Vincent Van Gogh. **BELOW:** *The Night Watch* at the Rijksmuseum.

Stained-glass portrait in the Rijksmuseum of the illustrious sculptor and architect Hendrick de Keyser.

Below: dolls' house at the Rijksmuseum

them to tell their own story and maintain their own special presence. Large-scale extensions and refurbishment, still ongoing in the case of the Rijksmuseum and the Stedelijk Museum, were designed to equip the museums for the 21st century.

The Rijksmuseum

The dominant building in Museumplein is the palatial **Rijksmuseum ❷** (State Museum, tel: 674 7000; open daily 10am–6pm; entrance fee). This, the most important museum in the Netherlands, has some seven million items in its collection. However, until the summer of 2008 almost all of the vast building is closed for renovation and rebuilding. Until then, in the Museum's Philips Wing (entrance at 1 Jan Luijkenstraat), a vastly scaled-down selection of the most outstanding works is on display under the title *The Masterpieces*. During the closure period, there are likely

to be temporary exhibitions at other locations in the city, covering different elements of the collection. It's indicative of the museum's wealth of treasures, in particular those from the Dutch Golden Age, that even this truncated display represents one of the highlights of a visit to Amsterdam. (In addition, there's the Rijksmuseum Schiphol pavilion, a museum annexe at Schiphol Airport, which holds 10 paintings by Old Dutch Masters.)

The gigantic Rijksmuseum building, designed by architect P.J.H. Cuypers to house the national art collection, first opened its doors in 1885. The opening exhibition was a collection from The Hague's National Art Gallery, brought to Amsterdam in 1808 by King Louis Napoleon. The facade, which looks like that of a medieval French chateau, reflects Cuypers' penchant for the Gothic style (he also designed Centraal Station and you

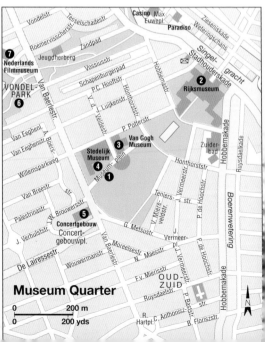

Museum Quarter

0 ———— 200 m
0 ———— 200 yds

can see the similarities between the two buildings in the towers and brick overlay).

On the ground floor of the Philips Wing, the first two rooms provide an insight into the Netherlands' rich heritage, with the emphasis on 17th- and 18th-century history: the Revolt against Spain, the early Dutch republic, and the brief but brilliant period of maritime supremacy. Paintings, weapons, costumes, documents, models of ships and memorabilia relating to Dutch seafaring history are the legacy of this turbulent period *(see pages 21–30)*.

The three remaining ground-floor rooms each cover a different theme. Dolls' houses are the unlikely highlight of Room 3. But these exquisite and fantastically detailed dolls' houses are modelled after real 17th-century houses and are fully furnished, complete with tiny Delft plates, paintings, copper plates, and precious silver, glass and porcelain objects, most of which were made by respected craftsmen. Comparable to the richly decorated cabinets of collectors, these dolls' houses

were clearly not playthings for children but for women of the regent and merchant classes. Room 4 has French-influenced 17th- and 18th-century furniture and furnishings, and a superb collection of Chinese-inspired Meissen porcelain. In Room 5 there is a beautiful collection of Delftware, with delightful pieces such as a polychrome pair of pointed, high-heeled shoes and a violin, among the more familiar jugs and plates.

The upper floor is where the museum's unsurpassed collection of Old Dutch Masters gets some space to breathe, if not quite to spread out. Still, there are some 400 paintings on display. The long Rooms 9 and 10 are where the late Rembrandts are hung, along with works by some of his eminent pupils. Contrary to what people believed for many years, Rembrandt received some important commissions in his last years, among them *The Sampling Officials of the Drapers Guild*. *The Jewish Bride*, now titled *Isaac and Rebecca*, is one of the great late works. Its heavily impastoed glowing golds

Map on page 148

ORIENTATION
This chapter covers all the sights centred on Museumplein beyond the canal belt, and Vondelpark, the green space that extends southwest of the Museum Quarter.

BELOW: Frans Hals' *The Marriage Portrait of Isaac Abrahamsz Massa and Beatrix van der Laen.*

In The Love Letter, *by Jan Vermeer, a moment of anticipation is caught in sidelong light with almost photographic precision.*

and reds evoke a mood of warmth and tenderness. Van Gogh was so enamoured of the painting that he once said he would give 10 years of his life to be able to sit in front of it with a loaf of bread.

Frans Hals, who today is one of the most admired Golden Age artists, gets the small Room 7 to himself. Hals's paintings make a radical departure from typical early 17th-century portraiture. Realistic portrayal of his subjects in works like *The Marriage Portrait of Isaac Abrahamsz Massa and Beatrix van der Laen* is unusual in showing the married couple posing together. Husband and wife more commonly had their own separate portraits. Hals has set the newly-wed pair in a fantasy garden with peacocks, which serve as a reference to the classical goddess Juno, the guardian of marriage. *The Merry Drinker,* painted in swift Impressionistic brush strokes, shows Hals's remarkable capacity to depict a fleeting gesture. This portrait is typical of his style at its most lively, and the sitter appeals to us largely through his smile and gestures.

There are only 30 known works by the Delft master Jan Vermeer *(see page 27),* and four of the most famous are in Room 10. They may well be familiar through reproductions, but no copy can do justice to these superb works in the flesh. His vivid interpretation of the street in Delft could have been painted in the present day. *Woman Reading a Letter* is a study of subdued emotion. Perhaps loveliest of all is *The Kitchen Maid,* a serene domestic scene of a woman pouring milk into a bowl. The beauty of the colour and the play of sunlight transforms an everyday chore into poetry.

The merry genre scenes in Room 11, typified by the bawdy tavern and chaotic household interiors of Jan Steen, are not just intended as realistic and witty portrayals of everyday life, although Steen took pride in being a storyteller by filling his paintings with cheery visual anecdotes. Like the still lifes of the 17th century, these works are frequently filled with symbolism and allegorical allusions which were evident to most literate Dutchmen of the time.

The Appeal of Rembrandt

Rembrandt Harmenszoon van Rijn is probably the most famous Dutchman in history. Although more has been written about him than perhaps any other prominent figure from Holland, the greatest painter of the Golden Age remains a mystery. In recent years efforts of the Rembrandt Research Project have helped to set the record straight on just how many paintings are credited to the master of chiaroscuro (light and shade). Not long ago there were thought to be more than 650 Rembrandt paintings, but authenticity studies have reduced that figure to around 300. *The Night Watch* remains his most famous painting. Rembrandt completed it in 1642 at the age of 36, when he was one of the most sought-after painters in Amsterdam. According to the Rijksmuseum, which was specially constructed with the painting as the centrepiece, it remains priceless. And yet it was highly criticised at the time for being too dark and for breaking rules. Even the title is misleading, because the figures in the painting are clearly not on watch duty. The painting has survived despite being cut down in the 18th century to fit into the old Town Hall on Dam Square and suffering a lunatic slashing in 1975. The pilgrimage of visitors continues.

His *Merry Family,* in which children are following the example of their parents by smoking, drinking and disporting themselves with abandon, warns against loose morals and bad upbringing. In his painting of *The Toilet,* the allusions are erotic – red stockings symbolise a whore; a dog on the pillow, candlestick on the chair and chamberpot on the floor are all indications of lust.

The most dazzling of Rembrandt's masterpieces occupies a whole wall of Room 12. The painting is a militia piece, an official portrait of the civic guard that defended the city. The subject matter is *The Company of Captain Frans Banning Cocq* and the captain is giving his company orders to march. Unlike the militia pieces that had gone before, in which the figures, seated or standing, looked stiff and lifeless, Rembrandt's painting portrays a group in action, each figure moving or about to move, and the overall activity is enhanced by the play of light. The layers of varnish and grime which had accumulated on *The Night Watch* led 19th-century experts to believe this was a night scene, hence the mistaken title.

Paintings from the later schools of Dutch art are set out in Room 6. These include works of Dutch Realism and feature landscapes and beach scenes painted around The Hague by Anton Mauve and H.M. Mesdag, as well as the Amsterdam Impressionists, known as the *Tachtigers* (Eighty-ers) because their movement began in the 1880s. Besides two early works by Van Gogh, there are several bold canvases by Georg Hendrik Breitner, considered Amsterdam's leading Impressionist.

Van Gogh Museum

A short stroll further down the street, to 7 Paulus Potterstraat, brings you to the **Van Gogh Museum ❸**, which has the world's largest collection of works by Vincent van Gogh (tel. 570 5200; open daily 10am–6pm; entrance fee). This is currently the only one of Museumplein's – and Amsterdam's – big three museums to be in place and intact. Designed by De Stijl

TIP

To check on the current status of the Rijksmuseum's renovation and on which elements of the collection are on view in the wing that remains open, visit the museum's website, www.rijksmuseum.nl

BELOW: *Merry Family* by Jan Steen.

The Van Gogh Phenomenon

In a letter to his brother Theo, penned in 1883, Vincent van Gogh encapsulated his artistic goals: "One thing I know, within a few years I must bring a certain work to completion... I am concerned with the world only insofar as I have, as it were, a certain debt and duty... and also because I want, out of gratitude, to leave behind a sort of remembrance in the form of drawings and paintings... not made in order to promote this or that trend, but on account of them having in them something that expresses a sincere human sentiment. That is the goal of my work."

During his entire lifetime Vincent sold only one painting. And yet today he is arguably the most popular, and certainly the most reproduced, of the modern artists. His paintings are famous for fetching world-record prices, with the last being sold at auction for approximately $80 million (£55 million). Unsurprisingly then, Amsterdam's Van Gogh Museum is one of the most popular tourist attractions in the Netherlands, receiving around 700,000 visitors each year.

Van Gogh's imagery continues to have an impact on people of all ages and backgrounds. The museum shop and its Museumplein annexe, shared with the Rijksmuseum, sells millions of postcards, as well as posters, calendars, diaries, pencils and paintboxes. At the Museumplein annexe you can buy even more collectibles – bath towels, coffee mugs, candles, mouse pads, refrigerator magnets and more – without having to pay the museum entrance fee.

What an irony that a man who was considered a failure and a misfit, and who died penniless and unrecognised, should become such a commercial phenomenon. What is it about this sensitive painter that continues to be celebrated in songs, poetry, books and films? More than 100 years after his death, new generations from all over the world continue to be inspired by his work: the homely ambience of *The Potato Eaters*, the pastoral landscapes of Holland and France, the sensual flowers, haunting self-portraits and turbulent skies of his final days at St Rémy and Auvers-sur-Oise. Perhaps it is the humanity that is seen and felt in these works, and the spirituality, which was such an important element of the troubled Van Gogh spirit.

Although his artistic career spanned only 10 short years (Vincent had first decided to become a minister but failed his theology exams), he produced close to 2,000 works. The paintings from Arles – amounting to a prolific 200 in 15 months – were produced in a frenzy of haste, as though he knew that the end was near. Some of his most famous canvases were dashed off between fits of depression and debilitating insanity. Yet, in his letters to his brother Theo, he writes with great insight about his deteriorating health and state of mind and describes his paintings in detail. Although Van Gogh's art was rarely praised during his lifetime, he achieved his humble goal and his legacy remains. ❑

LEFT: one of the many self-portraits in the Van Gogh Museum.

architect Gerrit Rietveld, it was built in 1973 as a permanent home for some 200 paintings and 500 drawings by Van Gogh, together with works by other 19th-century painters and sculptors. There are also 700 letters, all bequeathed by Van Gogh's nephew, who was also called Vincent. In 1999 the museum completed an extensive renovation and saw the completion of a striking new wing. Almost double its former size, and with major improvements to the facilities, including air-conditioning and better lighting, it is like a new museum, light and spacious, with whitewashed walls and open-plan floors.

The permanent collection features a selection of paintings by Van Gogh hung in chronological, and to a degree, thematic order – though the location of individual works may change from time to time. The first floor is designed to give an overview of the main developments in his œuvre. The early works, typified by scenes from the daily lives of peasants, show his early preference for heavy forms and dark, sombre colours. The numerous studies of peasants in the province of Noord-Brabant culminates in *The Potato Eaters*, a painting Van Gogh regarded as one of his finest but whose uncompromising ugliness did not impress friends or critics. His intent was not to idealise or sentimentalise, but to portray peasant life as he observed it.

Vincent's move to Paris in 1886 shows his vision transformed. Exposed to the rainbow colours and broad brush strokes of Impressionism and other new painting styles, he began to paint with a brighter palette. The intensity of his period in Brabant gradually disappears and gives way to lively Parisian street scenes, café interiors, windswept landscapes and vivid portraits of some of his friends.

Woman Sitting in the Café du Tambourin has the subject matter, the swift brush strokes of pure colour and the vivid effect of the Impressionists. It was a café he knew well; he took meals there, swapped canvases for food, was friendly with the Italian woman who

Sunflowers *is Van Gogh's most famous work.*

LEFT: looking across Museumplein to the Rijksmuseum.
BELOW: Van Gogh's boats.

Map on page 148

TIP

The Cobra Café in Museumplein pays homage to the post-war Cobra Movement (see page 194) in its decor and ambience.

owned it and used it as a venue to exhibit his collection of Japanese prints. Tiring of city life and passionate for "a full effect of colour", Van Gogh then moved to Arles. Enthused by the intense light and warm colours of the Mediterranean, he produced some of his most vivid landscapes and portraits, luminous, swirling masterpieces created with great speed and intensity.

The famous *Sunflowers*, one of a series of five pictures of this subject, shows his love of warm colour, light and simplicity. The predominant colours of this period are blazing yellows, ochres and oranges, as in *The Yellow House* (where Van Gogh lived), *The Harvest at La Crau*, *Self-Portrait with Straw Hat* and *Van Gogh's Bedroom, Arles*. Of this last picture, he wrote that the colour was "to be suggestive of rest or sleep in general. In a word, to look at the picture ought to rest the brain, or rather the imagination".

Following a quarrel with Gauguin, Van Gogh cut off a portion of his own ear and admitted himself to the asylum at St Rémy. He was physically and emotionally exhausted, had been drinking too much and was diagnosed with a form of epilepsy. The asylum offered him a refuge where he could be cared for and work in peace. His paintings of the landscapes around the asylum become bolder and more visionary, the canvases less colourful and heavily impastoed. Of *Olive Trees with Pink Sky* he writes: "What I have done is rather hard and coarse reality but it will give a sense of the country and will smell of the soil." In *Cypresses, St Rémy*, he shows the trees as swirling dark flames, reflecting his growing anguish and tormented sensibility.

In the final period at Auvers-sur-Oise in the north of France, the landscapes are similar but fiercer, painted in a frenzy of creation between fits of insanity. *Wheatfields with Crows* is the most ominous and desolate of the last works. "They are vast fields of wheat under troubled skies and I do not need to go out of my way to try and express sadness and extreme loneliness." A few weeks later, Vincent shot himself. He was 37. An

BELOW: face to face with Van Gogh.

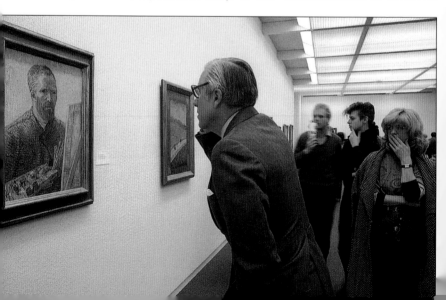

inevitable question mark hangs over the end of this sequence: what more might Vincent have accomplished and what recognition might he have achieved had he not cut short his own life? In his last 10 years he had produced more than 800 paintings and 1,000 drawings, as well as sketches and watercolours. Unfortunately, the drawings and letters are no longer on permanent display as they are too sensitive to light.

Works from the collection of 19th-century art are on show on the ground and third floors. These include paintings by Van Gogh's friends and contemporaries, and new acquisitions, and are displayed in rotation. Among these are works by Toulouse Lautrec, Gauguin and Emile Bernard, all of whom had an influence on Van Gogh. The second floor houses changing presentations of drawings and graphic art, and has a study area with computers where visitors can find out more about Van Gogh and the art of his time by viewing the reserve collection and the museum website (www.vangoghmuseum.nl).

The new wing of the Van Gogh Museum, designed by Japanese architect Kisho Kurokawa, was created to house a programme of changing exhibitions. This austere modern structure stands slightly apart from Rietveld's building, and almost two thirds of it is carved out below ground level. Its striking 21st-century form, inspired by such geometric elements as cones, ovals and squares, are moulded in granite, aluminium and titanium. The latter metal takes on surprisingly varied reflections and colours in the changing conditions of light and weather. The use of natural stone on the curved gable is another of the building's original gestures. A tranquil pond makes a strong Zen statement and serves as a resting place between the two buildings, linking old with new.

Situated in the middle of Museumplein is an annexe of the Van Gogh Museum shop, which is co-operative venture with the Rijksmuseum, selling an extensive range of gift articles and souvenirs relating to the two museums.

Map on page 148

In response to criticism about The Potato Eaters, *Van Gogh wrote: "I have tried to make it clear that those people, eating their potatoes in the lamplight, have dug the earth with those very hands they put in the dish, and so it speaks of manual labour, and how they have honestly earned their food."*

LEFT: staircase at the Stedelijk.
BELOW: the neo-Renaissance facade of the Stedelijk Museum.

A cellist plays for passers-by outside the Concertgebouw, acknowledged by many as the world's finest concert hall.

BELOW: the Concertgebouw.

Stedelijk Museum

As if things weren't bad enough for Museumplein at the start of 2004, with most of the Rijksmuseum shuttered *(see above)*, the modern art **Stedelijk Museum** ❹ (Municipal Museum, 13 Paulus Potterstraat) has closed its doors too, for renovation and extension. In this case, the museum – housed in a Dutch neo-Renaissance building embellished with gables and turrets – was due to reopen in May 2006. In the meantime, most of the collection is on display on three floors of the TPG Building *(see page 183)*, close to Centraal Station. In addition, elements of the collection are likely to be displayed at other venues, including the Van Gogh Museum, the Cobra Museum of Modern Art in suburban Amstelveen *(see page 194),* and the museum's own experimental gallery, the Stedelijk Museum Bureau Amsterdam, at 59 Rozenstraat in the Jordaan *(see page 122).*

The Stedelijk Museum's collection consists of more than 100,000 works of art, including works of applied art and industrial design. Of these, a mere fraction have been on display over the years, and the exhibition space of the museum has been devoted to rotating the permanent collection every few months, so that the Picasso you saw in January has been replaced by a different work in August. The museum's main challenge over the past two decades has been one of space, not for exhibition halls, but for art depots, and work and office space for personnel.

The eccentric Dowager of Jonkheer Lopez Suasso, whose heterogeneous collection of antique furniture, coins, jewellery, watches and trinkets filled the rooms of the Stedelijk when it first opened in 1895, might well be indignant if she set foot in the museum today. Her whole collection was cast out in 1975 in order to accommodate a large new collection of paintings, sculpture, applied art and industrial design, for the most part uncompromisingly "modern". What was created was a strikingly contemporary interior, in which walls were ripped down to create large open

spaces, ceilings were partially glassed and rooms whitewashed to offset large, colourful canvases.

Concertgebouw

Moving away from museums to the southern end of Museumplein, the **Concertgebouw ❺** (Concert Building) has the reputation of being acoustically among the world's finest concert halls, as well as one of the most beautiful. Designed by A. L. van Gendt and opened in 1888, it is home to the **Koninklijk Concertgebouworkest** (Royal Concertgebouw Orchestra). A golden lyre stands on the roof above the entrance, and the neo-classical colonnade is watched over by grave portrait busts of Beethoven, Sweelinck and Bach. Among the composers who have held court here are Brahms, Stravinsky, Strauss, Mahler, Ravel and Debussy. Famous European and US orchestras have performed here. The Concertgebouw's programme is not exclusively classical; past performers have included Philip Glass, Wynton Marsalis and an orchestra of 100 gypsy violins.

Under the baton of Riccardo Chailly, the Royal Concertgebouw Orchestra has earned a reputation for versatility and is considered one of the world's leading orchestras. There are two performance halls, the stately Grote Zaal (Large Hall), which seats 2,250, and the Kleine Zaal (Little Hall) on the upper level, which accommodates 450 for concerts with solo artists and chamber orchestras. Besides the regular concert schedule, popular Sunday concerts are held each week from 11am. On Wednesday lunchtimes (generally at 12.30pm) there is usually a free half-hour "surprise concert" where visitors get a chance to hear the resident (or guest) orchestra in rehearsal.

The stylish street outside the Concertgebouw is **Van Baerlestraat**, which runs just a few blocks and leads up to the Vondelpark *(see page 158)*. It has clothing, music and bookshops, and speciality shops selling perfume, cigars, coffee and language books. At the far end of the street at No. 52 is the **Small Talk Café**, a popular spot for visitors

Map on page 148

LEFT: *Composition in Grey* by Theo van Doesburg, 1919.

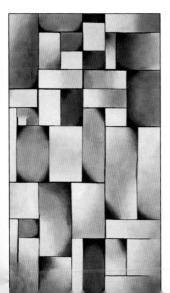

Mondrian and De Stijl

With his distinctive paintings of grid lines and blocks of primary colours, Piet Mondrian (1872–1944) was the leading figure of the Dutch De Stijl ("The Style") Movement. But it was the dogmatic and polemical magazine called *De Stijl*, founded and edited by Theo van Doesburg, that would start the rumblings of modern art in the Netherlands.

Its purpose was "to state the logical principles of a style now ripening, based on a pure equivalence between the age and its means of expression – we wish to pave the way for a deeper artistic culture, based on a collective realisation of the new awareness." Moving on from Cubism, De Stijl captured the Dutch imagination, across art and architecture.

Mondrian's premise was that bold colours and straight lines offered a "true vision of reality" by eliminating personal interpretation of the work. Another major artist in the De Stijl tradition was Bart van der Leck, whose work is distinctive for its use of triangles rather than squares. Mondrian himself abandoned De Stijl in 1925, producing even more abstract works before moving to New York, where he threw it all in to depict the lively world of jazz music.

between museums. Typical Dutch soups are served, which hit the spot on a cold day; in summer you can sit outside. One block further up is **Pieter Cornelisz Hooftsraat** (invariably shortened locally to "the P.C. Hooft"), considered Amsterdam's smartest shopping street, sporting designer names like Armani, DKNY and Hugo Boss.

Vondelpark

If you have, by now, grown weary of museum exhibitions and overpriced boutiques in this area, then it is time to take refuge in the green environs of **Vondelpark** ❻. The oldest and largest of Amsterdam's municipal parks is a year-round refuge for strollers, joggers, cyclists, dog walkers, music-makers, sunbathers, picnickers, frisbee-throwers and skaters. Plus you can buy cannabis-spiked "space cakes" here, if you prefer to see the park from above the trees. Amsterdammers love their green spaces, and make a great deal of effort to enjoy them at every opportunity afforded by time constraints and cli-mate. Vondelpark is the most popular of the lot, accessible from entrances all around the 45-hectare (120-acre) green oasis, the main one being on Stadhouderskade, close to Leidseplein.

Vondelpark sprang onto the scene during what came to be known as the "Second Golden Age", in the late 19th century. The park, whose gates first opened in 1865, was named after the 17th-century German-born poet and playwright Joost van den Vondel, who chose Amsterdam as his home. Vondel is often dubiously referred to as the Shakespeare of the Netherlands. He died of hypothermia at the ripe age of 92. A statue of Vondel was unveiled in the park two years after the grand opening, and another sculpture, *The Maid of Amsterdam*, stands at the main entrance.

Vondelpark's architects, J.D. and L.P. Zocher, made a deliberate move away from the symmetrical Dutch garden style when they drew up their plans back in the late 1850s. They aimed instead for a romantic English-style garden. On

BELOW: summertime in the Vondelpark.

completion, it served as a private park, paid for by the wealthy families who lived in the surrounding environs of Amsterdam South. In the 1960s and 1970s, Vondelpark was the happening place for great hordes of hippies.

For such a relatively small city as Amsterdam, Vondelpark is a sizeable stretch of ponds, lawns, woods and tennis courts – roughly equivalent in length to the distance between Centraal Station and Leidseplein. In typical Dutch fashion, the park is run through with water in the shape of long sinuous pools. In spells of warm weather crowds gather around these ponds to sunbathe.

During the summer months, Vondelpark hosts a series of daily concerts, theatre, comedy, puppet shows and dance performances in a small open-air theatre right in the middle of the park. In winter, if the ponds freeze over, there is also the possibility of ice skating. At other times of the year, one of the best-loved activities is rollerblading: skates are available for rent at the

Amstelveenseweg end of the park.

One of Vondelpark's primary focal points is the striking round form of **Het Blauwe Theehuis** (The Blue Tea House; *see listing below*), a café at the centre of the park. At the northeast corner is the **Nederlands Filmmuseum** ❼ (Netherlands Film Museum; tel: 589 1400; box office open daily; entrance fee for screenings), whose stated aim is to promote film culture by the collection, restoration and screening of film treasures (including hand-coloured silent movies). It serves as a cinema resource centre and offers regular screenings of historic and specialist films and documentaries. The museum is housed in a pavilion built in 1881, and the main hall is clad in the old interior of the Cinéma Parisien (1910), which was gutted in 1987.

Also inside the museum is a popular bar and restaurant, **Café Vertigo** *(see listing below)*, which features a wonderful open-air terrace on which there are free screenings on Saturdays throughout the summer months. ❑

Map on page 148

In Vondelpark street performers, an outdoor theatre and a flock of resident parrots keep the crowds entertained. Others doze on the grass with a book.

RESTAURANTS AND CAFES

Het Blauwe Theehuis
5 Vondelpark
Tel: 662 0254
Open: B, Br, L, D daily. €
Don't pay too much attention to the street address, since this circular café-restaurant (it used to have the Dutch word for "round" in its name) lies pretty much in the middle of Vondelpark. It's great for Continental breakfast and snacks, or just a drink, amid all the trees and fresh air.

Sama Sebo
27 Pieter Cornelisz Hooftstraat
Tel: 662 8146
Open: L, D Mon–Sat. €€
For classic, if not overly ambitious Indonesian food – the authenticity of which is complemented by a profusion of mats made from rushes and batik – visit this veteran and invariably busy establishment close to the Rijksmuseum. Their *rijsttafel* is among the best in town

and they also serve up excellent individual dishes.

Van Altena
Stadhouderskade (no street number)
Tel: 676 9139
Open: 11am–7pm
Tues–Sun. €
Something of a place of pilgrimage for the city's fans (their number is legion) of fresh raw herring and other seafood favourites, this fish stand at the Rijksmuseum adds more than a pinch of quality to the genre, and incorporates a few

tiny tables along with a nice line in chilled white wine – perfect for warm evenings.

Café Vertigo
Film Museum, 3 Vondelpark
Tel: 612 3021
Open: L, D daily. €€
The food is Mediterranean-inspired, and in good weather you can dine outdoors on one of the finest fresh-air terraces in town.

● ● ● ● ● ● ● ● ● ● ● ●
Prices are for a three-course meal for one, with wine and coffee
€ under €20, €€ €20–40,
€€€ €40–60, €€€€ over €60

AMSTERDAM'S BIKE CULTURE

From the moment one arrives in Amsterdam, generally at the entrance of Centraal Station, the first impression is of bicycles everywhere

At any time of the day or evening, as one walks the city or crosses town on a tram, the bicycle ballet unfolds before one's eyes: mothers with children on front and back; passengers on handlebars or on the shoulders of the cyclist; others sitting gracefully perched behind the rider; septuagenarians on their *oma fiets* (granny bike) with high handle bars. Some bicycles have trailers attached for easy transport. The bike of choice is basic, usually black, with no frills or gears – de rigueur for city life, although serious cyclists may invest in sleek, multiple-speed racing bikes.

For visitors, it often looks tempting to join the bicycle brigade, but in the city centre you do so at your own risk. Cycling in Amsterdam has become *levensgevaarlijk* (life-threatening) in recent years. The Dutch pride themselves on being "born on a bicycle", and weaving through traffic is second nature to them. But when that traffic also includes taxis who drive on tram tracks, aggressive drivers, skaters and pedestrians, then riding becomes a serious business. There seems to be a constant war between taxi drivers and cyclists and, in the anarchist style typical of Amsterdam, many cyclists run red lights. Still, many visitors do get around safely by bike in the city. If you are nervous, start out in a quiet area or at a quiet time such as early morning. And when crossing tram tracks go across them, *never* parallel, as the wheels get trapped and one is immediately aflight.

ABOVE: live in Amsterdam and you soon become a deft hand at puncture repairs. Still, pumping up a bicycle tyre beats jacking up the car. Such is life on the streets of Amsterdam.

LEFT: two's company in this soft-top child-carrier.

OVE: while most Amsterdammers shun flashy mountain bikes, y are not averse to adapting their traditional boneshakers. ld-carrying systems are common. Most use rear-mounted ld seats but some – at the expense of easy parking – opt for stom-made, roomier set-ups such as this.

OVE: bicycles are the principal form of transport for sterdammers, with over 600,000 in the city – that's almost one every man, woman and child. Obviously the lack of hills plays a t in the popularity of bicycles – though the Dutch do take their ironmental responsibilities very seriously, and cycling is a lot lthier than sitting behind the wheel.

UNDER LOCK AND KEY

Some say there are one million bikes sold in the Netherlands every year. Others say that one million are stolen. Which doesn't necessarily mean there are one million bikes, it just means there are often bikes that get stolen many times and, if you'll pardon the expression, recycled.

No matter how many sturdy, well-guaranteed locks one uses – generally two locks, one snap-on style for the back wheel and another chain style to link through the back tyre to whatever you are locking the bike to – the fact remains that there are clever thieves around who make an industry out of stealing bikes. One notorious fellow recently published a book about his exploits, which many booksellers refused to stock. There are also the local junkies needing cash for their next fix who roam the streets with their latest acquisition, offering to sell it for around $20 to passers-by, which probably led to another infamous saying in Amsterdam: "You buy your first bike and steal the rest."

Back in the 1960s an organisation called Provo decided to tackle the problem head-on. Wooed by the times, they proposed the White Bike Plan and introduced of a fleet of white bicycles to be owned "by everyone and no one". Predictably the plan failed. In recent years, however, a thief-proof alternative has proved more successful. Smart cards with PIN numbers release white bikes from their depots, while hidden microchips and electronic locks make them less appealing targets for would-be thiefs.

RIGHT: bicycles are used to transport a variety of objects, from a ladder or chair to huge bouquets of flowers or a small tree.

JODENBUURT AND PLANTAGE

Although little remains of the pre-war atmosphere and bustle, Amsterdam's Jewish quarter is today a sobering but fascinating memorial to its once thriving Jewish community

he **Jodenbuurt** (Jewish Quarter – also sometimes known as the Jodenhoek (Jewish Corner) – was once a lively, colourful and proud neighbourhood, poor but hard-working. Those days have gone for ever. During World War II, the Jewish community in Amsterdam, which had numbered 80,000, was reduced to only 5,000. Neglected and decrepit, the Jodenbuurt became a virtual ghost town. Jewish street life disappeared.

Since then it has been a victim again, this time of demolition for property development, road-building and Metro lines – look for the demolition ball inside Waterlooplein Metro station, a reminder of the destruction, and a typically Dutch indulgence in self-mortification. Stand at the broad junction of Mr. Visserplein and look at the dull concrete embankments flanking Jodenbreestraat to the north, the gaping underpass which leads traffic from Weesperstraat north towards the IJ tunnel, and the great square hulk of the Town Hall overlooking Waterlooplein, and you could be forgiven for thinking that Amsterdam is just another ugly modern city.

Yet the Jodenbuurt and the neighbouring Plantage have a powerful story to tell, and some element of the indomitable Jewish spirit remains. There are enough places of interest to visit to occupy a full day and, if you are interested in Amsterdam's Jewish past, careful exploration is rewarded.

Waterlooplein

Ironically, the thoroughly modern setting of **Waterlooplein** ❶ is an appropriate place to start exploring the Jodenbuurt. At Nos. 33–39, Amsterdam's first public synagogue was completed in 1639 (and demolished in 1931). This area was known

Map on page 165

LEFT: the Portuguese-Israelite Synagogue was the first large synagogue to be built in western Europe (1675). **BELOW:** the flea market at Waterlooplein.

Unusual decorative pieces can be found at the flea market on Waterlooplein.

BELOW: the flea market at Waterlooplein is the city's oldest.

as Vlooyenburg (Flood Town), a stretch of marshy ground regularly flooded by the Amstel, and was the site of the original Jewish Quarter. Two canals, Houtgracht and Leprozengracht, ringed Vlooyenburg to the north and east, creating an island. Here the Jews lived in poverty. In the 19th century, when Jews were allowed to practise trades for the first time, many small businesses were established in houses that were already too small and so conditions worsened. In 1882, the two canals were filled in to create Waterlooplein (the square takes its name from the Battle of Waterloo in Belgium in 1815, where Dutch troops played a prominent part in Napoleon's defeat). Markets on Sint-Antoniesbreestraat *(see page 97)* and Jodenbreestraat were transferred there, and the marketplace became the focal point of Jewish life in the area.

Jodenbreestraat (Broad Street of the Jews) was once the Jewish Quarter's business centre. Today you can do little more than imagine all that vanished colour and life. Modern buildings have torn the heart out of the Jewish Quarter. Construction of the Metro, which runs under Waterlooplein, and extensive redevelopment at the southern end of Sint-Antoniesbreestraat, further contributed to the changes that destroyed the area's character.

The Waterlooplein **flea market** (open Mon–Sat 9am–5pm), Amsterdam's oldest and best-known, is worth visiting as the last vestige of the once vital community life of the area. In the 19th century, the author Multatuli wrote of the market: "There were headless nails, toothless saws, bladeless chisels, locks without springs, keys without locks, hooks without eyes and eyes without hooks, buckles without prongs..." You may well find that nothing much has changed, and some of the goods on offer won't meet even these low expectations, but there are some genuine bargains to be had.

The Roman Catholic **Mozes en Aaronkerk** ❷ (Moses and Aaron Church) is proof that Waterlooplein was not exclusively Jewish. The building was completed in 1841, on the site of an earlier clandestine

church, where Catholics worshiped in secret to avoid antagonising the city's Calvinist authorities.

Opera and dance

If you enjoy opera and ballet, you could visit Waterlooplein in the evening, having bought tickets for the **Muziektheater** ❸ (tel: 625-5455). This is one half of the combined Stadhuis (Town Hall) and Opera Hall complex – hence **Stopera** – the centrepiece of Waterlooplein's redevelopment, and one of the most controversial property developments Amsterdam has ever seen. Opposition to the project was widespread. Many felt the area should be residential, and squatters battled against riot police and water cannons here in the 1980s. Austrian architect Wilhelm Holzbauer was responsible – guilty, some would say – for the plans for this huge structure. But attempts to stop the building failed, despite the clever battle-cry

"Stop the Stopera", and it was completed in 1986. The Muziektheater's main hall can accommodate an audience of 1,600, and its stage extends over 22 metres (70 ft).

From a tour boat on the Amstel you will likely need little persuasion that the architecture of the complex is totally out of keeping with the scale and style of buildings nearby. But the Muziektheater (if not the Town Hall) has at least brought a measure of charisma to the area, and is a star in the city's cultural firmament, if not quite a beloved one, at least not yet. Two resident companies perform here: the Netherlands Opera and the National Ballet, accompanied respectively by the Netherlands Philharmonic Orchestra and the Netherlands Ballet Orchestra. Together they quickly earned the Muziektheater a place on the international opera and ballet circuit. Acclaimed guest performers have included those of the Netherlands

Map below

The Muziektheater, a collusion of marble, bricks and glass on the banks of the Amstel. Medieval houses in the Jewish Quarter made way for this architectural oddity.

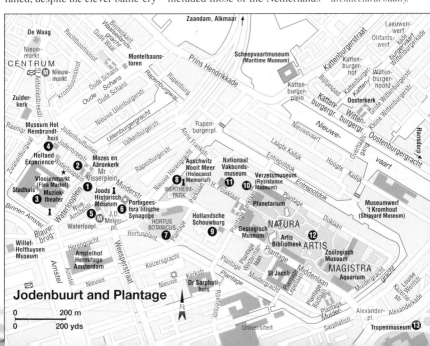

Jodenbuurt and Plantage

0   200 m
0   200 yds

Dance Theatre from The Hague, and also performances by Moscow's Bolshoi, London's Royal Ballet and New York's Martha Graham Dance Company.

Rembrandt's house

About the only surviving vestige of 17th-century Jodenbreestraat is also the most visited sight in the Jewish Quarter. The **Museum Het Rembrandthuis** ➍ (Rembrandt House Museum; tel: 520 0400; open Mon–Sat 10am–5pm; Sun 1–5pm; entrance fee), in a former home of Rembrandt's at Nos. 4–6, has been in the care of a foundation since 1906. It became a museum in 1911.

Rembrandt Harmenszoon van Rijn (1609–69), to give the artist his full name, was born in Leiden and came to Amsterdam in 1631. Soon after arriving he took lodgings in what was then known simply as Breestraat (Broad Street), later to be known as Jodenbreestraat. The artist lived for much of his life in the Jewish Quarter. In Rembrandt's day this was on the edge of the town; he was fond of walking out into the country,

eastwards to the village of Diemen, now an Amsterdam suburb. Along with Van Gogh and Vermeer, Rembrandt continues to be one of Holland's most beloved painters.

Rembrandt purchased the house in Jodenbreestraat in 1639, by which time he was a celebrated and successful artist. Even so, his comfortable new home (then just a two-storey building topped by a step gable) cost him dearly; he incurred substantial debts to pay for it, and his extravagant furnishings and running expenses contributed to his bankruptcy in 1656. Forced by his creditors to sell the house and many of his possessions, Rembrandt was nevertheless allowed to stay on until 1658, when he made a new home in the Jordaan (see page 121).

In 1998 Prince Willem-Alexander opened a new wing adjacent to the Rembrandthuis, doubling the available display space. This new wing has radically altered the role of the original house – intriguing as it was, it had become little more than a receptacle for Rembrandt's world-renowned prints and etchings. The new wing now houses the 250 drawings and etchings, and a display that explains the technique of producing them, along with a portrait of Jan Six, one of Rembrandt's patrons (portrayed as a refined art lover, instead of the ostentatious merchant he was). Among the finest works are the sensitive portraits of his wife Saskia and his homely portrayals of beggars, barrel-organ players and a rat-catcher. The trades have moved elsewhere, but Rembrandt's physiognomies are recognisable in the faces of present-day Amsterdammers. Entrance to the Rembrandthuis is via the new wing. This spacious and well thought-out building houses temporary exhibitions in addition to the above-mentioned art treasures. There are also video and slide presentations.

A startled self-portrait welcomes visitors to the Museum Het Rembrandthuis, the artist's home until 1658, following his bankruptcy. A bailiff's inventory gave researchers an accurate picture of Rembrandt's domestic set-up.

BELOW: Rembrandt's house on Jodenbreestraat.

The extension opened up an opportunity to restore the residence to its pre-museum role. Restoration has been carried out with scientific precision using, for example, floor and wall tiles of the same period and, where possible, using Rembrandt's own works as a guide. The greatest point of reference, however, was the bailiff's inventory drawn up at Rembrandt's bankruptcy declaration. As a result, the mansion contains some of the artist's own belongings and looks about as it would have done when Rembrandt lived and worked here. Visitors gain a new insight into his character.

The museum's entrance fee includes admission to the neighbouring **Holland Experience** (17 Waterlooplein; open daily 10am–6pm; entrance fee). It's hard to imagine what Rembrandt would have thought of this vision of his beloved Dutch landscape, which you "hurtle" through by way of a 3D film (complete with funny glasses).

Diamond life

On the opposite side of Jodenbreestraat from the Rembrandthuis, in the direction of the harbour, is another key part of the Jewish Quarter, bounded by Oude Schans and Valkenburgerstraat. In the 17th century there were two islands here, Uilenburg and Marken, thick with shipyards and wharves. When shipbuilding moved to the islands of Kattenburg, Wittenburg and Oostenburg, large numbers of poor Jews settled here, in a maze of back alleys and sweatshops.

Amsterdam claims to be the "City of Diamonds" (hardly justifiable when you consider that Antwerp's diamond trade is worth six times as much), and diamonds have been processed here for more than four centuries. The Cullinan diamond, the world's largest, was cut here in 1908 by the Asscher company.

The Amsterdam industry has always been dominated by Jewish families and was a major source of employment for Jewish residents. When this business was new to the city, it was not governed by any of the guild regulations that would have disqualified Jews from becoming involved *(see page 22)*. It has been calculated that in 1748 around 600 Jewish families earned their living from diamond processing. The great boom came during the Kaapse Tijd (Cape Age) when, around 1870, the first raw diamonds began to arrive from South Africa. The resulting surge in the supply broke the monopoly of the Diamond Cutting and Polishing Society. Soon there were more than 3,000 people working with diamonds in Amsterdam.

A Jewish success story, in the shape of the former Boas diamond-polishing factory, was founded here in 1878. The building still stands, overlooking the waters of Uilenburgergracht, and is home to the **Gassan Diamonds** company, at 173 Nieuwe Uilenburgergracht. Visitors, of course, are welcome.

Map on page 165

ORIENTATION
Jodenbuurt and Plantage extend eastwards from Waterlooplein as far as Muiderpoort.

The philosopher Spinoza is thought to have been born in 1632 in one of the houses demolished to make way for the building of the Moses and Aaron Church.

BELOW: Amsterdam's diamond industry has been important for centuries.

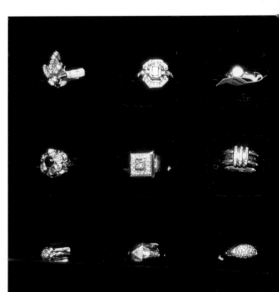

This area's principal attraction used to be the **Bimhuis** (73–77 Oude Schans). Housed in a rambling old warehouse, this is one of Amsterdam's best jazz venues, but it was due to move out at the end of 2004, along with the De IJsbreker contemporary music club. The smart new home is the Muziekgebouw concert hall, under construction at the time of writing on the south shore of the IJ channel, between Centraal Station and the cruise-ship Passenger Terminal Amsterdam *(see page 180).*

Jewish history and worship

While Waterlooplein was the embryo of the Jewish Quarter, its heart today is a short walk away in the **Joods Historisch Museum ❺** (Jewish Historical Museum; 2–4 Jonas Daniël Meijerplein, tel: 625 4429; open daily 11am–5pm, except on Yom Kippur; entrance fee). The museum, which had previously been housed in the Waag (Weigh House) in Nieuwmarkt *(see page 96),* occupies the Ashkenazi Synagogue Complex, which comprises four

synagogues built during the 17th and 18th centuries, restored after extensive destruction in World war II. The oldest, the Grote Schul, dates from 1671. When it moved here in 1987, Amsterdam's Jewish community achieved a long-standing ambition to have this major collection on Jewish life in a building where something of the Jewish spirit would reign. Its mission statement is to provide a "place of reference for those whose links with past generations were broken by the war". Be advised that it is an enormous, sober and serious collection. If you want to absorb it fully, you should give yourself a full morning or afternoon here.

Beginning in the domed New Synagogue, the exhibition traces the spread of Judaism through the Netherlands, from its humble beginnings to the years of prestige in the 18th century, the decimation of the community during the Holocaust, and up to the present day. Highlights include an 18th-century Ark, ritual baths, and wartime memorabilia. The detailed history of Zionism, collections of religious artefacts and insights into the lives of important Dutch Jewish personalities are part of a narrative. This is counterbalanced by exhibits of more general interest: paintings, books, household objects, the story of Jewish settlement in the Netherlands, explanations of Jewish dietary laws and photographs that depict Jewish life today.

Across the way, between Jonas Daniël Meijerplein and Muiderstraat, the **Portugees-Israëlitische Synagoge ❻** (Portuguese-Israelite Synagogue; open Sun–Fri 10am–4pm, except for Jewish holidays; entrance fee) was constructed between 1671 and 1675, around the same time as the Grote Schul synagogue *(see above).* Both buildings are important in that they were the first synagogues of any size to

TIP

On a lighter note than the Jewish Historical Museum's subject matter, the kosher café attached to the museum reputedly sells the best cheesecake in Amsterdam.

BELOW: exhibits in the Joods Historisch Museum.

be built in western Europe, and the former is said to have been the largest synagogue in the world in the 1670s. It was originally a "clandestine" place of worship, with the same unofficial but tolerated status as the "clandestine" Catholic churches. The synagogue's 17th-century interior was beautifully restored in the 1950s. A high barrel-vault and handsome furnishings of oak and Brazilian hardwood add to its richness of detail. Services are still held by the light of candles on a huge bronze candelabrum.

The Portuguese-Israelite Synagogue is so large that it dominates the junction of busy Mr Visserplein even today; in the 17th century the effect would have been more dramatic. When wealthier Jews went to live in the extensions to the Gracht-engordel – the new canals to the east of the Amstel – this locality became the new centre of the Jewish Quarter. Paintings of the area soon after the synagogue was constructed depict tranquil scenes on Muider-gracht, a wide canal that passed through what is now Jonas Daniël

Meijerplein. (The canal is now partly submerged, reappearing at the east end of Plantage Middenlaan).

The dockworker

This triangular "square" flanking the Portuguese-Israelite Synagogue is named in honour of Jonas Daniël Meijer (1780–1834), who graduated as a Doctor of Law at the age of 16 and in the same year, 1796, became the first Jew to be admitted to the Bar. It proved to be an auspicious year for the community as a whole, for Jews were also granted equal citizenship rights for the first time.

Sadly, Jonas Daniël Meijerplein is today associated more with the annihilation of most of the city's Jews during World War II. Following the German invasion in May 1940, anti-Jewish measures were at first introduced only gradually. The stakes were raised in early February 1941 when the Germans ordered the Jewish Council to be set up, supposedly to maintain order among the Jewish people. Following a disturbance on 19 February, the German chief of police decided to make an

Map on page 165

The huge copper candelabrum at the Portuguese-Israelite Synagogue.

BELOW: the impressively large Portuguese-Israelite Synagogue dominates J.D. Meijerplein.

Jews in Amsterdam

Jews first settled in the Netherlands in large numbers in the late 16th century. The 1579 Treaty of Utrecht stipulated that no one should be persecuted for their religious beliefs. This was a reaction to Spain's repression of Protestantism (*see page 21*) and did not necessarily have the Jews in mind, but nevertheless the new republic seemed to offer Jews a freedom they did not enjoy elsewhere in Europe.

The first Jews to settle in Amsterdam were relatively prosperous and well-integrated Marranos – Sephardic Jews from Spain and Portugal who had been forced to convert to Christianity. By the 17th century, up to 10 percent of Amsterdammers were Sephardic Jews. From 1620, the pattern had changed. Most Jews coming to Amsterdam were now Ashkenazi – refugees of German or Polish origin. They settled in the east of town and, unable to speak Dutch, turned to menial ghetto jobs around Sint-Antoniesbreestraat.

Amsterdam's tolerance of its Jewish immigrants was not unbounded. In 1598 the city magistrates determined that the Portuguese merchants could purchase citizenship provided they did not worship openly. A more serious restriction prohibited Jews from becoming members of the guilds. Since nearly all trades were run by guilds, the Jews were in effect excluded from most occupations. They were forced to pursue guild-free activities: banking, diamond polishing, sugar refining, silk manufacture, tobacco twisting and printing (*see page 22*). Jews were also forbidden to own shops, while a later measure decreed that they should not attempt to convert Christians or have relations with Christian women.

It is hardly surprising, therefore, that Jews settled in the city's poorest neighbourhoods. In 1795, after two centuries of Jewish immigration, the vast majority of Jews received poor relief. But 1796 was a year of emancipation for the Jews. With the dissolution of the guilds by the French, all occupations were open to them. Furthermore, they were free to settle anywhere and they obtained the right to vote. As a result, the Jewish community grew substantially, though the "boundaries" of the city's Jewish Quarter had been established: Jodenbreestraat, Sint-Antoniesbreestraat, Uilenburgergracht and Waterlooplein. When the Grachtengordel was completed, wealthier Jews moved to the new canals and by the end of the 19th century, Plantage Middenlaan was an affluent extension of the quarter. By the early 20th century, some 95 percent of Jodenbuurt's residents were Jewish, and they played a visible role in Dutch society until World War II, when their numbers had grown to 80,000.

During the war, the area became a sealed ghetto, and over 70,000 Jews were sent to their deaths in Auschwitz, Sobibor and Bergen-Belsen. At the end of the war there were only 5,000 survivors and the Jodenbuurt was in ruins (*see page 163*). It was one of the darkest eras in the city's history. Amsterdam, once known as the "Jerusalem of the West", today has a Jewish population of about 25,000. ❑

LEFT: display at the Joods Historisch Museum.

example and on 22 and 23 February, 425 young Jewish men were forcibly arrested, herded together and taken away in trucks.

What happened in this square sparked off the first organised Dutch resistance against the Nazi Occupation. In the face of further round-ups the following day, the communists called for a general strike in protest. The dockworkers were among the first to respond and the strike spread through Amsterdam, only to be broken up violently the following day. Even if the strikers' slogan, "Keep your dirty hands off our rotten Jews", expressed what might be described as an ambivalent attitude, it was a courageous stand and a unique protest in occupied Europe against Nazi inhumanity towards the Jews. Mari Andriessen's bulky bronze statue, *De Dokwerker (The Dockworker)*, in Jonas Daniël Meierplein, unveiled in 1952, commemorates the February strike and is one of Amsterdam's most important war memorials.

The strike merely delayed the inevitable. German policy against the Jews gathered pace in 1942. In January of that year, Jews from Zaandam were the first to be moved from their home town, and Amsterdam was used as the collection point. The Nazis used the Jewish Council, whose headquarters were on Nieuwe Keizersgracht, to co-ordinate the deportations. They evaded resistance by claiming that the deportees were being sent to work in German factories.

Botanical garden

The **Plantage** (Plantation) district begins to live up to its name as soon as you cross over Nieuwe Herengracht. The **Hortus Botanicus ❼** 2a Plantage Middenlaan, tel: 625 9021; open Feb–Nov Mon–Fri 9am–5pm, Sat–Sun 10am–5pm; Dec–Jan Mon–Fri 9am–4pm,

Sat–Sun 10am–4pm; entrance fee) is a medley of colour and scent, and a relaxing place for a stroll. This is one of the world's oldest botanical gardens, founded in 1638 as the Hortus Medicus, a nursery for apothecaries' healing plants. It moved to its current location in 1682 and now houses something like 250,000 flowers and 115,000 plants, shrubs and trees, from more than 8,000 different species. It owes plenty to the treasure trove of tropical plants the Dutch found in their former colonies of Indonesia, Suriname and the Antilles, and not a little of its popularity to the national infatuation with flowers – not only tulips.

Among the garden's highlights are the **Semicircle** behind the entrance, a reconstruction of part of the original layout from 1682, and the **Palm House**, whose collection includes the world's oldest recorded palm tree. Most impressive of all is the **Tri-Climate House**, a greenhouse completed in 1993. Under its immense glass roof you can stroll through a subtropical section, a desert section and a tropical section,

Map on page 165

A black marble memorial at Waterlooplein, at the heart of the Jewish Quarter, commemorates the Holocaust.

BELOW: view across Herengracht from the Hortus Botanicus.

Despite being thoroughly out-gunned by the new Tri-Climate House, the Palm House (1912) is home to the oldest recorded palm in the world, a 400-year-old cycad (a type of palm fern).

BELOW: the striking Holocaust Memorial at Wertheim Park.

with a gallery that can take you 5 metres (16 ft) high through the "jungle". Of historical interest are plants that were brought to the Netherlands by the United East India Company in the 17th and 18th centuries. The **Orangery**, constructed in 1870, has been converted into an airy café where you can order simple meals and snacks; in the summer you can enjoy tea on the terrace under the pleasant scent of citrus trees.

Across the street, the 19th-century Wertheim Park, named after a leading Jewish banker, became the focus of much attention in 1993 when a new **Holocaust Memorial** ❽ was unveiled. Entitled *Auschwitz Nooit Meer (Auschwitz Never Again)*, a collage of broken mirrors jaggedly reflects the sky, alongside a reminder in Dutch and English of the atrocities suffered by the Jewish community during the war. The monument was designed by Dutch writer and sculptor Jan Wolkers.

Between here and Artis Zoo *(see below)* is a prosperous 19th-century Jewish enclave. Doorways here are occasionally adorned with pelicans.

According to Jewish legend, in adversity the pelican will feed its starving young with its own blood. More positive are the Portuguese nameplates – Coelho, Quendo, d'Oliveira – which tell of Jewish blood returning to the quarter.

In remembrance

A little further down Plantage Middenlaan, at No. 24, is another sad reminder of World War II. The facade of the **Hollandsche Schouwburg** ❾ (Holland Theatre; open daily 11am–4pm; free) has been preserved not for architectural reasons but as a memorial. In September 1942, the theatre was appropriated by the Germans as an assembly point for Jews prior to deportation. Their length of stay varied but their route out was always the same: by train to Westerbork, the Dutch transit point for the death camps of Auschwitz, Sobibor and Bergen-Belsen. Through the doorway of this building is a quiet courtyard and a stark obelisk that stands as a monument to the 104,000 Dutch Jews murdered by

the Nazis. A small educational exhibition tells the story of the Jewish community's gradual isolation.

The brightly coloured building opposite is the **Moederhuis** (Mothers' House), dating from 1978, a home for single mothers and their children, designed by Aldo van Eyck. During the war, its predecessor housed a kindergarten for the adjacent Reformed Church Teacher Training College. Some children of those awaiting deportation in the Hollandsche Schouwburg were smuggled across the street and into the kindergarten, where staff helped rescue them. The building still exists and bears a plaque dedicated to all those who helped in the rescues.

At 61 Plantage Kerklaan, the **Verzetsmuseum** ❿ (Resistance Museum; tel: 620 2535; open Tues–Fri 10am–5pm, Sat–Sun noon–5pm; entrance fee, except 5 May) gives a well-balanced account of the struggles and achievements of the Dutch resistance movement during World War II. It is difficult to imagine the circumstances in which the resistance came into being, especially when you consider that at the outbreak of war Dutch society was made up of four main persuasions: Catholics, Protestants, liberals and socialists – subcultures that were not necessarily trusting of each other.

The permanent exhibition conveys chronologically the inevitable social changes and developments in a small country living under progressively worsening conditions imposed not only by an occupying enemy, but also by the horrors of an extreme winter that led to starvation in many areas. Of particular interest are the many interactive exhibits, such as a radio you can tune in, desk drawers you can open to read documents, and the doorbell of a "safe house". Strolling through these corridors of time, you get not only an insight into the dangerous underworld of the resistance but also an appreciation of the pressures that caused many people to end up collaborating with the Germans.

Education is one of the museum's key objectives, and its many facilities include a documentation and study room. In the foyer you'll find temporary exhibitions on present-day resistance to human injustice.

A visit to a museum that details the history of the Dutch trade unions would likely be of interest only to those with a passion for the history of the international labour movement. But Amsterdam's **Nationaal Vakbondsmuseum** ⓫ (National Trades Union Museum; 9 Henri Polaklaan; open Tues–Fri 11am–5pm, Sat 1–5pm; entrance fee), around the corner from the Resistance Museum, might prove the exception. It's in the Diamond Workers' Union building of 1900, designed by architect Hendrick Petrus Berlage, who also designed the Beurs van Berlage *(see page 83)*. This beautiful temple of socialism, replete with coloured decorative tiles and socialist murals,

Map on page 165

The colourful Moederhuis stands opposite the the sombre Hollandsche Schouwburg.

BELOW: wartime heroism remembered at the Verzetsmuseum.

reflects the wealth of the workers' brotherhood that paid for it, and the sensibility of the then new-wave Amsterdam School of architecture.

A zoo and more

The extensive terrain of **Artis Zoo** ⓬ (38–40 Plantage Kerklaan; tel: 523 3400; open daily 9am–5pm; entrance fee), founded in 1838 as Natura Artis Magistra (Nature, Mistress of Art), encompasses the oldest zoo in the Netherlands. There are of course the usual lions, tigers, leopards, gorillas, elephants, camels, peacocks, polar bears, seals and more that no self-respecting zoo can be without, along with a reptile house and an aviary.

In 1998 a huge three-phase expansion programme was begun, in addition to refurbishment of several areas within the existing 10 hectares (25 acres) of gardens. Phase one of this expansion, the African Savannah, opened in 1999. In keeping with the zoo's fanaticism for authenticity, this is a microplain, home to zebras, wildebeests, ostriches and other savannah birds

– the only things to remind you you're in Amsterdam are the surrounding 18th-century warehouses.

In addition to the main part of the zoo, and included in the entry fee, there is a **Planetarium**, a **Geological Museum** and a **Zoological Museum** with exhibits on the evolution of various animal species, and tropical greenhouses. The refurbished **Aquarium** is well-presented, particularly the sections on the River Amazon, coral reefs and Amsterdam's own canals. Artis's garden layout and range of tree and plant species comes close to rivalling Hortus Botanicus *(see page 171)*. You can rest for a while with a snack or lunch at **Artis Restaurant**.

Topical tropical museum

Just across Singelgracht from Artis, at 2 Linnaeusstraat, you can visit one of Amsterdam's most interesting cultural experiences, the **Tropenmuseum** ⓭ (Tropical Museum; tel: 568 8215; open daily10am–5pm; entrance fee), which started life in the early 20th century as the Koninklijk Instituut

BELOW: children can join in at the Tropenmuseum.

voor de Tropen (Royal Tropical Institute). At that time it was unashamedly a celebration of Dutch colonial rule in the East Indies, but all that changed during the 1970s when the museum switched to a politically correct track and abandoned its "white-man's burden" ethos. Today it is an authoritative showcase for the lifestyles, and some of the problems, found today in many of the world's developing countries.

It is housed in a palatial 19th-century building, a symbol of imperialism writ large, yet once inside you encounter a thoroughly modern and often provocative museum, in which you can lose yourself profitably for hours. After entering a magnificent hall with a high glazed dome, you will discover on the main floor and surrounding galleries some 10 separate displays depicting daily life in towns and villages of West Asia, North Africa, Southeast Asia and Latin America. It's easy to become absorbed in the ambience of sights, sounds and scents, as if you have been transported to some exotic

location. Other rooms are devoted to themes such as clothing, music, dance, ecology and appropriate technology. Part of the museum is aimed at children aged 6–12. This so-called **Kindermuseum T.M. Junior** aims to bring elements of an already fascinating (and far from dry and dusty) collection even more to life for kids, by going that extra, hands-on mile.

Cultural performances are frequently held in the museum's main hall. These include *gamalan* orchestra music from Indonesia, Japanese drum music, fiery salsa or sensual tango sounds from Latin America, and evocative Andean pan pipes. Appropriate – and tasty – cuisine is served up at both the **Ekeko** café and the **Souterijn** restaurant, which features a diverse menu of fish, meat and vegetarian dishes from more than a dozen countries.

Just east of the museum is a block of streets with evocative names: Javastraat, Balistraat, Celebesstraat and others recall the former Dutch colonies in what is now Indonesia. ❑

From animals to rocks to planets; a ticket to the Artis Zoo includes entry to the Geological Museum and the Planetarium.

RESTAURANTS AND CAFES

Kilimanjaro
6 Rapenburgerplein
Tel: 622 3485
Open: D Tues–Sun. €€
This could easily have been a disaster – Africa with hollandaise sauce – but in fact the Dutch enthusiast owner has created a small wonder, a little slice of that multifaceted continent in an uncluttered space. The cuisine ranges across several countries' specialities, but here's an emphasis on Ethiopia and francophone Africa.

Tom Yam Fusion Cuisine
22 Staalstraat
Tel: 622 9533
Open: D Tues–Sat. €€–€€€
Once a highly regarded Thai restaurant, Tom Yam reinvented itself as a ... Thai restaurant. And lots more besides. Now the designer setting is matched by designer food that runs the gamut of international styles, mixed and matched on the plate. Recom-

mended, but perhaps a tad pricey.

Bierbrouwerij 't IJ
7 Funenkade
Tel: 622 8325
Open: 11am–midnight daily. €
You can take care of two activities in one place here: visit a working windmill – the De Gooier mill – and quaff some of the excellent craft beers that the microbrewery on the premises produces. If you have doubts about Heineken's and Amstel's pedigrees, try some of these. The outdoor terrace is very popular.

Café de Sluyswacht
1 Jodenbreestraat
Tel: 625 7611
Open: 11am to 1am daily. €
Dating from 1695, this is one of the oldest and most atmospheric brown cafés in Amsterdam, not so much for its interior, which is pretty so-so, but for its street terrace beside a lock on the Oude Schans canal, from where you have a fine view.

● ● ● ● ● ● ● ● ● ● ● ●
Prices are for a three-course meal for one, with wine and coffee
€ under €20, €€ €20–40,
€€€ €40–60, €€€€ over €60

THE WATERFRONT

Amsterdam grew up around its maritime prowess and,
although one of the least visited areas of the city,
the harbour gives a fascinating historical insight
into this seafaring nation

From its earliest days as a fishing village, Amsterdam has turned its face towards the sea. In the late 16th and early 17th centuries, the city's phenomenal growth was built on its role as a mighty centre of shipping and world trade. Dutch maritime prowess was founded on the fishing industry; a Dutchman discovered a recipe for curing fish and pickling herring, which then became important commodities. Dutch sailors opened up scores of new routes to the Far East and the Americas, and Amsterdam's port became the world's busiest. Unfettered access to the sea continued to be vital, and in 1824 the Noordhollandskanaal (North Holland Canal) opened, creating a connection through the entire length of Noord-Holland province to the naval base at Den Helder. The Noordzeekanaal (North Sea Canal) followed in 1876, connected to the sea via the locks at IJmuiden.

The port and its associated activities of shipbuilding and repair are still an important factor in the city's economy, providing jobs and creating wealth. But they no longer occupy Amsterdam's own waterfront. The modern commercial harbour has moved away to the big industrial docks west of the city, along the North Sea Canal.

Amsterdam's history as a port can still be traced along its waterfront in what is known as the Nautisch Kwartier (Nautical Quarter), even if some of the surviving sites hardly count as scenic corners of Amsterdam: Prins Hendrikkade, the Eastern Docks and Oostenburgstraat can look rather forlorn. No matter. Amsterdam's Golden Age wealth came in on ships, and you cannot hope to understand what made this city tick without knowing a little more about its seafaring past.

Map on page 178

LEFT: the past lives on along today's waterfront.
BELOW: *Amsterdam Harbour*, depicted in the 17th century by W. van der Velde.

Amsterdam North

A walk to the rear of **Centraal Station ❶** brings you to the edge of the IJ channel. There are 18 piers here, with various "partyships", Rhine and IJsselmeer cruise boats, and the hydrofoil service to IJmuiden dock. Commuters shuttle back and forth on passenger-only ferries across the IJ between Centraal Station and **Amsterdam-Noord** (North). These ferries afford visitors a brief and – amazingly, for Amsterdam – free sightseeing trip. Both the number of ferries and the routes they serve have increased, a process likely to continue as the old harbour waterfront opens up for new housing developments.

One ferry route goes straight across to Buiksloterweg, which looks about as uninviting as it sounds, and takes just two minutes to get there. Another angles slightly eastwards, to dock at IJplein, and takes a few minutes longer – one good reason for taking this ferry is that IJplein is close to the excellent **Wilhelmina-Dok** waterside café-restaurant (*see page 187*). Both ferries transport bikes. On the way across the busy channel you will probably intersect the wakes of barges, canal-tour boats, yachts and other pleasure boats, perhaps even a visiting warship or an ocean-going cruise liner. Look out for the Royal Dutch Shell office tower to the west on the north bank – its windows are laced with gold dust and they sparkle in the sun. There isn't a lot to see in Amsterdam North, which is a modern residential area, but since ferries come and go every few minutes, you can take refreshment at the tollhouse café before returning to Centraal Station. More ambitiously, you could go for a stroll along the North Holland Canal.

Ferries that ply the longer routes are not free, but a trip on one gives you a great view of the old harbour and the new developments that are transforming it.

BELOW: commuter ferries across the IJ channel are free.

Eastern Islands

For a slightly longer trip you could take a ferry to **Java-Eiland** ❷ (Java Island) and **KNSM-Eiland** ❸ (KNSM Island). These are part of a romantic-sounding cluster of islands, the **Oostelijke Eilanden** (Eastern Islands), in the eastern reaches of the harbour, which have undergone extensive redevelopment in recent years to provide innovative modern housing for people wishing to live just outside the city centre. These two islands were once separate but have been joined together. KNSM Island was the domain of the Royal Dutch Steamship Company, and takes its name from the Dutch initials of the line's name. Most of the old cargo warehouses on the two islands have been demolished to make way for residential projects and there are many interesting modern buildings to look at. The "new" joined island is like a modern-architecture exhibition, combining traditional and new elements.

When you disembark from the ferry, on Sumatrakade on the Java Island section, walk along this northern quay. As you proceed you'll notice some of the older buildings. When you get to the end, there's a good viewpoint from Venetiëkade, which takes in the entrance to the Amsterdam-Rijnkanaal (Amsterdam-Rhine Canal) and to the Oranjesluizen (Orange Locks) that connect Amsterdam to the IJsselmeer lake (formerly the Zuiderzee).

From this viewpoint, follow the shore around to Levantkade on the south, where there are café terraces to enjoy a drink and look out over the barges and docks – one of the best of these is **Kanis en Meiland** *(see page 187)*, at No. 127, a clever Dutch wordplay on KNSM-Eiland. If you're not returning by ferry, take bus 32 back to Centraal Station, past old warehouses in various states of repair and restoration – this entire area is currently undergoing massive redevelopment – boasting their former trading glories in massive letters: AFRIKA, INDIA and others.

Bus 32 also takes you across the bridge over the Erts-Haven to the other cluster of Eastern Islands that

Map on page 178

ORIENTATION
The Amsterdam Waterfront borders the northern fringe of the city, from the new residential developments on the Eastern Islands to the old man-made Western Islands, which are further downstream on the IJ and northwest of the centre.

BELOW: fishermen still trawl the waters west of the harbour.

Gable stones in the harbour area graphically illustrate the maritime heritage.

are part of the grand harbour redevelopment. **Sporenburg** (Rail Town), the northernmost, took its uninspiring name from the fact that it was the principal railhead and marshalling yard for this part of the docks, though no tracks remain among the more or less nondescript new housing blocks. The next island south, **Borneo-Eiland**, has more of the same, as has **Zeeburg**, but Borneo Island does have at least one fascinating street. Each of the houses in Scheepstimmermanstraat, which backs on to the water, is individually designed but on identically sized plots, in an occasionally bizarre architectural case study of unity in diversity.

Further out east, a group of newly created artificial islands in the IJmeer, a southern bay of the IJsselmeer lake, is being developed under the name **IJburg** to provide homes for 20,000 residents.

A new terminal

The growing size of luxury cruise liners and the steadily increasing number of such vessels calling at Amsterdam led to a decision to build a new facility, the **Passenger Terminal Amsterdam** ❹, at 9 Oostelijke Handelskade, just east of Centraal Station. It has room for 2,500 passengers in a building occupying 35,000 sq. metres (377,000 sq. ft), and facilities include a convention centre, boardrooms, restaurants, banks and shops. The terminal's official opening in 2000 coincided with *Sail Amsterdam*, the city's week-long maritime festival held every five years.

In an area that is being redeveloped at breakneck speed, one of the most interesting new buildings springing up is the **Muziekgebouw** ❺ (Music Building), at 1 Piet Heinkade, on the westernmost tip of the waterside peninsula just east of Centraal Station. Under construction at the time of writing and due to open early in 2005, the Muziekgebouw will complement the classical-music emphasis of the Concertgebouw *(see page 157)* by focusing on modern music. Two music operations that are due to move here from their present bases are the Bimhuis jazz club *(see page 224)* and De IJsbreker *(see page 223)* experimental music club. There will also be visiting musicians from around the world.

Inner harbour

Heading east from Centraal Station, you don't need to go far along Prins Hendrikkade before you arrive at the **Schreierstoren** ❻ (Tower of Tears) at Nos. 94–95. This is the oldest surviving tower in Amsterdam and was built in 1482 as part of the city walls. The tower got its name from the sailors' wives and lovers who would stand here sadly as they watched their menfolk depart on voyages that could last months or years, and who might learn of the death of their partners when their ship returned.

The Schreierstoren stands at the head of a pretty canalside outlook, down Oudezijds Kolk towards Zeedijk, and along Geldersekade towards Nieuwmarkt. Today it houses an atmospheric bar – it could hardly be otherwise, given the setting – called the **VOC Café**, which takes its name from the Dutch initials for the United East India Company. It has attached to it three clues to Amsterdam's nautical past. A 1927 tablet from the Greenwich Village Historical Society commemorates Henry Hudson's departure from here in 1609, the beginning of a long voyage to what is now New York and the Hudson River. Another tablet, from 1569, shows a weeping woman and a ship weighing anchor. The third was placed in 1945 and reads: *Eerste schipvaart naar Oostindi' 1595* (First voyage to the East Indies, 1595).

Further along Prins Hendrikkade, across Waals-Eilandsgracht, is the massive and exuberant **Scheepvaarthuis** ❼ (Maritime House), an appropriate name for a building that overlooks the Oosterdok (Eastern Dock), even if it doesn't date from the city's seagoing heyday. Built in 1915, it was designed as shipping-company offices by Jo van der Mey, an architect of the Amsterdam School that flourished in the early 20th century *(see pages 66–67)*. This was not only the building that launched the style, it is also one of its finest expressions. Internally and externally, the building's lively, imaginative and humorous seafaring motifs and decorations recount Amsterdam's maritime history in delightful detail. Bas-reliefs of ships, chains, anchors, whales, dolphins, seals and mermaids ornament the facade, and the railings ripple like waves. Four female forms on the cornices represent the cardinal compass points, and above the entrance is an image of the constellation Ursa Major (the Great Bear, or the Plough). The edifice now houses offices of the municipal transport company, GVB Amsterdam, but there are plans afoot, though not yet approved, to turn it into a luxury hotel.

Admiral Michiel Adriaensz de Ruyter (1607–76), a naval hero

Map on page 178

With a crew of 20 and a ship called Half Moon, Henry Hudson set sail for North America from the Schreierstoren, a medieval tower once part of the city walls.

LEFT: an old salt.
BELOW: the new Muziekgebouw, a major music venue.

Montelbaanstoren, fortification-cum-clocktower.

BELOW: climb the steps on top of NEMO for a commanding view.

credited with making the Dutch navy powerful enough to overcome British and French fleets, lived at 131 Prins Hendrikkade. A frieze over the front door commemorates him. De Ruyter is buried in the Nieuwe Kerk.

Landward from here, on the south side of Waals-Eilandsgracht was an important area known as the Lastage, the site of the city's earliest ship-building yards. These lay outside the now vanished defensive walls. You can pinpoint this locality by visiting the **Montelbaanstoren** ❽, in a scenic location a short walk along the west bank of Oude Schans. This tower was constructed in 1512 as a fortification to protect the Lastage, which was a vital element in the prosperity of a town that depended so much on shipping and shipbuilding. Its decorative spire was added in 1606 by Hendrick de Keyser, the architect responsible for many of Amsterdam's other pinnacles, not to mention some of its finest buildings.

Behind the tower is the old Lastage area. Along the narrow Recht Boomsloot canal are con-verted warehouses that display some fine examples of spout, neck and bell gables. At No. 22, a monumental stairway leads to a ware-house that in 1714 was converted to an Armenian church. Binnen Bantammerstraat leads across Geldersekade into the Red Light District *(see page 103)*.

Science centre

Once a busy harbourside, Prins Hendrikkade is today a major road taking traffic in and out of Amsterdam via the IJ Tunnel. Unattractive as it may sound – and look – to a pedestrian, a stroll to the entrance of this tunnel is worth the effort. Above the entrance, at 2 Oosterdok, is a giant, fantastical, patina-sheathed building which, seen from the north, has the appearance of a large ship's prow. From Prins Hendrikkade you can ascend to its roof. At the top you are standing on a ter-race with a panoramic view over the Eastern Dock and the IJ. From this point you can see many of the places mentioned in this chapter, as well as shipping, Rhine barges and local har-bour traffic.

The building is the **NEMO Science and Technology Centre** ❾ (tel: 0900 919 1100; open July–Aug daily 10am–5pm; Sept–June Tues–Sun 10am–5pm; entrance fee), designed by architect Renzo Piano and opened in 1997. This science museum, whose motto is "A world wherein you are the greatest miracle", lives up to its promise. Nearly all the exhibits are interac-tive, from refilling radio-controlled model oil tankers to conducting light and sound experiments and carrying out your own investigation in a laboratory. You create your own voyage of discovery in six depart-ments on four floors. All exhibits are in Dutch and English, and the place is child-friendly.

Walking between Prins Hendrikkade and NEMO, you can hardly

Map
on page
178

miss the collection of vintage vessels along the quayside: they are all registered as floating monuments, and lovingly restored with plaques on the quay detailing the history and working life of each boat.

A pedestrian walkway connects NEMO with the Oosterdokskade area just to the east of Centraal Station. From May 2004, the TPG Building at 3–5 Oosterdokskade beside Centraal Station has been the temporary home of Amsterdam's modern art museum, the **Stedelijk Museum** ❿ (Municipal Museum; tel: 573 2737; open daily 11am–5pm; entrance fee). Its regular home at Museumplein is closed until mid-2006 for renovation and extension *(see page 156)*.

Housed in an appropriately futuristic building between NEMO and the Maritime Museum, and designed by René van Zuuk, is **ARCAM**, the Architectuur Centrum Amsterdam (Amsterdam Architecture Centre; 600 Prins Hendrikkade, open Tues–Sat 1–5pm; free), a resource centre devoted to the city's fast-changing architectural landscape. It hosts educational seminars and discussion groups, and organises exhibitions on topical architectural and urban development themes.

Maritime Museum

One of Amsterdam's highlights, which both documents and celebrates Holland's seafaring history, is the **Scheepvaartmuseum** ⓫ (Maritime Museum; tel: 523 2222; open Tues–Sun, daily during school holidays, 10am–5pm; entrance fee), beside the water at Kattenburgerplein. Even the most ardent of landlubbers will consider an hour or two here well spent. This rich collection occupies the old Zeemagazijn, the Amsterdam Admiralty arsenal, built in 1656. From this building, sails, ropes, cannons, cutlasses, food and fresh water were supplied to the newly built ships launched at the adjacent yard, and to the fleet moored in the port. In the 20th century the Dutch navy moved its bases to harbours with direct access to the North Sea and the Zeemagazijn lost its original function. The building was renovated in the 1970s and a

BELOW: the unmistakable profile of the NEMO Science and Technology Centre.

first-class museum was born. There's a pronounced emphasis on the 17th century, when the country was one of the world's great sea powers. The models and paintings are of the same period as the ships and events they represent.

The museum charts a detailed course through Amsterdam's and Holland's maritime achievements, starting with the V-shaped timber of a small medieval vessel found in the reclaimed land of the former Zuiderzee and finishing with glimpses into the lives of passengers cruising to South America, the United States, Asia and Australia on the luxurious liners of the early and mid-20th century. Between these two points, the collection provides colourful insights into the development of the 16th-century three-masted sailing ships that opened the way to the uncharted oceans; Holland's many naval wars; and how, in the 17th century, Amsterdam was the world centre of marine cartography, producing the first sea-atlas.

One of the highlights – particularly for children – is a full-size

BELOW: maritime history at the Scheepvaartmuseum.

replica of a 17th-century Dutch East Indiaman, the *Amsterdam,* which ran aground off Hastings in England on her maiden voyage. The ship has a "crew" of actors dressed in period naval costume and is moored at the museum's landing-stage. It presents a fantastic sight, a squat yet elegant mountain of timber surmounted by three tall masts and threaded with a tracery of rigging. When a breeze roils the water, or the wake from a passing boat rolls by, the recreated *Amsterdam* sways gently at her moorings. Below decks, in the crew quarters and cargo hold, the ship's timbers creak and groan alarmingly, creating an evocative impression of conditions on such a craft on water.

East of the museum is an archipelago of man-made islands projecting into the IJ, and dating from the 17th century. Originally the three Eastern Islands – **Kattenburg**, **Wittenburg** and **Oostenburg** – were created to help Holland in its battle for maritime trading and naval supremacy against Great Britain, which started around 1650. Providing building space for warships and ocean-going merchant vessels, these islands were lined with harbours and bisected with wide canals. The United East India Company's Oostenburg shipyard was perhaps the world's largest industrial complex at the time. Consecrated in 1670, the **Oosterkerk** (Eastern Church) stands near the old island harbour.

New uses

There is no shortage of buildings in this area surviving from the days when Amsterdam was a centre of world commerce. Going inland from Kattenburgerplein, a walk along the Entrepôtdok reveals a line of warehouses built by the United East India Company, and recently converted into apartments. At the western end, the grand gateway emblazoned with the dock's

name looks sadly out of place surrounded by the seedy bars and cafés of Kadijksplein. But go through the gate and walk along the waterside and you can picture just how many shiploads laden with exotic eastern cargoes once used these waterways. Today the buildings have been turned into stylish offices and apartments. Tucked between them are quiet bars that provide welcome ports of call as you retrace the footprints of Amsterdam's seafarers.

Just over halfway along Hoogte Kadijk, which runs parallel to and north of the Entrepôtdok, the **Kromhout Shipyard**, one of 30 shipyards established here by the end of the 17th century, still survives. The name Kromhout was first mentioned in 1757 in relation to a forge on the site of the present-day shipyard. A shipwright, Doede Jansen Kromhout, developed the site. In the 19th century a new owner, Daniël Goedkoop, equipped the yard for building iron ships, and his son turned it into the city's biggest and most modern shipyard.

One of his investments, an iron canopy over the slipway, stands today and is a protected monument. Moves to preserve the Kromhout yard for the future were first made in 1970 and later gained the support of the city's Maritime Museum. The yard was later placed on Amsterdam's list of protected monuments. Still an operating shipyard, it now restores and repairs historic vessels.

A modest museum here, the **Museumwerf 't Kromhout** ⓬ (Kromhout Wharf Museum; tel: 627 6777; open Tues 10am–3pm; entrance fee), consists mostly of old ships' engines, pumps, models of old steamers – things that are only likely to appeal to people with a penchant for marine engineering. Some of the framed engravings on display, depicting the Nieuwe Vaart as a busy artery of floating repair platforms and ships at anchor, serve only to emphasise that the docks here have long been dead commercially. There are plans to install a permanent exhibition that will paint the full picture of shipbuilding on the city's Eastern Islands and of the

Map on page 178

Free ferries provide a convenient service for pedestrians and cyclists who live on the north bank of the IJ. Thrifty tourists can also hop aboard for a tour of the waterfront.

BELOW: actors bring the past to life at the Scheepvaartmuseum.

people who lived and worked here. But the Kromhout Shipyard currently lacks the money to do justice to the heritage of this sleepy corner of Amsterdam, and a visit here is currently for aficionados only.

Western Islands

To get to the old, man-made **Westelijke Eilanden**  (Western Islands) west of Centraal Station, take bus 35 from outside the station to Van Diemenstraat. You could also walk there, along waterfront De Ruijterkade and Westerdoksdijk – the road is not exactly a pleasure itself, but it does have a scenic view of the harbour. South of Van Diemenstraat is a serene, cramped but character-rich neighbourhood of 17th-century warehouses, many of which have been converted to residential use, docks, small boatyards and other harbour installations.

The three islands – **Realeneiland**, **Bickerseiland** and **Prinseneiland** – are artificial, originally constructed in the 17th century to house shipyards. The yards profited from a shipbuilding boom caused by the United East India Company's policy of granting trading licences to companies that used Dutch ships. They were also used for storing inflammable items at a safe remove from the city. Warehouses are today the most visible surviving legacy of this maritime zone. Many have been converted into chic apartments. Unimproved warehouses, now scarce, are favoured by artists because of their space and character.

To get a sense of this area without traipsing up and down every one of its streets, go down waterside Houtmankade, past a children's playground in Zoutkeetsplein, to the end of the canal. Turn left into Schiemanstraat and its continuation, Sloterdijkstraat. Cross the narrow bridge over Prinseneilandsgracht into Galgenstraat, then cross the bridge over Bickersgracht. At the far end of Bickersgracht is a **children's farm** where city kids get acquainted with nature. Finally, by way of Bickersstraat and Jonkerplein, head under the railway arch towards busy Haarlemmer Houttuinen.

The Kromhout Shipyard Museum is virtually all that remains of the shipbuilding industry that once flourished on the Eastern Islands.

RIGHT: 17th-century engraving of Ambon harbour in the Moluccas, fabled spice islands of the east.

The United East India Company

In 1595, a Dutch expedition reached the East Indies for the first time, by way of the Cape of Good Hope and the Indian Ocean. Voyaging as far as Australia, they opened up the legendary spice route and began to displace the Spanish and Portuguese as rulers of the waves in these parts. The trade in tropical products became one of the largest sources of income for Amsterdam.

The Vereenigde Oostindische Compagnie (United East India Company), or VOC., was founded in Amsterdam in 1602. Shares in the company were traded in the Mercantile Exchange. A Westindische Compagnie (West India Company) was later founded to maintain trade with the Americas. In 1609, when an Exchange bank was established to facilitate trade, Amsterdam was well on its way to becoming the most important trading centre in Europe.

The VOC soon fulfilled its aim to secure a monopoly of the eastern spice trade. Its trading posts became colonies, and by 1730 the VOC was the world's largest trading enterprise, even creating its own coinage. Although it lost its leading position after 1750, its influence lasted much longer. The Dutch empire in the East Indies remained intact until Indonesia gained independence in 1949.

Map
on page
178

Culture Park

From here, you can go west past Haarlemmerplein to the **Cultuurpark Westergasfabriek ⑭** (Western Gasworks Culture Park, 8–10 Haarlemmerweg). Based in a disused gasworks, this monument of restored industrial archaeology from 1885 reopened in 2003 as a budding new star in the city's cultural firmament (some elements had already been open for years on the site, and others have yet to be completed). The complex covers 13 hectares (32 acres). The park alone – a combination of lawns, grass, trees, elongated and circular ponds, water-gardens and even artificial hills – is an attractive and more than respectably sized addition to the city's roster of green spaces. There are pavement and indoor cafés, a cinema, a dance club and arts-and-crafts workshops. Some of the city's top festivals, such as the Drum Rhythm Festival and the Holland Festival, take place here.

Returning to Haarlemmer Houttuinen, a good way back to Centraal Station is to turn into Oranjestraat and Haarlemmerdijk. You will notice a gradient here, which serves to remind you that you're now on top of an old dyke that used to face the sea. Turn left to the next bridge, which provides a neat view along Prinsengracht all the way to the Westerkerk *(see page 118)*. Cross over into Haarlemmerstraat, a lively street full of interesting small shops, cafés and restaurants. On the right is West Indisch Huis *(see page 113)* and at No. 105 you pass the **Café Prinsesse-Bar**, an archetypal brown café. Look out too for the ship's winch embedded in the pavement.

On one side of the bridge over Singel, on a pedestal, is a ship's propeller, which marks the boundary of the Nautisch Kwartier. The brick building to your left is the Amsterdam School of Architecture, formerly a school for barge skippers' children. Cross over the bridge, which is sandwiched by lock gates that used to separate the city from the sea, and pause, if you like, to partake in the delights of fresh raw herring from the prize-winning stall on the bridge. ❏

LEFT: daily specials at Wilhelmina-Dok.

RESTAURANTS

Wilhelmina-Dok
1 Noordwal
Tel: 632 3701
Open: L, D daily. €€
Surprisingly, for all Amsterdam's lengthy harbour waterfront, there's a paucity of restaurants to take advantage of such a prime location. This slightly rough and ready place in Amsterdam-Noord (you can get there for free by ferry across the IJ from Centraal Station) has a wonderful, if windy, waterside terrace and some acceptable Mediterranean food.

Kanis & Meiland
127 Levantkade
Tel: 418 2439
Open: L, D daily. €
Unless you speak Dutch, or say it fast, the clever pun in the café's name might not be clear – it's on KNSM-Eiland (Island) in the redeveloped eastern harbour, and has a fine waterside terrace on a former dock to prove it. The interior is instant-brown café. Bar snacks are served.

● ● ● ● ● ● ● ● ● ● ● ● ● ● ●
Prices are for a three-course meal for one, with wine and coffee
€ under €20, €€ €20–40,
€€€ €40–60, €€€€ over €60

AMSTERDAM SOUTH

If you venture by foot, tram or bus just south of the
city centre, you will experience a very different
Amsterdam, with characterful neighbourhoods and
peaceful green expanses

Population growth during the 19th century forced Amsterdam to expand its old boundaries and spread south. As a result, if you venture just a short distance beyond the semicircle traced by the Singelgracht canal, which forms a moat around the old city, there are numerous new neighbourhoods worthy of discovery. In the far south is a wonderful park that offers a welcome green refuge from the centre's busy sightseeing trail.

Brewing traditions

Just beyond Singelgracht, a place to visit for a barrel of fun is **Heineken Experience** ❶ (Stadhouderskade 78; tel: 523 9666; open Tues–Sun 10am–6pm; entrance fee; under 18s not admitted), even if you are forced to swallow a substantial mouthful of Heineken's marketing message along the way. The beer's popularity was the brewery's undoing, in that demand forced Heineken out of Amsterdam in 1988. The Amsterdam plant was able to produce a mere 80,000 bottles an hour, and Amsterdam on its own consumes beer at the same rate. Heineken's Den Bosch plant has a capacity of 350,000 bottles an hour and the one at Zoeterwoude manages a hefty 700,000 (when demand requires, production can surge to a million bottles).

The Experience opened in 2001 on the site of the decommissioned Heineken Brewery dating from 1867, most of which has been demolished. It replaces an earlier nostalgic and sedate traipse through the old brewing facilities – copper vessels, antique brewing paraphernalia, malt silos and cellars. But then some bright spark decided that the practice of donating the then modest entrance fee to charity made about as much business sense as pouring beer down the drain. Nowadays, you get to pay a

LEFT & BELOW: inside the Heineken Brewery.

Flowers and Dutch-style statuettes are just some of the finds at Albert Cuypmarkt.

lot more to be persuaded, in a variety of fast-moving, hands-on, interactive, multimedia, and occasionally ingenious ways, that Heineken is the greatest thing since sliced bread. In one of these, you "tour" Amsterdam virtually aboard an old horse-drawn dray wagon. At the end of your visit you receive two "free" glasses of beer – and an empty Heineken glass.

A street market

At the centre of Amsterdam's first suburb, **Oud Zuid** (Old South), an area that sprang up in the late 19th century, is a place that pulls the crowds. The **Albert Cuypmarkt** ❷, Amsterdam's busiest street market, attracts some 20,000 people on weekdays, and one estimate puts the number of visitors on any Saturday at 50,000 – more than six percent of Amsterdam's population. The market, and the long street on which it stands, takes its name from an important 17th-century Dutch land-scape painter, Albert Cuyp, some of whose works can be seen in the Rijksmuseum. The market starts at Ferdinand Bolstraat and stretches east to Van Woustraat. As you walk through, keep your wits about you – this is a notorious haunt of petty thieves. Otherwise, do what the locals do and buy fresh raw herring to nibble on while you stroll.

The construction of housing beyond Singelgracht – often of poor quality – had begun around 1870. A new working-class neighbourhood emerged around Gerard Doustraat, Govert Flinckstraat and Albert Cuypstraat, dubbed "De Pijp" (The Pipe) after the long, narrow streets of three- and four-storey tenements. The Albert Cuypmarkt originated soon afterwards, gaining momentum in 1905 when a local law allowed a greater range of goods to be sold.

The arrival of industry in Amsterdam in the 19th century brought with it thousands of immigrant

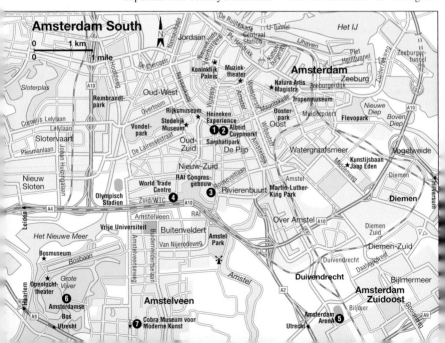

workers, many of whom settled in De Pijp. A second wave of foreign workers following World War II widened the variety of ethnic groups represented here, hence the Turkish and Surinamese restaurants. The fortunes of the Albert Cuypmarkt wavered in the early years but today it is a long, crowded, noisy and fascinating market. If you want to rub shoulders with a sizeable proportion of Amsterdam's multicultural population, this is the place to do it.

A. Van Moppes & Zoon (tel: 676 1242) is located at 2–6 Albert Cuypstraat, at the western end of the street. It is one of several prominent diamond workshops that have an open-door policy, allowing you to see diamonds in raw form and learn something of how the cutting industry took root here.

Social architecture

If the De Pijp district shows Amsterdam pushing back its boundaries with little concern for visual style, elsewhere in the suburbs – especially in **Nieuw Zuid** (New South) – there are strong examples of a much more inspirational kind of architecture. One of the best known of the city's architectural movements is the Amsterdam School, which emerged in the early part of the 20th century. The term was used for a group of socialist architects who developed a radically new style of building (*see pages 66–67*).

The work of the Amsterdam School has been described as "solid but rather playful housing... a kind of domestic sculpture in brick". Even though the style lasted for just a decade it has become a well-known ingredient in Amsterdam's street scene. An important piece of legislation in 1901, which introduced municipal subsidies into the construction of working-class housing, paved the way for buildings in the distinctive style of the Amsterdam School.

If you want to pursue examples around here, go to Pieter Lodewijk Takstraat, a few minutes' walk south of Sarphatipark, to see apartment blocks designed by architect P.L. Kramer. Nearby, on Henriëtte Ronnerplein to the east, and on Thérèse

Map on page 190

ORIENTATION
This chapter covers the southern suburbs, which lie just beyond the limits of the city centre, an area bound by the semicircular Singelgracht. The extensive woodland of the Amsterdamse Bos lies several kilometres further afield.

BELOW: a busy Saturday at Albert Cuypmarkt.

Schwartzeplein to the west, are good examples of the work of M. De Klerk, another accomplished Amsterdam School architect.

Southern efficiency

As the city grew beyond the cramped confines of its historic core, new suburbs were built, both residential and commercial, and beyond them, entire new towns.

Visitors negotiating the traffic around the vast **RAI Congresge-bouw** ❸ exhibition centre might find it hard to believe that this was once open polderland. The RAI's complex of glass-and-steel exhibition halls has been expanding and modernising on its present location since 1961. Now it takes all kinds: religious revivals, Aids congresses, performances by Amsterdam's Concertgebouw Orchestra, the Modern Homes Exhibition, Jumping Amsterdam (a horse-jumping event), cat shows, dog shows, fashion shows, car shows, boat shows. The complex, located just a matter of minutes by train from Schiphol Airport, has more than 30,000 sq.

The blue glass of the World Trade Centre towers above surrounding office buildings.

BELOW: the suburbs are well serviced by a modern rail network.
RIGHT: peaceful Amsterdamse Bos.

metres (320,000 sq. ft) of halls, its own railway and Metro station, express tram links, a bus station, vast underground and above-ground car parks, and even its own harbour linked to the city's canal network.

Just one train and Metro stop west of the RAI is the cluster of office towers of Amsterdam's **World Trade Centre** ❹, dubbed *De Blauwe Engel* (The Blue Angel) for its oceans of blue-tinted glass. This emphasis on business carries over into the extensive commercial zones of **Amsterdam Zuidoost** (Southeast), where the modern architecture is often award-winning, notably the organic architecture of the ING Bank Building (1987). Zuidoost's Bijlmermeer district is the location of the **Amsterdam ArenA** ❺. This superlative stadium of the city's football aces Ajax (and the national team) doubles as a venue for concerts by international superstars and supergroups. An entire entertainment complex of cinemas, theatres, museums, restaurants and cafés has grown up around the ArenA, and further expansion is planned.

Amsterdam Forest

Amsterdammers like to get away from the irritations of the busy city centre and grab a big gulp of fresh air at the **Amsterdamse Bos ❻** (Amsterdam Forest), way out on the southern fringes. This large, wooded park is the country on the city's doorstep. Bring along a picnic if the weather is fine.

Although it now seems entirely natural, the Amsterdamse Bos, like much of Holland, is artificial. The decision to turn a wide stretch of open polderland on the city's southern edge into a park to meet the growing demand for leisure space was made by the city council in 1928. When work on the Amsterdamse Bos began, it provided welcome jobs to many men who had become unemployed as the Depression years began. It was, literally, a man-made landscape – the work was done not by machine but by men and horses. The fruit of their labours was an 800-hectare (2,000-acre) park that draws people in their thousands all year round. With around 48 km (30 miles) of bicycle paths and close to 160 km (100 miles) of footpaths, there is room for everybody. The trees and plants are now firmly bedded in, and the park has become an important home for birds, insects and small animals.

There is plenty to do and see. The **Bosbaan** rowing course, which exceeds the international competition length of 2,000 metres (6,600 ft), also provides a venue for canoe, speedboat and swimming races. At the eastern end of this long, straight stretch of water is a cluster of rowing stations and pavilions, and a café, the **Café Bosbaan**, with a terrace overlooking the course. On most days there will be competition-rowing enthusiasts setting up and plying their craft, and a long line of anglers on the shore.

Various performances take place on summer evenings at a 1,500-seat open-air theatre, and there's a children's farm, stables, playgrounds, a campsite, a pancake house, a wildlife preserve, a large pond called the **Grote Vijver** on which you can hire boats, and even an artificial hill to provide a focus to the

Map on page 190

Holland's premier football stadium, the Amsterdam ArenA, illustrates the point that Amsterdam is a civilised, grown-up sort of place – restaurants, theatres, museums and cafés have all mushroomed in its vicinity.

BELOW: the legendary Johann Cruyff.

Dutch Football

In the early 1970s, one of the finest football teams ever assembled began to take shape in the distinctive orange of the Dutch national side. Cruyff, Neeskens, Krol, Haan et al showed the world a new dimension to the beautiful game, so-called "total football". The concept was that each of the 10 outfield players could, in theory, play in any position, interchanging at will in a fluid style the like of which had never been seen. Yet the brilliance somehow failed to translate into trophies – the Dutch reached the 1974 and 1978 World Cup Finals, but lost both. Since then there have been setbacks and an improbable number of internal squabbles, but the team has largely retained its quality, and is respected by all.

Map
on page
190

Watching the world go by at Amsterdamse Bos.

BELOW: *Dry Zen Garden* sculpture at the Cobra Museum.

landscape. A small ferry takes visitors on trips across the **Nieuwe Meer**, a surprisingly tranquil lake considering that it lies on the edge of the busy A10 ring road and close to Schiphol Airport. The view of the water will probably be enlivened by pleasure boats and fishermen.

At the new **Bezoekerscentrum** (Visitor Centre; 5 Bosbaan, open daily noon–5pm; free) you can trace the story of the park's creation and learn about its wildlife. Exhibits reel off the statistics with pride: hundreds of species of birds, trees, herbs, fungi and beetles (more than 700 of the latter). A rustic restaurant, the **Boerderij Meerzicht**, is a good place for pancakes.

In the summer, on Sundays and public holidays, a novel way of getting to Amsterdamse Bos is by antique tram from the old **Haarlemmermeerstation**, just north of the 1928 **Olympisch Stadion** (Olympic Stadium) at Stadionplein. The service is provided by the **Electrische Museum Tramlijn** (Electric Tramline Museum), which has collected and renovated old trams

from around Europe. Otherwise, take the No. 16 tram from Centraal Station to the Stadionplein terminus, then hop on any outbound bus. Or catch direct buses (170, 171, 172) from Centraal Station.

Cobra Museum

Just beyond the city limits, in the nondescript new town of Amstelveen, is an intriguing museum. The brilliantly white **Cobra Museum of Modern Art** ⑦ (Cobra Museum voor Moderne Kunst; 1–3 Sandbergplein; open Tues–Sun 11am–5pm; entrance fee) opened here in 1995. It focuses on Karel Appel, Constant, Corneille and other members of the controversial post-war Cobra Movement, which took its name from the first letters of three European capitals – Copenhagen, Brussels, Amsterdam – where its members were based. Their works drew inspiration from folk art, naive painting, primitivism and the drawings of children and the mentally ill, and many incorporated text. To get there, take tram 5 from Centraal Station to the end of the line. ❏

RESTAURANTS

Restaurants

Continental

De Kas
3 Kamerlingh Onneslaan
Tel: 462 4562
Open: L, D Mon–Fri; D Sat.
€€€
You get a great outside view from inside this restaurant, a converted greenhouse dating from 1926, and the brightly lit interior makes good viewing too. Its changing fixed-price Continental menus, which emphasise Mediterranean flair and eco-friendly ingredients, are endlessly popular, despite the far-out location and high prices.

De Vrolijke Abrikoos
76 Weteringschans
Tel: 624 4672
Open: D daily. €€
The "Happy Apricot" is a slightly unusual mixture, a "vegetarian" restaurant where delectable organic food shares space on the menu with some meat and fish dishes. There's a large non-smoking section – something that's a rarity in smoke-happy Amsterdam.

La Rive
Amstel Inter-Continental Hotel, 1 Professor Tulpplein
Tel: 520 3264
Open: L, D Mon–Fri; D Sat.
€€€€
This elegant riverside hotel restaurant with two Michelin stars specialises in elaborate modern French and Mediterranean cuisine, served at tables that are intimate yet widely spaced for maximum privacy. The service, which is on the formal side, is flawless – unless you consider a superfluity of super-attentive waiters to be a flaw.

Wildschut
1–3 Roelof Hartplein
Tel: 676 8220
Open: B, Br, L, D daily. €–€€
Permanently trendy, this café-restaurant stands on a curving street corner that catches enough rays from the late-afternoon sun to make its pavement terrace hallowed ground in good weather for recently liberated office workers. The food ranges from bar snacks to well-prepared international dishes.

Italian

L'Angoletto
18 Hemonystraat
Tel: 676 4182
Open: D Sun–Fri. €–€€
Pasta, pizza and other Italian dishes every bit as tasty as mamma used to make them, and for a reasonable price, are the unique selling point of this plain but authentic eatery in the multi-ethnic De Pijp district. That's enough to bring the crowds, so you may have to wait a bit to get served.

Japanese

Yamazato
Okura Hotel, 333 Ferdinand Bolstraat
Tel: 678 8351
Open: B, L, D daily. €€€€
This elegant restaurant's reputation for having the finest Japanese food in the Netherlands is merited, not only for the usual offerings like sushi and tempura, but also for its changing theme menus, which feature lobster and game in season. After you've dined, head up to the lounge on the 23rd floor for drinks, with superb views across the city.

Yoichi
128 Weteringschans
Tel: 622 6829
Open: D Thurs–Tues. €€€
Through-and-through traditional Japanese, with family owners and waitresses in kimonos, but with a style that's far from stiff, Yoichi has been going strong for more than 30 years. It's not cheap, but Japanese food rarely is, and quality is high. Try to get a seat upstairs.

PRICE CATEGORIES

Prices are for a three-course meal for one, with wine and coffee
€ = under €20
€€ = €20–40
€€€ = €40–60
€€€€ = over €60

RIGHT: a typical Dutch dish of herring salad.

BEYOND THE CITY

For a change of scenery from the busy city, a day trip
offers a completely different ambience: historical
towns such as Haarlem or Delft, Dutch cheese
centres or traditional windmills

L ike any major city, Amsterdam does not necessarily reflect the nation of which it is a part. The residents of this "cosmopolitan village" take pride in being more free, tolerant, outspoken, outrageous and independent than their Dutch counterparts in other cities. But enthusiasm can begin to wane when one's spirit starts to crave a bit of peace and a respite from dodging trams and bicycles. There is life beyond Amsterdam, and it is rewarding to discover on many levels: climbing inside a windmill; walking along a historic canal that inspired the young Rembrandt; or eating pancakes in a pastoral village.

Some of these side destinations are served by package coach tours, though you can find your own way by bus, train, bicycle or rented car. All are within unhurried day-trip range of Amsterdam.

Zaanse Schans

On the River Zaan, less than half an hour outside the centre of Amsterdam, you can appear to travel back in time to Holland's Golden Age. **Zaanse Schans** ❶ is not, as you might imagine, an open-air museum but a typical "dyke-village", complete with working windmills, traditional wooden homes, merchants' stone mansions and warehouses.

Its picture-postcard appearance belies the fact that Zaanse Schans was the heart of the Zaanstreek (Zaan District), one of the world's first industrial areas at a time when windmills, not smokestacks, cluttered the skyline. After the invention around here of the first sawmill in 1592, more than 200 windmills were built on this site, and more than 1,000 in the entire Zaan District, engaged in the production of linseed oil, paint, snuff, paper and mustard, and sawing timber for the

Map
on page
200

PRECEDING PAGES:
Zaanse Schans
windmills.
LEFT: Volendam
harbour.
BELOW: Noord
Hollander in
traditional clothing.

Decorative clogs are popular souvenirs.

Zaan shipyards. Eight still function at Zaanse Schans today.

Beside them stand buildings that were relocated here in the 1950s with the aim of preserving a residential quarter typical of the district. Quaint shops are housed in well-preserved, authentic old monuments. You can buy hand-painted skates, timeless pewter objects, wooden toys, Delft pottery and clogs – all made in the traditional way. Each shop and windmill has its own ambience. At the cheese farm you can taste before you buy. And don't leave without a pot of the cel-

ebrated piquant Zaanse mustard, produced in a mill by a family business that dates back to 1786. There is also a historical museum, a clock museum, a bakery museum and an antique costumier. Along the 8-hectare (20-acre) terrain with its tiny bridges and cobblestoned walkways is a pancake house, a bakery and a Michelin-starred restaurant. The **Zaans Museum** (open Tues–Sat 10am–5pm; Sun noon–5pm; entrance fee) features locally themed collections. There is also a *rondvaart* (round-trip) cruise along the waterways. For further informa-

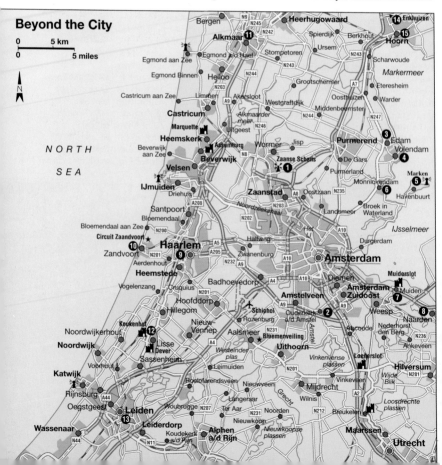

Beyond the City

tion, contact the Zaanse Schans Visitor Centre (tel: 075 616 8218).

Ouderkerk aan de Amstel

No matter what form of transport you take to **Ouderkerk aan de Amstel** ❷ – boat, bicycle or bus – the riverside village just 4 km (2½ miles) south of Amsterdam is simply too beautiful to miss. Its scenic land- and waterscapes remain a popular destination for cyclists and boating enthusiasts alike, who travel along pleasant roads and waterways bordered by farms and elegant country estates. Located at the spot where the Bullewijk, a picturesque tributary, joins the Amstel, this romantic village of windmills and wooden-shoe factories dates back to the 12th century, making it the oldest village in the Amstelland region.

Its name derives from the reformed church which was founded in the area in AD 1000 and which now neighbours a row of houses from 1733. One of these is home to the **Oudheidkamer** (open Tues–Fri 10am–noon; Sun 1–3pm), which hosts exhibitions and provides historical information. Just next door is the **Out Bakery**, a century-old family-operated business offering a host of delectable confections made from recipes as old as the bakery itself. Across the bridge is the **St Urbanus Catholic Church** (1867), a stately masterpiece by P.J.H. Cuypers, architect of the Rijksmuseum *(see page 148)* and Centraal Station *(see page 85)*. The village's churches can be viewed by appointment only.

Edam

Within easy reach of Amsterdam there are four villages on or near the great lake called the IJsselmeer (the former Zuiderzee): Edam, Volendam, Monnickendam and the island village of Marken. The northernmost, **Edam** ❸, less than 24 km (15 miles) from Amsterdam, is a cheerful, interesting little place with attractive canals crossed by narrow wooden bridges. Like many towns in this district, Edam was once an important whaling centre, as the quay named Groenland (Greenland) recalls. In the 17th century it was an important port too, with large shipyards on the waterway to the east of the town. With its picturesque canals, narrow bridges and 17th-century exteriors, the small village has done well not to give in to some of the worst excesses of tourism.

The distinctive balls of Edammer cheese, wrapped in a protective skin of red wax for export, which are produced by farms on the fertile Beemster and Purmer polders, have spread the name of Edam to many parts of the world. Today the **Kaasmarkt** (Cheese Market) and the 16th-century **Waag** (Weigh House) ensure the town's continuing prosperity. If cheese alone isn't enough to attract you, there are historic buildings too. One of the main draws is the curious **Edams Museum** (1 and 8 Damplein; open late Mar–Oct 1.30–4.30pm;

Map on page 200

ORIENTATION

The destinations featured in this chapter are in the provinces of Noord-Holland or Zuid-Holland – to the north, west and southwest of Amsterdam; all lie within easy reach of the city, and are ideal for leisurely day trips.

BELOW: Nederlandsche Spoorwegen (Dutch railways) travel poster from the 1930s.

The cheese market at Alkmaar.

BELOW: world-famous Dutch cheese.

entrance fee). It occupies a late-Gothic house wth a curious floating cellar that rocks to and fro as you walk across it. Opinions differ as to its purpose. The romantic theory is that it was built by a retired ship's captain to remind him of the sea; a more prosaic explanation is that it was built this way to keep it dry in times of flooding. The museum proudly displays portraits of three eccentric local characters: Jan Claeszoon Clees, who was extremely fat; Trijntje Cornelisdochter Kever, who was very tall; and Pieter Dirkszoon Langebaard, who (as his name suggests) had an extremely long beard. "Long Beard" toured the country displaying his facial hair to raise money for the local **Weeshuis** (Orphanage), which still stands in Kerkstraat.

Damplein, in which the museum stands, is an unusual square, built in the form of a long, arched bridge to allow ships to pass beneath. South of here stands a solitary tower, the leaning **Speeltoren** (Playing Tower), a remnant of the 15th-century Kleine Kerk (Small Church), with a beauti-ful carillon of bells from Mechelen. Further south, you come to Edam's most attractive canal, the Schepenmakersdijk (Shipbuilder's Dyke), with curious tea houses at the water's edge on one side.

Overlooking Damplein is the **Raadhuis** (Town Hall), built in 1737, with an elaborate stucco interior complete with antique furniture. For a traditional Dutch treat, stop at the pancake house on the main street. In Kerkstraat, the **Grote Kerk** (Great Church) also dates from the 15th century, though what you see today is the result of a reconstruction in 1602 following a fire. In addition you will find 16th-century almshouses belonging to the Beguine sisterhood, the same group associated with Amsterdam's Begijnhof *(see page 89)*.

Volendam, Marken and Monnickendam

The IJsselmeer, a large freshwater lake north of Amsterdam, was created in 1932 by the enclosure of the saltwater Zuiderzee, which had been open to the North Sea. Once a quiet

fishing port, today **Volendam** ❹ is the most commercialised village on the IJsselmeer and could learn much from its neighbour Edam. A few fishing boats still use the small harbour, but it does not take much to see that Volendam has now put all its faith in the tourist trade. No doubt this provides a more reliable source of income than fishing ever did, but Volendam is still reputed for its fish, and there are several good restaurants and herring stands along the harbour. Volendam's next greatest asset is its distinctive local style of costume, especially the winged lace caps of the women. On the seafront there are shops inviting you to dress up in traditional costume so that you can have your picture taken.

The boat service from Volendam to **Marken** ❺ takes you swiftly away from the crowds. At one time this village did not sit on the edge of the IJsselmeer – it was an off-shore island in the Zuiderzee. Before 1957, when a short causeway was built, the only way in and out of the village was by boat. Then there were just 70 families living in

Marken, and they enjoyed being isolated from the mainland. Today the population is more than 2,000. Even so, Marken still hasn't lost its insularity, and the inhabitants like to keep themselves to themselves. The narrow streets have no name and there are no doorbells or knockers to be seen. One of the concessions to tourism is the Marken Museum, and some of the female inhabitants still wear traditional costume *(klederdracht)* consisting of 10 pieces, including corset, bodice, skirt, cap and clogs. Marken remains the quietest, prettiest and maybe the most eccentric of the IJsselmeer villages and you can't help feeling that the locals are going to keep it that way.

Monnickendam ❻ is equally unspoilt and, with Amsterdam just 13 km (8 miles) away, it makes for an easy day's excursion – a bus departs from just outside Centraal Station. A 15th-century church, a 16th-century belltower, a 17th-century weigh house (now a restaurant) and an 18th-century town hall account for just some of this village's charm.

Map on page 200

The Aalsmeer Blomenveiling (Flower Auction), held five days a week, is the world's largest flower auction. Just a 45-minute bus ride from Centraal Station, an annual 200,000 spectators come to view the lightning-speed transactions. The auction begins at 6.30am. Arrive at this time if you can – most of the action is over by 9am.

BELOW: the island village of Marken.

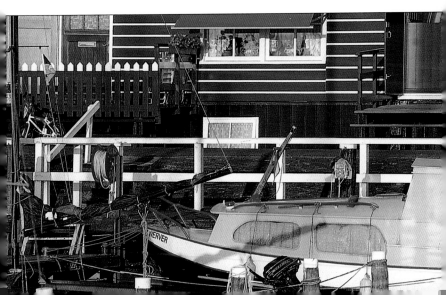

Castles and poets

To the east of Amsterdam there are two towns within easy reach by car or bus (and in summer by boat). At **Muiden** ❼, you can take a guided tour of red-brick **Muiderslot** (open for tours Apr–Oct Mon–Fri 10am–4 pm; Nov–Mar Sat–Sun 1–3pm; Dec 18–27 noon–5pm; other public holidays 1–4pm), a moated brick castle built in 1285 by Count Floris V of Holland, the founder of many Dutch towns. It stands at the point where the River Vecht flows into the IJsselmeer. Floris was murdered here in 1296 by nobles who opposed his policy of encouraging urban development. The castle as it stands today dates mainly from the 14th century. The interior, however, is a recreation of the castle as it appeared when it was occupied by the poet and historian P.C. Hooft in the 17th century, when it became the meeting place of the illustrious Muiderkring (Muiden Circle) of poets and writers. Members of the circle included the jurist Hugo Grotius, and poets Constantijn Huygens, Joost van den Vondel and Maria Tesselschade.

The fortification theme continues at **Naarden** ❽, a little further to the east. This town's impressive double line of ramparts was built at the end of the 17th century. Naarden had already suffered its worst attack a century earlier, when, in 1572, Spanish invaders massacred its inhabitants, an event that's commemorated by a 17th-century stone tablet on a building at 7 Turfpoortstraat. The Spanish conquerors demolished the town's fortifications and Naarden temporarily became a ghost town.

More advanced defences were erected in the 17th century. These fortifications still completely encircle the town and are fascinating to explore. Their history is explained in the **Vestingmuseum** (Fortress Museum; open mid-June–Aug Mon–Fri 10.30am–5pm; Sept–mid-Dec noon–5pm; entrance fee). This is housed in the bastion at 6 Westwalstraat, connected to underground passages and cannon-equipped casemates, which are now home to the **Arsenaal**, a complex of upmarket restaurants and shops.

TIP

If the Aalsmeer auction has just given you a taste for this method of selling, you might want to visit the Broeker Veiling, an auction in the nearby village of Langedijk, where boats laden with vegetables are navigated through the auction sheds.

BELOW: raw herring is a Dutch delicacy.

Haarlem

Just 15 minutes west of Amsterdam by train, **Haarlem** ➒ is one of the Netherlands' gems. This historic town on the River Spaarne has clung to its ancient character more than any other town in the Randstad (Rim City), the great conurbation also known as the "big village" that stretches south from Amsterdam to Rotterdam, embracing The Hague, Leiden, Utrecht, Delft and Gouda. Haarlem, the capital of Noord-Holland province (to which Amsterdam belongs), is small and manageable, and still seems very much under the sway of sober 17th-century virtues. Once you are in the old city at the Grote Markt, a central square with elegant Renaissance and Gothic architecture, there are many side streets to discover filled with galleries, antiques shops and cafés.

Walk from the railway station – a handsome art nouveau building that is a worthwhile destination in its own right – towards the Grote Markt and the tower of the imposing **Grote Kerk** (Great Church) or **Sint-Bavokerk** (St Bavo's Church). The city's principal landmark, it was built during the 15th century, with an ornate bell tower and 16th-century embellishment. The enormous Gothic church, a favourite subject of 17th-century artists such as Pieter Saenredam and Gerrit Berckheyde, is an intricate jumble of roofs and gables. Several low buildings are attached, including the **Vishal** (Fish Hall), once a fish market and now used for art exhibitions, and several tiny 17th-century houses along the south wall that are rented out by the church authorities to raise revenue.

The entrance to the church is through one of these little shuttered houses, which adds to the dramatic impact of the vast nave. Inside, a magnificent vaulted cedar ceiling is supported by 28 columns. Though the church seems rather empty, it contains many fascinating features, including curious medieval misericords, and decorated graves of shoemakers in the ambulatory. Superlatively grand is the famous Christian Müller organ, one of the world's largest, with 5,068 pipes, said to have been played by Joseph Haydn, Franz Liszt and a precocious 10-year-old prodigy, Wolfgang Amadeus Mozart. Frans Hals is buried here, as is Laurens Coster, who Haarlemmers claim was a co-inventor, with Gutenberg, of printing in 1423.

Haarlem's impressive main square, the **Grote Markt** ➊, is worth more than a few minutes of your time. It still looks very much as it did in the 17th-century townscapes of Gerrit Berckheyde in the Frans Hals Museum (but not as it did in an earlier period, when it was a tournament field of the Counts of Holland). The **Vleeshal** (Meat Hall) on the

The Stadhuis in the centre of Haarlem.

**Maps:
Area 200
City 205**

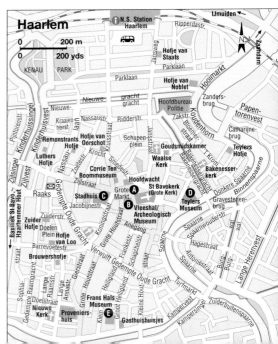

Detail from De Verrijzenis *by G. David (1460–1523) at the Frans Hals Museum.*

BELOW: Amsterdam isn't alone in the beauty of its canals – Haarlem has them too.

south side, dating from 1602, was designed by Haarlem's Flemish city architect Lieven de Key in a crowded Dutch Mannerist style, with a giant ox's-head emblem to indicate the building's function. In the basement is the **Archaeological Museum** Ⓑ (open Wed–Sun 1–5pm; entrance fee), and the building also functions as an annexe to the Frans Hals Museum *(see below)*. Opposite, exhibiting the more restrained classicism typical of the mid-17th century, is the **Hoofdwacht** (Guard House). The **Stadhuis** Ⓒ (Town Hall) on the west side of the square, on the site of a banqueting hall of the Counts of Holland, is an attractive mixture of buildings dating back to the medieval and Renaissance periods. There is also a statue of Laurens Coster on the square, another tribute to Haarlem's local printer hero.

If you leave the Grote Markt by Damstraat and walk down to the River Spaarne, you come to the **Teylers Museum** Ⓓ (16 Spaarne, tel: 023 531 9010; open Tues–Sat 10am–5pm, Sun noon–5pm; entrance fee). The Netherlands' old-

est museum is also one of its most eccentric. Housed in a number of interconnecting buildings, it is based on the collections of Pieter Teyler van der Hulst, a wealthy Haarlem silk merchant who died in 1778. This magnificent relic of the Dutch Enlightenment boasts a priceless collection of prints, mostly Dutch (including works by Rembrandt) and Flemish but also containing works by Michelangelo and Raphael. There are fossils and bones, crystals, coins and a marvellous array of gadgets and scientific instruments. The round entrance hall of the museum, with its marble statues and bas-reliefs depicting the sciences, has all the grandeur of a country mansion. More splendid still is the **Oval Hall**, a two-storey neo-classical hall built in 1779.

On the opposite bank of the Spaarne is a jetty from where the boats of **Woltheus Cruises** (tel: 023 535 7723) leave every hour or so for a cruise around the town's canals.

To the south, in a quiet 17th-century *hofje* at 62 Groot Heiligland, is the **Frans Hals Museum** Ⓔ (tel:

023 511 5775; open Tues–Sat 11am–5pm, Sun noon–5pm; entrance fee). This occupies a Dutch Renaissance building dating from 1608. It was designed by Lieven de Key as a hospice for old men, but two years later was converted to an orphanage. The museum contains several attractive period rooms and a detailed dolls' house, but its principal treasure is the collection of eight group portraits by Frans Hals, one of the great Dutch portrait artists, who was probably born in Antwerp but lived most of his life in Haarlem and died here in 1666.

Zandvoort

No more than a short bus or train ride west of Haarlem is the brassy North Sea resort of **Zandvoort** ⑩, where you can see what Amsterdammers get up to at the beach. After Scheveningen, near The Hague, this is the most popular of the Netherlands' coastal resorts. In summer Amsterdammers flock here, but there is space enough for everybody. On a hot, sunny day, you might want to pack swimming gear and suntan lotion. When you arrive at Zandvoort Station, it's a five-minute walk to the beach. Topless bathing in summer is pretty well de rigueur, and the southern end of the long stretch of sand is where naturists congregate – try to avoid shocking them by wearing clothes. Beach bums hang out either here or at the areas frequented by windsurfers and catamaran enthusiasts.

Even in bad weather, many Amsterdammers like to go for an invigorating stroll along the 8 km (5 miles) of beach before retiring to one of the resort's cafés or restaurants for something restorative. In summer, the beach is lined with dozens of *paviljoenen* (temporary beach cafés), where the food is mostly, but not exclusively, of the burgers-and-fries variety. In com-

pensation, the mobile seafood stalls that trundle down to the water's edge are generally good.

Zandvoort is a great place to hike as well as swim. Away from the beach you can tour the **Nationaal Park De Kennemerduinen** (Kennemer Dunes National Park), where rolling dunes form a vital part of Amsterdam's sea defences.

Alkmaar

A modest inland town, some 40 km (25 miles) north of Amsterdam, **Alkmaar** ⑪ had its moment of glory in 1673, when it successfully withstood a Spanish siege. It's now a busy market town where a "traditional" cheese market is staged on Friday mornings during the tourist season. The yellow-skinned cheeses are piled on to wooden sledges by porters wearing traditional garb, before being taken to the **Waaggebouw** (Weigh House). This was a chapel before being converted to a weigh house in the 16th century by the addition of a Renaissance gable and a jaunty bell tower. It contains a small museum of cheese-making techniques.

Maps:
Area 200
City 205

The white sands and beachside bars of Zandvoort are within easy reach of Amsterdam.

BELOW: Zandvoort is the Netherlands' second-largest beach resort.

Keukenhof is ablaze with colour in the summer months – a must for any flower lover.

BELOW: cycling amongst the tulip fields.

To explore Alkmaar on foot, take Stationstraat from the railway station, then follow the moat to the right, which brings you to a bridge leading to the **Grote Kerk**. This imposing 15th-century church was built of mellow Brabant limestone by the Keldermans family of Mechelen. Its 17th-century organ was designed by Jacob van Campen, the architect of Amsterdam's Town Hall.

Heading into town along Langestraat, you come to the **Stadhuis** (Town Hall), of which the east wing and tower were built in late-Gothic style around 1510; the baroque west wing was added in 1694. North of here is the **Stedelijk Museum Alkmaar**, the municipal museum, which has a local collection of guild group portraits, antique toys, tiles and paintings. Located in the attractive Renaissance guild house of the archers, it is worth a visit just to see the panoramic view of the *Siege of Alkmaar*, painted by an unknown master in the 16th century, and including nice touches of typical Dutch humour, such as a drunken soldier, and a couple making love while the battle rages on.

Keukenhof

The next place to visit after Haarlem (between March and May) is **Keukenhof** in the village of **Lisse** ⑫ (en route to Leiden). Keukenhof (open Mar–May daily; entrance fee) has been a tradition since 1949 when a group of prominent Dutch bulb-growers from the region created an annual exhibition showcasing the variety of the Dutch bulb-flower industry. The spectrum of flowers consists not only of tulips, in all their Technicolor glory, but daffodils, narcissi, hyacinths and other small varieties. The main paths are surrounded by stately beech and oak trees planted in 1830. Fountains, canals and streams make a watery chorus, and there are benches everywhere to encourage visitors to sit down and smell the flowers while listening to birdsong. At the season's height, this expanse explodes into a rainbow of colour. The two-month exhibition enables visitors to enjoy the beauty of the plants during their entire flowering period.

Leiden

The rich history and university atmosphere of **Leiden** ⑬ make for an interesting visit. Just a half-hour by train from Amsterdam, this medieval city, famous for its cloth-making and brewing industries, joined the Dutch Revolt against Spain and was besieged. It eventually rallied after the dykes were broken and the land was flooded, enabling a rescue fleet to sail directly across the countryside and save the city. Rembrandt was born in Leiden as well as other Dutch Masters such as Gerrit Dou, Jan Steen, Gabriel Metsu and Jan van Goyen. This is also where the Pilgrim Fathers formed a community

Map on page 200

in 1608, seeking refuge from Spain. Leiden University is probably the most prestigious in the Netherlands, with alumni including René Descartes and the 17th-century international lawyer, Hugo Grotius.

Visit the **De Valk windmill** on Binnenvestgracht, which today functions as a museum, and the **Museum De Lakenhal** on the Oude Singel, with its fascinating rooms illuminating Leiden's history. The inner city is ringed by two concentric canals, so a stretch of water is never far away and there are many bridges to cross. Make your way to the marketplace where the old and new Rhine meet and where open markets are held on Wednesday and Saturday. Then cross the bridge to the Old Rhine and turn right where you will find the **Burcht**, Leiden's 12th-century castle, which continually takes visitors by surprise. Have a drink at the Koetshuis in the courtyard. The **Botanical Gardens** along the Wittesingel are also worth a visit after an afternoon of sightseeing. The Leiden tourist office offers special guided walking tours with recorded commentary.

Zuiderzee Museum

The Zuiderzee's fascinating history is vividly presented at the **Zuiderzee Museum** (open Apr–Oct daily 10am–5pm; entrance fee) in **Enkhuizen ⓮**. This is largely an open-air, living museum, though part of it is housed in a Dutch Renaissance waterfront complex dating from 1625. The building began life as a local merchant's combined home and warehouse. Later, the Enkhuizen Chamber of the United Dutch East India Company acquired it, and it became known as the **Peperhuis** because of the company's lucrative trade in Indonesian pepper.

A large hall houses an extensive collection of traditional Zuiderzee fishing boats and pleasure craft. It is interesting to see how different styles of boat-building developed in fishing towns only a short distance apart. Local furniture also varied in style from one town to the next. But the greatest diversity is in costume, as you can see in a series of furnished rooms illustrating the local styles of Terschelling Island, the industrial Zaanstreek, West-Friesland, Hindeloopen (famous for hand-painted furniture), Marken, Urk, Spakenburg and Volendam.

The only way to reach the nearby open-air section of the museum is by boat, either from the pier near the railway station or from a car park at the beginning of the dyke road to Lelystad. The inconvenience of this arrangement is outweighed by the thrill of arriving by boat, though the landing-craft boats built for the museum look out of place alongside traditional, brown-sailed boats in Enkhuizen harbour.

Around 130 buildings were rescued from towns around the Zuiderzee to feature at the museum. Many are furnished in period style, with tea trays set out in front rooms

BELOW: De Valk Windmill, Leiden.

Map on page 200

A new form of windmill; the Dutch are keen to promote green energy as far as possible.

BELOW: marina in the centre of Hoorn.

as if the occupants might return at any time. A grocery shop in Harderwijk quarter sells delicious smoked sausage and boiled sweets, and a baker's shop on the main canal sells traditional cakes. Demonstrations of local trades are given in some buildings, such as the painter's shop and the steam laundry. The museum has three restaurants in historic buildings: one occupies the Landsmeer cheese warehouse, another a tiled interior from a restaurant in Zandvoort, but the most attractive is a dyke house with a gleaming tiled interior from Hindeloopen.

You need a day to visit both parts of the museum, and ideally another day for Enkhuizen. This modest, well-preserved town was Holland's foremost herring port during the 17th century – hence the three herrings motif on its coat of arms. The fishing industry is not quite dead, and a small fish auction still takes place on **Buitenhaven**.

Hoorn

Hoorn ⑮, 19 km (12 miles) to the south, was one of the Dutch republic's great seafaring towns. Among the many famous mariners born here were Abel Tasman, the first European to reach Tasmania, and Jan Pietersz Coen, founder of the Dutch trading post Batavia (now Jakarta). Another Hoorn native, Willem Schouten, named Cape Horn after his home town. Although nowadays the town is effectively a suburb of Amsterdam, many mementoes of its maritime history have survived.

The harbour quarter to the south of **Grote Oost** is particularly interesting to explore, with the best view from south of Binnenhaven towards a row of step-gabled merchants' houses on Veermanskade. Three curious 17th-century houses on Slapershaven, named the **Bossuhuizen** after a Spanish admiral, are decorated with colourful friezes depicting a sea battle off Hoorn in 1573.

A magnificent Dutch Mannerist building overlooks the **Rode Steen**. Built in 1632 for the College of the States of West-Friesland (the seven towns Alkmaar, Edam, Enkhuizen, Hoorn, Medemblik, Monnickendam and Purmerend), it houses the **Westfries Museum** (open Apr–Sep Mon–Fri 11am–5pm, Sat 2–5pm, Sun noon–5pm; Oct–Mar Mon–Fri 11am–5pm, Sat–Sun 2–5pm; entrance fee) of local history, filled with the confidence of the Dutch Golden Age, and containing furniture, guild group portraits, ship models and period rooms.

Opposite, the **Waag** is a handsome, Dutch classical weigh house of 1609. Streets north of Rode Steen contain other relics of Hoorn's glorious past. These include the Dutch Renaissance **Statenpoort** from 1613 at 23 Nieuwstraat, former lodgings of the representatives of the States of West-Friesland. In Muntstraat opposite is the Hoorn Chamber of the Dutch East India Company, completed in 1682. ❏

RESTAURANTS

Restaurants

Edam

Hotel-Restaurant De Fortuna
3 Spuistraat
Tel: 0299 371671
Open: D daily. **€€**
The highly regarded in-house restaurant of this hotel, which consists of six 17th-century houses, boasts an excellent mix of French, Dutch and international cuisine. There's an outside terrace at the canal's edge and in good weather you can dine in the garden.

Haarlem

De Pêcherie Haarlem aan Zee
10 Oude Groenmarkt
Tel: 023 531 4848
Open: L, D Mon–Sat; D Sun. **€€–€€€**
An excellent choice for lovers of seafood. The marine decor and ambience are both redolent of the Brittany coast – or perhaps more prosaically of a fine-weather day on the beach at nearby Zandvoort – and most of the fish is fresh from the quays at IJmuiden.

Lezer
37 Spaarne
Tel: 023 533 5525
Open: D Wed–Mon. **€€–€€€**
Just across from the Teylers Museum, and with a waterfront view

along the River Spaarne, this restaurant serves French and Mediterranean cuisine and is one of the finest in Haarlem. The imaginative menu has vegetarian offerings, as well as fish and meat, and there is an extensive and impressive wine list.

Ma Brown's
31–33 Nieuwe Groenmarkt
Tel: 023 531 5829
Open: D Wed–Sun. **€€**
Considering the traditional English nature of the cooking, the cuisine served here is surprisingly sophisticated. Inspiration for the cuisine dates from "before the French influence", according to the proprietor and chef. Reservations are a must.

Hoorn

De Hoofdtoren
2 Hooft
Tel: 0229 215487
Open: L, D daily. **€€**
In a town that specialises in traditional Dutch character and charm, there is no place more replete with either than the restaurant in this historic defensive tower thadates from 1532. From inside you have a fine view over the IJsselmeer. The menu features old Dutch favourites and complements this with Continental options.

Leiden

Jill's
6–9 Morsstraat
Tel: 071 514 3722
Open: D Mon–Fri; L, D Sat–Sun. **€€**
This brasserie situated in the heart of the city – part of a Dutch chain that's still small enough not to have lost the personal touch – offers different Continental menus in adjoining facilities, both with a Burgundian ambience, for either a quick lunch or a more leisurely three-course dinner. It has both friendly service and a pleasing atmosphere.

Stadscafé van der Werff
2 Steenstraat
Tel: 071 513 0335
Open: B, L, D daily. **€–€€**
Housed in a beautiful art deco building on the edge of the old town, this café has an eclectic menu, featuring Indonesian snacks, sandwiches, fish, vegetarian choices and traditional Dutch favourites.

Marken

De Taanderij
1 Havenbuurt
Tel: 0299 602206
Open: L, D Tues–Sun. **€–€€**
From spring to autumn, the outdoor terrace here, which has an unmatched view of Marken harbour, is always busy. At all other times, the tea-room style interior is the place

to sample anything from coffee and apple pie to a modest meal.

Volendam

Hotel Spaander
15–19 Haven
Tel: 0299 363595
Open: B, L, D daily. **€€**
The main dining room at this old-fashioned but excellent little hotel serves traditional Dutch food in an ambience that's quintessentially IJsselmeer. There's an open-air terrace beside the harbour that fills up fast in fine weather.

Zaanse Schans

De Hoop op d'Swarte Walvis
15 Kalverringdijk
Tel: 075 616 5629
Open: L, D Mon–Sat. **€€€**
Right beside the River Zaan in the recreated village north of Amsterdam is one of the area's premier restaurants, owned by the Albert Heijn supermarket chain. Despite this pedigree, it serves primarily French cuisine. The name translates "For the Hope of the Black Whale".

PRICE CATEGORIES

Prices are for a three-course meal for one, with wine and coffee
€ = under €20
€€ = €20–40
€€€ = €40–60
€€€€ = over €60

TRANSPORT

GETTING THERE AND GETTING AROUND

GETTING THERE

By Air

Schiphol Airport, 14 km (9 miles) southwest of Amsterdam, is one of Europe's busiest airports, with connections to 250 cities in 100 countries. It is also relatively user-friendly, with spacious terminals, shops, casino, business centre, two hotels and a children's play area, along with a reputation for efficiency. Overland transport links are good to all parts of the Netherlands. *For information on getting into the city from the airport, see page 213.*

From the UK

Taken together, British Airways, KLM Royal Dutch Airlines and British Midland operate an almost hourly service during the day between Amsterdam and the UK from London Heathrow and East Midlands airports. Easy Jet has several daily flights to Schiphol from London Gatwick, Stansted and Luton. Services from regional airports are covered by various British and Dutch airlines. From Ireland, Aer Lingus flies from Dublin to Amsterdam.

The Amsterdam Travel Service and Tours, with offices in the UK and in Amsterdam, offers specially priced excursion packages to Amsterdam and many other cities throughout the Netherlands (see page 234).

From other places

There are direct daily flights between Schiphol and destinations across the USA and Canada. Daily flights also operate from various points in Australia and New Zealand. There are regular links with all major European airports

AIRLINES

British Airways:
Tel: 346 9559 (Amsterdam)
Tel: 0870 850 9850 (UK)
www.britishairways.com
BMI:
Tel: 601 5459 (Amsterdam)
Tel: 0870 6070 555 (UK)
www.flybmi.com
EasyJet:
Tel: 023 568 4880 (Netherlands)
Tel: 08706 000 000 (UK)
www.easyjet.com
KLM Royal Dutch Airlines:
Tel: 474 7747 (Amsterdam)
Tel: 08705 074 074 (UK)
www.klmuk.com
Aer Lingus:
Tel: 517 4747 (Amsterdam)
Tel: 0818 365 000 (Ireland)
www.aerlingus.com

By Train

There are good rail connections to all parts of the Netherlands from Brussels, Paris, Antwerp, Cologne, Berlin and the North Sea ports. The Eurostar Channel Tunnel train goes direct from London's Waterloo station to Brussels, from where trains run to Amsterdam. The total journey time from London is about six hours. The Thalys high-speed train (reservation required) connects the city with Brussels, Paris and Cologne.
Eurostar: Tel: 08701 606 600 (in UK); www.eurostar.com
Rail Europe: Tel: 0870 584 8848 (in UK); www.raileurope.co.uk
Thalys: Tel: 0900 9296 (in the Netherlands); www.thalys.com

By Coach

This is generally the cheapest way of getting to the Netherlands. From the UK Eurolines (tel: 08705 808 080; www.eurolines.com) operate frequent coach services to Amsterdam.

By Sea

From the UK, Stena Line operates two ferries a day (for passengers with vehicles) from Harwich to Hoek van Holland:

crossing time is around 8½ hours. P&O Ferries has a daily sailing from Hull to Rotterdam, taking 13 hours. DFDS Seaways has a daily overnight car-ferry service from Newcastle to IJmuiden: crossing time is 14 hours.

Stena Line: Tel: 01255 242 000 (UK); www.stenaline.com
P&O Ferries: Tel: 08705 202 020 (UK); www.poferries.com
DFDS Seaways: Tel: 08705 333 000 (UK); www.dfdsseaways.co.uk

By Car

From the UK, the Channel Tunnel provides a 35-minute drive-on service between Folkestone and Calais, from where there is a straightforward motorway connection to Amsterdam up through Belgium. Journey time from Calais is about four hours (not allowing for stops or traffic jams).

From Hoek van Holland (8½ - hour crossing) to Amsterdam, driving time is roughly 2½ hours. There are also the shorter cross-Channel ferry routes: Ramsgate–Dunkirk (2½-hour crossing plus 4-hour drive); Dover–Calais (1- or 1½-hour crossing plus 4-hour drive).

To drive in the Netherlands, you must carry a current EU or national driving licence (an international licence is not necessary), vehicle registration document, insurance and a warning triangle for use in the event of an accident or breakdown. The Netherlands has an excellent network of roads and signposting is good. However, once you are in the cities, a car is often more of a hindrance than a help. And do be aware that in most large cities you are required to buy parking tickets at specially posted vending machines on the streets, marked with a "P". It is notoriously difficult to find a parking space in Amsterdam, and the city is known for high fines, parking clamps and an enthusiastic parking-enforcement team.

AMSTERDAM PASS

The Amsterdam Pass gives free entry or substantial discounts to all the most important museums in the city and various tourist attractions such as the Museum Boat and Canal Bus *(see page 214)*. The Pass costs €31, €41 and €51 for one, two and three days respectively, and can potentially offer savings of up to €150. It can be purchased at any of the VVV offices in Amsterdam and at many of the hotels in the city. It is an alternative for visitors to the Museum Year Card, which is used mainly by local residents.

GETTING AROUND

From the Airport

There is a 24-hour rail service from Schiphol to Amsterdam Centraal Station, with up to six trains an hour at peak times, and in late evenings around once an hour. Trains also depart frequently to Amsterdam RAI Station and Amsterdam Zuid/WTC (South/World Trade Centre) Station. The journey time to Centraal Station is about 20 minutes. Taxis to the city centre leave from in front of Schiphol Plaza and cost around €45.

Connexxion operates a hotel shuttle bus from the airport, serving 16 city-centre hotels every 20–30 minutes from 7am–9.30pm. It costs more than twice the price of the train.

Orientation

Thanks to its size and layout, the centre of Amsterdam is easily covered on foot. Main streets radiate out from Centraal Station, crossing a more or less regular pattern of concentric canals. It all looks very simple on paper but the canal system can be tricky to negotiate if you are a first-time visitor. It's eas-

ier if you remember that *plein* means square, *straat* street and *gracht* canal.

The most prominent landmarks are the three main squares, the Dam, Rembrandtplein and Leidseplein. The best way to get your bearings is to start out from Centraal Station.

Public Transport

Amsterdam's public transport network consists of tram and bus routes and four Metro lines. All operate from 6am until midnight, after which there are night buses.

One-day or multiple-day tickets are valid on all public transport lines within the city and can save you time and money. Otherwise, use a *strippenkaart* – strip ticket; the more strips you buy, the cheaper they come. These are valid for one hour's travel, and the amount you use depends on the number of public transport zones you cover. The city is divided into zones and you cancel one strip more than the number of zones you will be travelling within – two strips for one zone, three strips for two zones, and so on. It sounds complicated, but in practice everything works well.

Tickets are available from the GVB Tickets & Info office next to Centraal Station, as well as at railway stations, tourist offices, post offices, some tobacconists and at major hotels. Tickets purchased on trams and buses cost more than those bought in advance.

Trams

Within the city centre the blue and grey trams (also a few yellow ones survive) are the best means of getting around. Tickets must be

PHONE NUMBERS

All local Amsterdam numbers in this guide are listed without the city's area code (020). All other numbers, in the Netherlands and elsewhere, appear with their relevant area code.

stamped by the conductor at, or towards, the rear, or in the machines that are usually located next to the doors. If you have no ticket, enter through the front door (doors open automatically if you press the "Deur Open" button), state your destination and buy a ticket from the driver. If the tram has a conductor, enter at the rear, where there is a small counter.

On busy tram routes such as Nos. 2 and 5 to the Museum Quarter, teams of *zakenrollers* (pickpockets) are active, especially in summer months and holiday periods. Be aware of your personal property at all times.

Buses, Metro and trains

You are unlikely to use buses or the Metro system unless you are travelling outside the city centre. Both are clean and efficient. On the Metro you must stamp your ticket in the machines provided – these are usually found close to the steps leading to the platforms.

Overground rail lines connect with nearby attractions such as Volendam, Alkmaar and Haarlem, as well as Schiphol Airport.

Boats

Canal Buses

The Canal Buses are modern, glass-topped launches which pick up passengers at 11 major points along three different routes. They take you through some of the loveliest parts of Amsterdam en route to various museums and tourist attractions. Day passes, which enable you to hop on and off at your whim, are available.

The Museum Boat service stops at nine major museums at 75-minute intervals – well worth considering if you intend doing a lot of sightseeing. You can buy a day ticket from the office opposite Centraal Station, where the boat service starts. The Canal Bus 52-seat cruiser provides a regular service between Centraal Station and the Rijksmuseum, with three stops on the way. For further information, tel: 623 9886.

Using the Canal Bus or Museum Boat gives reduced entrance fees to many museums.

Canal tours

The traditional *rondvaart*, or canal boat tour, is a delightful way to discover the city from a watery perspective, and gives a duck's-eye view of the elegant 17th-century houses which overlook the canals. There are several companies in front of Centraal Station, along Rokin, by the Rijksmuseum and Heineken Brewery, which offer a basic hour to hour-and-a-half tour. Lovers operates canal boat cruises as well as the Water Taxis – more expensive custom-made voyages that can last from an hour to a full evening and offer a more intimate approach to exploring the city's waterscape.

Boat hire

It is also possible to hire small motorboats and navigate the canals yourself. Be aware that there are safety rules, and that canal boats and flocks of swans always have the right of way! Electric-powered boats can be rented from:

Canal Motorboats: by Café De Jaren opposite 141 Kloveniersburgwal, tel: 422 7007.

Sesa Rent a Boat: 2 Stuurmankade, Borneo-Eiland, tel: 509 5052.

Duba Electra: 34 Prinseneiland, tel: 624 6424.

DAY TRIPS

Amsterdam makes a good base for day trips. Distances to towns of interest are short and easily covered. An extensive and very efficient rail service operates throughout the country. Fast electric trains link Amsterdam with most Dutch towns on an hourly or half-hourly basis. It is well worth finding out about excursion fares, which include entrance fees to museums and other attractions as well as the return rail fare.

Coach excursions are organised by Lindbergh Excursions. Most popular are the bulb fields at Keukenhof *(see page 208)*, the traditional eel-fishing villages of Volendam and Marken *(see page 203)*, the cheese market at Alkmaar *(see page 207)*, the cheese-making centre of Edam *(see page 201)*, and the pretty city of Leiden *(see page 208)*. Lindbergh Excursions, 26 Damrak, tel: 622 2760.

CAR HIRE

Renting a car is worth considering if you want to explore cities and regions beyond Amsterdam. Roads are good and signposting is clear. Try the following agencies:
Avis:
380 Nassaukade
Tel: 683 6061
Budget:
121 Overtoom
Tel: 612 6066
Europcar:
197 Overtoom
Tel: 683 2123
Hertz:
333 Overtoom
Tel: 612 2441
Kuperus BV:
175 Middenweg
Tel: 693 8790

Ferries

An increasing number of ferries ply the waterfront of the city's old harbour area. Most of them depart from jetties at the rear of Centraal Station, and carry foot passengers and bikes and other two-wheeled vehicles only. The short journey across the IJ channel to Amsterdam-Noord is free.

Taxis

Cabs cannot be flagged down (though they do stop sometimes), but should be hired from ranks at key locations throughout the city (in front of Centraal Station, and at Rembrandtplein, Leidseplein, Museumplein, the Dam, Waterlooplein and many other locations, for example outside public buildings such as Concertgebouw), or by dialling 0900 677 7777 (50 cents per minute). Meters are used and the cost is calculated according to the zone and the time of day. On longer journeys it is always wise to establish the cost before you set off. You can also make use of the Water Taxi in front of Centraal Station (tel: 622 2181).

Driving

Driving within the city is best avoided. Parking is prohibitively expensive, spaces are hard to find, and the aggressive meter brigade clamps wheels and issues tickets with a vengeance. Always be on the lookout for cyclists (who travel at speed and seem to appear from nowhere) and take particular care on the narrow canal streets (often blocked by delivery vans). Other hazards are the complex one-way systems, and trams which always have right of way.

If you arrive by car, leave it in a car park and either walk or use public transport. There is a large underground car park in front of Centraal Station by the Lovers Excursion Boat office, as well as the underground car park by the Museumplein. The multi-storey Europarking at 250 Marnixstraat in the west of the Jordaan district usually has space and is within walking distance of the city centre.

Within a built-up zone, the maximum speed is 50 kph (30 mph). In residential areas, indicated by signs of a white house on a blue background, vehicles may be driven only at walking pace. Outside the built-up area, the speed limit is 80 kph (50 mph). A speed limit of 120 kph (75 mph) applies on motorways (snelwegen), and a limit of 100 kph (60 mph) on most major roads. Lower limits are sometimes indicated.

The Dutch National Automobile Club (ANWB) has maps and other travel information. They also offer a breakdown service. You'll find them at 5 Museumplein, 885 Osdorpplein or 1001 Bijlmerplein.

Bicycles

Being a city of cyclists, Amsterdam has numerous bike lanes. Cycling is a fun way of getting around but bear in mind that there are 600,000 other cyclists

in the city, and a lot of chaotic traffic with which to contend. Locals run the red lights, taxis drive on tram tracks. Be careful of tram tracks – they should only be crossed at right angles!

Two of the main places for renting cycles are Damstraat Rent-a-bike and MacBike. Bicycle theft is rife (hence high deposits on rentals), so lock up at all times – wherever possible attaching your bike to railings or some other immovable object. If you prefer safety in numbers, why not take a Yellow Bike tour of the city? For tours outside of the city try Let's Go or Mike's Bike Tours.
Damstraat Rent-a-bike: 11 Pieter Jacobsz Dwarsstraat, tel: 625 5029.
MacBike: 2 Mr Visserplein, tel: 620 0985.
Yellow Bike: 29 Nieuwezijds Kolk, tel: 620 6940.
Let's Go: tel: 600 1809.
Mike's Bike Tours: tel: 622 7970.

Waterbikes

Canal pedalos for two or four are fun for exploring the canals. Detailed maps and suggested routes are provided by the hire companies, located opposite the Centraal Station, Anne Frank's House, by the American Hotel and opposite the Rijksmuseum.

On Foot

The compact centre of Amsterdam is well suited to walking provided you don't object to cobbled streets, chaotic cyclists and an inordinate amount of dog dirt. From Centraal Station to the Museumplein) area is roughly 30 minutes' walk. Most of the hotels are within walking distance of the centre – notable exceptions are those in the south and southeast, and the business hotels near the World Trade Centre and RAI Congress Centre. There are several walking tours to be enjoyed.

ACCOMMODATION

ACTIVITIES

A - Z

LANGUAGE

A CCOMMODATION

SOME THINGS TO CONSIDER BEFORE BOOKING YOUR ROOM

Choosing a Hotel

For most visitors, the areas south-west of the centre are the favoured places to stay in Amsterdam. The canal belt (Grachtengordel) around the three picturesque canals of Herengracht, Keizersgracht and Prinsengracht is always popular, as is the area around the Museumplein. There are plenty of hotels to choose from in these areas and most are quieter than those in the central Dam/Damrak area.

Roughly half the total number of beds in Amsterdam are in de luxe or first-class hotels, but tourists tend to go for the small, family-run hotels, which are not only cheaper and more charming but are often in better locations. Many of these lower-category hotels are converted from narrow old town houses overlooking canals, but the disadvantages are very small rooms and steep stairs – many hotels don't have a lift.

The busiest times of year, when you need to book well in advance, are the flower season (April and May), Easter, the summer months and Christmas and New Year. Low season, when packages and hotel prices are at their cheapest, is from October to March (excluding Christmas and New Year). The VVV tourist office publishes a useful brochure called *Amsterdam Accommodation Guide,* available from their offices locally and abroad.

Reservations

Reservations can be made via a travel agency or through the **Amsterdam Reservation Centre**. 5 De Ruyterkade, 1013 AA Tel/fax: 201 8800; E-mail: reservations@amsterdamtourist.nl; www.amsterdamtourist.nl

For reservations outside of Amsterdam, contact **The Netherlands Reservation Centre** 2 Plantsoengracht, 1441 DE Purmerend, tel: (029) 968 9144; fax: (029) 968 9154; www.hotelres.nl. The centre offers special winter packages known as "Amsterdam, the Amsterdam Way", a deal which includes lower-rate accommodation (from budget to luxury hotels) plus, for example, free entrance to the Rijksmuseum, free drinks in certain bars and a free canal cruise.

Bed & Breakfast Holland tel: 615 7527; fax: 669 1573; www.bbholland.com. Good-value accommodation at locations throughout the city, though not necessarily in the centre. Besides bed & breakfast rooms, they also offer studios with kitchens for those who want self-catering. They work only via fax and email and take no last-minute bookings as they are generally full, especially in holiday periods and summer months.

If you do arrive in the city on spec there is a free telephone reservation service at the airport, or you can ask the VVV

APARTMENT AND HOUSEBOAT RENTALS

Staying at a self-catering studio, apartment or residence is becoming a more popular choice in Amsterdam. And in this city of canals there's also the special option of a houseboat rental. Among the reputable companies who do both land and water accommodation are: Amsterdam House, 7 's-Gravelandseveer, 1011 KN Amsterdam, tel: 626 2577; fax: 626 2987; www.amsterdamhouse.com. The company provides moderately priced housing in 30 apartments and eight houseboats for short or long rentals. Rooms are comfortable and fully equipped, with many overlooking the canals.

offices at Centraal Station to make a reservation for you – a small booking fee will be charged. If you want to stay with a family in a private house – which works out a lot cheaper than opting for a hotel – the VVV will also be able to help.

Immediately around Centraal Station you will find many so-called "Youth Hotels" and "Hostels" offering accommodation at rock-bottom prices, and in summer you may be approached by touts as you arrive at the station. Cheap they may be, but they are also fleapits, often located above a noisy all-night disco or café, and you will be expected to share rooms as well as bathrooms. They are best avoided, but if you use them, never leave any of your valuables unattended.

Prices & Booking

(See also Budgeting for your Trip, page 229). Prices are quite high, and in recent years the emphasis has been on the top end of the market, a trend the city is trying to reverse. Bear in mind, however, that breakfast is normally included in the price (the choice of cheeses, cold meats, cakes and rolls, if rarely something to write home about, will keep you going for a good part of the day).

All hotels in the Netherlands are graded from 1 to 5 stars according to their facilities (or lack of them). As a general rule the quality of accommodation is high, but you get what you pay for. Prices vary depending on the season. Winter rates are commonly 30–50 percent lower than the published rates. But you need to ask for a discount – it won't be offered automatically.

You can book directly with the hotel; invariably the person who answers the phone will speak English. And at an increasing number of hotels you can book directly through their website. You'll often get the best available rate by doing so – but not always. It may be worthwhile to compare the internet rate with the one you get from a direct call to reception or reservations accompanied by a request for a discounted rate.

CENTRAL AMSTERDAM

HOTELS

De Luxe

Grand Sofitel Demeure Amsterdam
197 Oudezijds Voorburgwal
Tel: 555 3111
Fax: 555 3222
www.thegrand.nl
This unique property has a history going back to 1400 when it was a convent and eventually a royal hostelry and a town hall. The rooms are comfortable and feature all amenities. The Café Roux is under the culinary direction of master chef Albert Roux.

Hotel De l'Europe
2–8 Nieuwe Doelenstraat
Tel: 531 1777
Fax: 531 1778
www.leurope.nl

Grand late-19th-century hotel overlooking the River Amstel and the Mint Tower. Facilities include swimming pool, open-air terrace, meeting rooms, fitness centre and two restaurants.

Expensive

NH Barbizon Palace
59–72 Prins Hendrikkade
Tel: 556 4564
Fax: 624 3353
www.nh-hoteles.com
Nineteen old houses converted into a luxury hotel overlooking Centraal Station. The interior is a pleasing combination of old Dutch, French and postmodern styles. Facilities include fitness centre and congress hall. Fine restaurant with Michelin star.

NH Grand Hotel Krasnapolsky
9 Dam
Tel: 554 9111
Fax: 554 7010
www.nh-hoteles.nl
This historic hotel boasts comfortable rooms on the Dam facing the Royal Palace. Breakfasts are served in a glass-roofed winter garden. Congress centre and short-term apartments are some of the extras.

Radisson SAS
17 Rusland
Tel: 520 8300
Fax: 520 8200
www.radissonsas.com
Deep in the heart of old Amsterdam, this stylish Scandinavian hotel incorporates old buildings that date as far back as the 17th century, and offers an eclectic range of design in its guest rooms.

Map p78

Swissôtel Amsterdam Ascot
95–98 Damrak
Tel: 626 0066
Fax: 627 0982
www.swissotel.com
Efficient, ultra-modern Swiss-run hotel in city centre, very close to the

PRICE CATEGORIES

Price categories are for a double room with breakfast:
De Luxe: over €300
Expensive: €200–300
Moderate: €100–200
Inexpensive: under €100

Royal Palace and the Dam. Sound-proofed rooms and suites and excellent in-house restaurant.

Moderate

Amsterdam
93–94 Damrak
Tel: 555 0666
Fax: 620 4716
www.hotelamsterdam.nl
You're not likely to forget the name of this fine medium-sized hotel near Centraal Station, opened in 1911 but thoroughly modernised.

De Gerstekorrel
22–24 Damstraat
Tel: 624 1367
Fax: 623 2640
Located just off the Dam on the edge of the Red Light District, this bright, clean and cheerful hotel

is operated by a Finnish family. Rooms are comfortably furnished. 24-hour reception desk to assure security.

Estheréa
305 Singel
Tel: 624 5146
Fax: 623 9001
www.estherea.nl
A 17th-century canal house two minutes from the Dam. Steep stairs but there is a lift. Ask the friendly management for a room with a view.

Tulip Inn Dam Square
Gravenstraat 12–16
Tel: 623 3716
Fax: 638 1156
www.tulipinndamsquare.com
Housed in a converted distillery behind the Nieuwe Kerk by the Dam, this unique hotel is on a charming, almost hidden street with cafés and wine and liqueur tasting rooms.

Inexpensive

Amstel Botel
2–4 Oosterdokskade
Tel: 626 4247
Fax: 639 1952
www.amstelbotel.com
This boat hotel is moored between

Centraal Station and the Maritime Museum. Rooms are comfortably furnished and half of them have a view over the water. Late at night the location can be dicey, so it is better for couples rather than single women.

Sint-Nicolaas
1a Spuistraat
Tel: 626 1384
Fax: 620 0979
www.hotelnicolaas.nl
A friendly and comfortable family-owned establishment in a converted rope factory near Centraal Station. Rooms are a little basic, but the atmosphere and location compensate.

Winston
125–129 Warmoesstraat
Tel: 623 1380
Fax: 623 2308
www.winston.nl
This has been described as similar to New York's Chelsea Hotel, attracting artists and musicians. Some rooms are basic and low-priced while others have been decorated by artists and are more expensive.

HOSTELS

Amsterdam has a good choice of hostels open to people of all ages. Most offer dormitory accommodation only but some have private rooms and family facilities. If you are not a member, a card can usually be issued on the spot. For a list of hostels throughout the Netherlands, contact NJHC, 2 Prof. Tulpstraat, Amsterdam, tel: 551 3133, fax: 623 4986, www.njhc.org. The official YHA hostels in Amsterdam are:

Stayokay Amsterdam Stadsdoelen
97 Kloveniersburgwal
Tel: 624 6832
Fax: 639 1035
www.stayokay.com/stadsdoelen
On a canal, 10 mins' walk from Dam Square and close to the Red Light District. Bar and snacks, recreation room. The quality is high for a hostel. Groups are not allowed and people being overly noisy is not encouraged.

THE CANAL BELT (GRACHTENGORDEL)

HOTELS

De Luxe

Amstel Inter-Continental
1 Professor Tulpplein
Tel: 622 6060
Fax: 622 5808
www.intercontinenti.com
Lavishly furnished 19th-century hotel (20 mins' walk from the centre)

which is popular among visiting celebrities. High-class cuisine in 2-Michelin-star La Rive restaurant. Plush bedrooms and suites, efficient service, delightful terrace in summer.

Blakes I
384 Keizersgracht
Tel: 530 2010
Fax: 530 20 30
www.blakesamsterdam.com
This former theatre (later it was an

almshouse) is now an exclusive hotel (and restaurant) under the same management as its London counterpart. There are 41 uniquely furnished rooms with all the chic accoutrements.

Expensive

Ambassade
341 Herengracht
Tel: 555 0222
Fax: 555 0277

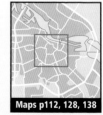

Maps p112, 128, 138

www.ambassade-hotel.nl
A hospitable, exclusive hotel created from a series of 17th- and

18th-century canal-side houses. Lots of antiques, paintings, steep steps and spiral staircases. Popular with visiting authors.

Crowne Plaza Amsterdam-American
97 Leidsekade
Tel: 556 3000
Fax: 556 3001
www.amsterdam-american.crowneplaza.com
Outstanding art nouveau building located on the lively Leidseplein. The Americain has comfortable, well-equipped bedrooms – and the eternally popular Café Américain, famous for Tiffany-style decor and colourful clientele, cocktail bar with terrace *(see page 135).*

Dikker & Thijs Fenice
444 Prinsengracht
Tel: 620 1212
Fax: 625 8986
www.dtfh.nl
Small enough to retain an individual character that complements its tasteful looks, this gem of a hotel is adjacent to the busy Leidsestraat shopping street, but you'd never guess as much from the tranquil oasis inside.

NH Schiller Hotel
26–36 Rembrandtplein
Tel: 554 0700
Fax 624 0098
www.nh-hoteles.com
As much an art gallery as a hotel, having been built during the *fin de siècle* period by an artist who filled it with his own creations and others by artists he particularly liked. The Café Schiller has long been one of Amsterdam's chic hangouts.

Pulitzer
315–331 Prinsengracht
Tel: 523 5235
Fax: 627 6753
www.luxurycollection.com
Terrace of 17th- and 18th-century canalside residences and warehouses, converted into a hotel of considerable charm and character. Exposed brick, beams, antiques and beautiful furnishings. Sophisticated bedrooms overlooking canals or gardens.

Moderate

Amsterdam Wiechmann
328–332 Prinsengracht
Tel: 626 3321
Fax: 626 8962
www.hotelwiechmann.nl
Attractively located canal-side hotel in two 17th- and 18th-century houses north of Leidseplein. Antique furnishings adorn the higher-priced rooms with a view on the canal, but those at the back are nicely furnished too.

Best Western Eden
144 Amstel
Tel: 530 7888
Fax: 623 3267
www.edenhotelgroup.com
This moderately priced

riverside hotel is big, sporting no fewer than 410 rooms, which means there's almost always a chance of finding one available. And it lacks nothing when it comes to the local character of its 17th-century merchants' houses. Guest rooms are furnished in modern style, and the inevitably named Garden of Eden brasserie is a good place for Dutch food.

Canal House
148 Keizersgracht
Tel: 622 5182
Fax: 624 1317
www.canalhouse.nl
American-owned hotel, expertly converted from three 17th-century merchant houses on a quiet canal. Lots of antiques and a charming breakfast room and cosy bar. Lift.

Mercure Amsterdam Arthur Frommer
46 Noorderstraat
Tel: 622 0328
Fax: 620 3208
www.accor-hotels.com
Popular hotel in quiet courtyard location not far from art museums and Rembrandtplein. Comfortable rooms built round private courtyard (where you can park free of charge).

Seven Bridges
31 Reguliersgracht
Tel: 623 1329
The owners give their guests the kind of attention that stems from pride. All furnishings and fittings, many of them antiques, have been chosen with a view to harmony and enhancing the atmosphere. You can see seven canal bridges from the hotel.

Toren
164 Keizersgracht
Tel: 622 6352
Fax: 626 9705
www.toren.nl
Cosy canal-side hotel located in two 17th-century buildings close to the Jordaan and the Anne Frank House. In-house bar and lovely garden. Ask for a room with a view. A recent renovation installed a lift.

Tulip Inn Dam Square
Gravenstraat 12–16
Tel: 623 3716
Fax: 638 1156
www.tulipinndamsquare.com
Housed in a converted distillery behind the Nieuwe Kerk by the Dam, this unique hotel is on a charming, almost hidden street with cafés and wine and liqueur tasting rooms.

Inexpensive

Acacia
251 Lindengracht
Tel: 622 1460
Fax: 638 0748
www.hotelacacia.nl
This fine small hotel in the Jordaan district has guest rooms that are plain but comfortable, and a definite plus in two houseboats moored on the adjacent canal.

Arena
51 's-Gravesandestraat
Tel: 850 2410
Fax: 850 2415
www.hotelarena.nl

PRICE CATEGORIES

Price categories are for a double room with breakfast:
De Luxe: over €300
Expensive: €200–300
Moderate: €100–200
Inexpensive: under €100

TRANSPORT   ACCOMMODATION   ACTIVITIES   A – Z   LANGUAGE

This unusual establishment in a monument building near the Tropenmuseum began as a youth hostel many years ago and has evolved into a trendy "cultural centre" hotel with a popular disco, terrace and restaurant.

De Admiraal
563 Herengracht
Tel: 626 2150
Fax: 623 4625.
Adjacent to a pretty, tree-shaded square, Thorbeckeplein, De Admiraal is in a building with 17th-century character and has even been in the movies, as a set in Alistair Maclean's Amsterdam-set *Puppet on a Chain*. The guest rooms are not quite as good as all this would suggest, but are by no means bad for the money.

Hans Brinker
136 Kerkstraat
Tel: 622 0687
Fax: 638 2060
www.hans-brinker.com
This no-frills establishment on a quiet street near Leidseplein calls itself the "most exclusive budget hotel".

Hoksbergen
301 Singel
Tel: 626 6043
Fax: 638 3479
www.hotelhoksbergen.com
Good quality and good deals are not easy to come by in canalside hotels in desirable locations. The Hoksbergen manages this seemingly difficult feat by keeping things simple while retaining both character and comfort.

Keizershof
618 Keizersgracht
Tel: 622 2855
Fax: 624 8412
www.hotelkeizershof.nl
With just six rooms, this great little canal-side hotel presents the obvious difficulty of finding a room free. You are well advised to reserve as far ahead as possible. If you get in, you'll find the De Vries family to be great hosts and their property to be virtually a home away from home.

Orfeo
14 Leidsekruisstraat
Tel: 623 1347
Fax: 620 2348
www.hotelorfeo.com
Popular with the city's many gay visitors, this hotel just off Leidseplein has simple but clean rooms and a friendly character. The breakfast room is a bit bland but Orefeo nevertheless represents good value.

Prinsenhof
810 Prinsengracht
Tel: 623 1772
Fax: 638 3368
www.hotelprinsenhof.com
Although somewhat rough and ready in places, the Prinsenhof is constantly being improved by its enthusiastic owners, who seem always to be engaged in laying down a new carpet here, or installing a new shower there. They retain an atmosphere of casual Amsterdam that is what many travellers – and not just budget ones – are looking for.

THE MUSEUM QUARTER AND VONDELPARK

HOTELS

De Luxe

Okura Amsterdam
3 Ferdinand Bolstraat
Tel: 678 7111
Fax: 671 2344
www.okura.nl
Essentially a hotel for business travellers, not far from the RAI building and with car-parking space for guests and their visitors. Facilities include swimming pool and fitness centre, congress facilities and several highly-regarded restaurants. The Ciel Bleu restaurant and bar on the 23rd floor offers a panoramic view of the city.

Moderate

AMS Hotel Amsterdam
23 Tesselschadestraat
Tel: 638 1811
Fax: 616 0320
www.ams.nl
Friendly, with small, pleasant rooms and basic amenities, quietly located by the Vondelpark. Bar on premises.

De Filosoof
6 Anna van den Vondelstraat
Tel: 683 3013
Fax: 685 3750
www.hotelfilosoof.nl
Situated at the Vondelpark within walking distance of Leidseplein and the museums. The individually furnished rooms are inspired by the great philosophers, as is the owner, a philosopher herself.

Bilderberg Hotel Jan Luyken
58 Jan Luijkenstraat
Tel: 573 0730
Fax: 676 3841
www.janluyken.nl
Late 19th-century building close to Museumplein. The personalised service attracts returning guests. Quiet rooms and apartments.

Prinsen
36–38 Vondelstraat
Tel: 616 2323
Fax: 616 6112
www.prinsenhotel.demon.nl
Converted 19th-century houses form this recently renovated hotel situated on a quiet street between the Vondelpark and Leidseplein.

Map p148

Inexpensive

Acro
44 Jan Luijkenstraat
Tel: 662 5538
Fax: 675 0811
Good-value budget hotel close to the art museums. Pleasant furnishings, in good condition.

AMS Hotel Holland
162 P.C. Hooftstraat
Tel: 683 1811
Fax: 616 0320
www.ams.nl

Quiet location at the far end of Amsterdam's chic shopping street in the Museum Quarter, right next to the Vondelpark.

AMS Hotel Trianon
3–7 J.W. Brouwersstraat
Tel: 638 1811
Fax: 616 0320
www.ams.nl
Charming hotel behind the Concertgebouw near the museum and shopping quarters. The rooms are comfortable and well equipped. Bar and Italian restaurant.

Concert Inn
11 De Lairessestraat
Tel: 305 7272
Fax: 305 7271
A friendly, family-run hotel opposite the Concertgebouw that has clean and cosy rooms with basic amenities.

Hotel Fita
37 Jan Luijkenstraat
Tel: 679 0976
Fax: 664 3969
www.fita.nl
This renovated hotel in the Museum Quarter is quiet and comfortably furnished with large bathrooms. Management is friendly but slow.

Parkzicht
33 Roemer Visscherstraat
Tel: 618 1954
Fax: 618 0897
www.parkzicht.nl
Reasonable rates and a location overlooking the Vondelpark attract young travellers who don't mind not being in the centre of things. The decor is old Dutch and the welcome is friendly.

P.C. Hooft
63 Pieter Cornelisz Hooftstraat
Tel: 662 7107
Fax: 675 8961
This hotel might seem a bit like a fish out of water – a budget lodging on Amsterdam's

most prestigious shopping street. Yet there it is, and the owners have long resisted the urge to go upmarket, relying instead on plainer virtues to keep their customers satisfied.

Piet Hein
52 Vossiusstraat
Tel: 662 7205
Fax: 662 1526
www.hotelpiethein.com
Mostly located in a converted mansion beside the Vondelpark (there is also an adjacent annexe), the Piet Hein offers comfortable accommodation in a quiet area.

Van Ostade Bicycle Hotel
123 Van Ostadestraat
Tel: 679 3452
Fax: 671 5213
www.bicyclehotel.com
In a way it's surprising that nobody in this bike-mad city thought of this before, but great ideas are often hidden in plain sight. Anyway, the youthful proprietors translate a commitment to environmentally friendly transport – you can rent bikes cheaply – into a comfortable hotel for cyclists.

Wynnobel
Vossiusstraat 9
Tel: 662 2298
Cheap and cheerful, with views of the Vondelpark. No private bathrooms. Near public transport, shopping quarter and museums.

HOSTELS

Stayokay Amsterdam Vondelpark
5 Zandpad, Vondelpark
Tel: 589 8996
Fax: 589 8955
www.stayokay.com/vondelpark
Quiet, well-equipped hostel in the Vondelpark. All rooms with shower and toilet; recreation rooms, meals and snacks, bar and family rooms.

CAMPING

Camping is permitted only on official campsites. The VVV office can provide a list of sites near the city but cannot make reservations. Most sites are easily accessible by bus from Centraal Station.

Amsterdamse Bos: 1 Kleine Noorddijk, Amstelveen, tel: 641 6868, fax: 640 2378, is a quiet site and suitable for families. One of the closest to the city.
Vliegenbos: 138 Meeuwenlaan, tel: 636 8855, fax: 632 2723. A short ride from the city centre, located in the middle of 25 hectares (60 acres) of woods, with cabins as well as tent and shower accommodation. The following three campsites are not so easy to get to, but the site's management can fax directions:
Zeeburg: 2 Zuider Ijdijk, tel: 694 4430, fax: 694 6238.
De Badhoeve: 10 Uitdammerdijk; tel/fax: 490 4294;
Gaspercamping: 7 Loosdrechtdreef, tel: 696 7326; fax: 696 9369.

PRICE CATEGORIES

Price categories are for a double room with breakfast:
De Luxe: over €300
Expensive: €200–300
Moderate: €100–200
Inexpensive: under €100

A CTIVITIES

THE ARTS, NIGHTLIFE, FESTIVALS, SHOPPING AND SPECTATOR SPORTS

THE ARTS

Museums & Art Galleries

Amsterdam has more than 40 museums, ranging from some of Europe's finest art collections to a host of small, specialist museums reflecting the diversity of the city's culture. The top two attractions, the Rijksmuseum and the Van Gogh, are conveniently located next to each other on Museumplein; however, the Rijksmuseum is undergoing major renovation work which will not be completed until 2008 – it remains open but much reduced in scope *(see page 148)*. The city's major modern art museum, the Stedelijk, is in the process of an even larger restructuring, which means that its Museumplein site will be closed to the public until 2006 – some exhibits have been moved to a temporary location on the Waterfront *(see page 183)*.

If you intend spending a large proportion of your time visiting museums, buy an Amsterdam Pass *(see page 213)* which gives free entry or substantial discounts to all the most important museums, a free canal cruise and discounts to tourist attrac-

tions. This is a viable alternative to the Museum Card (available at main museums and the VVV), valid for a year and entitling you to free entry to approximately 350 museums in the Netherlands, 16 of them in Amsterdam. The price of the Museum Card is such that you need to visit at least 10 museums before you make a saving, therefore making it more attractive to locals.

Most museums are closed all day Monday. They are generally open Tues–Fri 10am–5pm, Sat–Sun 11am–5pm.

Music, Opera, Ballet & Theatre

The chief venue for classical music is the Concertgebouw *(see page 157)* which holds special Sunday morning concerts, as well as other events including

free lunchtime concerts (12.30–1pm) on most Wednesdays. Chamber music is often performed in the city's historic churches, and there are student performances at the Music Conservatory (Conservatorium) at 27 Van Baerlestraat. The IJsbreker café/concert hall at 23 Weesperzijde is a popular venue for contemporary music played by many international and local artists.

The beautiful old Stock Exchange building (Beurs van Berlage; *see page 83)* near the Dam is now a twin-hall concert venue and home to the Netherlands Philharmonic Orchestra and the Netherlands Chamber Orchestra.

The impressive 1,600-seat Muziektheater, overlooking the River Amstel by Waterlooplein, is home of the National Ballet and

BOOKING TIPS AND WHAT'S ON

For the majority of theatre, music, ballet and opera performances, seats can be booked in advance at the Amsterdam Uit Buro (AUB), 26 Leidseplein, tel: 0900 0191; www.uitlijn.nl, open daily 10am–6pm. You can also book through the VVV *(see page 234)*.

For information on what's on, consult the English guide *Amsterdam Day by Day*, available from the tourist office and main hotels *(see page 232)*, or the monthly Uitburo publication, *Uitkrant*, published in Dutch, but easy to comprehend in terms of dates and events.

Netherlands Opera *(see page 165)*. There are usually free half-hour performances on Tuesday afternoons. The ballet, under the direction of Wayne Eagling, offers a varied repertoire of classics as well as modern work by today's top choreographers. As artistic director of the opera for more than a decade, Pierre Audi has helped it achieve worldwide renown with its mixed repertoire of classic and modern productions, from Monteverdi to Robert Wilson.

For something louder, take in a big-name concert at Amsterdam ArenA, the Ajax stadium in Amsterdam-Zuidoost (southeast).

Free concerts, dance and other events take place on summer afternoons and evenings in the Vondelpark, mostly in the amphitheatre.

The Holland Festival is an annual event each June, featuring international opera, theatre, music and dance *(see page 56)*. The main venue is the Stadsschouwburg theatre on Leidseplein.

Over the last weekend in August, theatre, dance and music companies from around the country perform extracts from their year's forthcoming programme in the streets of the city, during the Uitmarkt.

Most theatre performances are in Dutch but during the Holland Festival foreign companies perform in different languages. Amsterdam is putting on more English-speaking events year round. The VVV publishes brochures promoting these Amsterdam Arts Adventures in summer and winter.

Musicals are popular in the Netherlands. Several companies tour the country with Dutch productions and adaptations from foreign musicals, which are presented mainly at the 19th-century Theater Carré, on the River Amstel.

Fast-paced improvisational comedy rules at Boom Chicago, Leidseplein Theater, on busy Leidseplein.

Cinema

The largest cinemas are located around Leidseplein, Rembrandtplein and Haarlemmerplein. Due to the popularity of the large multiplexes, small art-house cinemas are becoming more scarce, but there are still some thriving, notably The Movies, Kriterion, Rialto, Desmet and Uitkijk.

All films are shown in their original language with Dutch subtitles. In the larger cinemas, many films are stopped halfway to encourage custom at the snack bar. Listings of screening times and venues are posted in most cafés and in front of cinemas.

Literary Events

Amsterdam is a literary kind of place, and there are a correspondingly large number of bookshops. There are occasional book signings for a foreign author at local stores such as Athenaeum or Scheltema, and that often means the author might be giving a reading somewhere.

The John Adams Institute for American Literature offers a reading series throughout the year at various venues in the city. Authors have included John Irving, Paul Theroux, Peter Matthiessen and Carol Shields. For information, tel: 624 7280. Winston Kingdom, a cultural centre/hotel holds poetry evenings on Monday around 10pm *(see page 224)*.

NIGHTLIFE

Nightspots

Amsterdam is well known for its nightlife. After dark, entertainment focuses on three main areas: Leidseplein, for lively discos and nightclubs; Rembrandtplein for clubs, discos, cabarets and strip shows pandering to older tastes; and the Red Light District, notorious for scantily

clad females sitting in windows *(see page 103)*.

Strip shows, porn videos and sex shops centre on the main canals of Oudezijds Voorburgwal and Oudezijd Achterburgwal. The smaller, sleazier streets leading off these two canals are best avoided – and don't take photographs. On a different note, you could take a candlelit canal cruise, with wine and cheese or full dinner provided *(see page 214)*, or try a brown café, or one of the new-wave bars with cool, whitewashed and mirrored walls, an abundance of greenery and a long list of cocktails.

Music Venues

Akhnaton
161 Nieuwzijds Voorburgwal
Hosts salsa, tango and world-music-themed evenings. Performances as well as dance nights.
Bourbon Street
6 Leidsekruisstraat
Blues, rock and Latin bands perform during the week.
De IJsbreker
23 Weesperzijde
Tel: 668 1805
This café-venue beside the River Amstel is the place to go for the latest in pioneering musical sounds. Set to move during 2005 to the new Muziekgebouw, just east of Centraal Station.
Last Waterhole
12 Oudezijds Armsteeg
Live music of all kinds is offered nightly.
Maloe Melo
163 Lijnbaansgracht
Tel: 420 4592
Mellow blues are played nightly at Amsterdam's "home of the Blues", in a suitably dark and smoky atmosphere.

GAMBLING

The main venue for gambling in Amsterdam is Holland Casino Amsterdam, 62 Max Euweplein, close to Leidseplein. A passport or ID card is necessary for entry.

Melkweg
234a Lijnbaansgracht
Long-standing offbeat arts centre-cum-club, with concert hall, disco, experimental plays (some in English) and art exhibitions. Cannabis and space cakes for sale.

Paradiso
6–8 Weteringschans (just off Leidseplein)
A hot spot for rock, reggae and pop concerts, attracting top international headliners as well as new talent from all around Europe.

Winston Kingdom
123 Warmoesstraat
The essence of cool, with live music, art and poetry happenings being offered during the week.

Jazz Bars

Bamboo Bar
66 Lange Leidsedwarsstraat
Live jazz and blues in a pleasingly exotic setting.

Bimhuis
73 Oudeschans
The in-place for jazz music, featuring top international players as well as locals. Moving in 2005 to the new Muziekgebouw, just east of Centraal Station.

Café Alto
115 Korte Leidsedwaarstraat
Jazz from 9pm. No admission fee.

Cotton Club
5 Nieuwmarkt
Live jazz at weekends in this local landmark.

Nightclubs

Casablanca
26 Zeedijk
Some nights they have a disco with top local DJs, and other nights live jazz, blues and more.

Club Arena
51 's-Gravesandestraat
A popular disco out of the city centre that attracts a mixed crowd.

Dansen Bij Jansen
11 Handboogstraat
A popular student disco that also attracts non-students.

Escape
11 Rembrandtplein
Big disco with variety of music and theme nights and a mixed crowd.

ANNUAL FESTIVALS

The following are the main events that take place in the city:

1 January: New Year's Day.
25 February: Commemoration of the "February Strike", led by the dockers in 1941 against the Nazis' treatment of the Jews, held on J.D. Meijerplein (see page 169).
February and March: Amsterdam Carnival.
March: On the Sunday closest to 15 March there is a silent procession through the city – the Stille Omgang – which celebrates the "Amsterdam Miracle", a 14th-century communion wafer which was supposedly impossible to destroy in fire (see page 20).
Late April: Keukenhof Floral Parade at Keukenhof Gardens, 30 km (19 miles) southwest of Amsterdam (see page 208).
30 April: Koninginnedag (Queen's Day). Street markets, street parties, fireworks and festivities throughout the entire city until the early evening (see page 56).
4 May: Dodenherdenking (National Remembrance Day).
5 May: Bevrijdingsdag (Liberation Day) is celebrated by a smaller version of Queen's Day, held primarily in the Vondelpark.
June: The Netherlands feast of culture, the Holland Festival, is held throughout most of the month at the Stadsschouwburg and other nearby venues. It features major theatrical, operatic, dance and musical events, many for an English-speaking audience (see page 56).
July–September: Free concerts and theatre are held on summer afternoons and evenings at the open-air pavilion in the Vondelpark, while classical music is performed by internationally renowned musicians on a barge in front of the Pulitzer Hotel.
Early August: Gay Pride, exuberant festival run by the city's large gay community, culminating in the colourful carnival parade on Prinsengracht (see page 57).
Late August: On the last weekend of the month, the annual Uitmarkt takes place in Museumplein. This popular event, which attracts thousands, celebrates the opening of the cultural season in the Netherlands. There are mini-performances by dance, theatre and musical groups as well as hundreds of stalls which provide information on the various events.
Early September: The annual Bloemencorso (Flower Parade) winds its way from Aalsmeer to Amsterdam in the first week of the month.
Mid-September: Jordaan Festival. Weekend in the Jordaan district devoted to a number of events, including brass bands and smartlap (tear-jerker music) choirs, and more.
Mid-November: The parade of St Nicolaas is held on a Saturday in the middle of the month. St Nicolaas (the Dutch version of Santa Claus) arrives by steamer at Centraal Station, together with his Moorish helpers (the Zwarte Pieten), who distribute pepernoten (spice biscuits) to the city's children along the parade site (see page 56).
5 December: Shops close early so that families can celebrate Sinterklaas or Pakjesavond (gift evening), exchanging presents and poems in honour of Saint Nicholas's birthday on 6 December (see page 56).
31 December: Firework displays take place around Amsterdam harbour and around the Nieuwmarkt/Chinatown area at midnight. Try some oliebollen (doughnuts without the hole) which is an Oudejaars (New Year) tradition.

Havana
17 Reguliersdwarsstraat
Club for gay clientele and people who like to party hard.
House of Soul
32a Amstelstraat
This place lives up to its name with various DJs on hand keeping things swinging and soulful.
Ministry
12 Reguliersdwarsstraat
Offers something for everyone from Groove to Soul and hip-hop.
Odeon
460 Singel
Elegant 17th-century house converted into a disco and café, with a mixed, suitably smart clientele as well as students.
Sinners in Heaven
3 Wagenstraat
This attracts a more "upmarket" crowd who come to see and be seen and dance the night away.
Soul Kitchen
32 Amstelstraat
Tel: 620 2333
As its name implies, this place rustles up some tasty soul, plus other kinds of music, with emphasis on the 1960s and 70s.
Trance Buddha
216 Oudezijds Voorburgwal
Stylish and relaxed club.
Vakzuid
35 Olympisch Stadion
In the southern part of the city, this new spot is the place to lounge, attracting a mix of creative and city types. The Quincy Lounge on Sunday afternoon is where people begin dancing early.
West Pacific
Westergasfabriek, 8–10 Haarlemmerweg
Tel: 488 7778
Dance to latin and hip-hop rhythms at this trendy spot in a sprawling redeveloped gasworks complex west of Centraal Station.

Comedy Cafés

Live comedy has become popular in Amsterdam in recent years. There are places to go which offer English-speaking entertainment, from stand-up comedy at two local clubs to the improvisational techniques of the Boom Chicago comedy troupe.
Boom Chicago Theater
12 Leidseplein
Tel: 423 0101 for reservations. Restaurant on the premises.
Comedy Café
43 Max Euweplein
Tel: 638 3971
Many comedians from the US, UK and Canada, and an occasional "open mike" evening.

SHOPPING

What to Buy

Bargains are a rarity in Amsterdam but browsing is fun, particularly in the markets and specialist shops. Avoid the tourist areas and high streets, where you won't find anything you can't find at home. Instead, try the nine small streets which run adjacent to Prinsengracht and Herengracht canals, between Leidsestraat and Raadhuisstraat. There are boutiques specialising in buttons, candles, custom-made handbags and wallets, erotic lingerie, kites and much more.

Most museums have good gift shops, especially the Jewish Historical Museum, Amsterdam Historical Museum, Maritime Museum, NEMO and the Nieuwe Kerk. The Rijksmuseum and Van Gogh Museum have a shared gift shop on Museumplein.

Where to Buy

Antiques

Nieuwe Spiegelstraat is lined with small antiques shops selling a fascinating range of items: old Dutch tiles, copper and brass, glass, pewter, Russian icons, prints and paintings, Delftware, period jewellery, Asian objets d'art, art deco, medical instruments, snuff boxes, clocks and dolls. The dealers have a lot of expertise as well as international reputations and welcome interested browsers *(see page*

132). In markets, beware of imitation antique copper and brass.

Art and reproduction

The major museums and art galleries sell excellent reproductions of their paintings, particularly the Rijksmuseum and Van Gogh Museum.

Numerous small commercial galleries sell original oil paintings, watercolours, drawings, engravings and sculpture. For old prints and engravings, try the Antiekmarkt de Looier, 109 Elandsgracht.

Books

The city has an exceptionally large choice of books, both new and second-hand. For second-hand English-language books, try the Book Exchange, 51 Kloveniersburgwal, or Book Traffic at 50 Leliegracht. For new English-language books try The American Book Center, 185 Kalverstraat, or Waterstone's, 152 Kalverstraat. Scheltema in Koningsplein boasts six storeys of books, including an antiquarian section and a café. The Athenaeum Boekhandel & Nieuwscentrum, 14–16 Spui, has a superb selection of literature in a splendid art nouveau setting and a competent staff. Architectura & Natura (22 Leligracht) specialises in books on architecture, nature and gardens. Premsela (78 Van Baerlestraat), Art Book (126 Van Baerlestraat) and Neighof & Lee (13A Staalstraat) all specialise in art and artists. The specialist travel book shop Pied à terre (Singel 393) was established in 1977 and offers an extensive range of maps and guides. At 62 Damrak is Allert de Lange, one of the city's finest bookshops.

There are many antiquarian booksellers in the streets around the Spui, where it is possible to get a list of the city's antiquarian shops. Every Friday on Spui, an antiquarian book market is held from 10am–6pm. In summer there are book markets held one Sunday a month at either the

Dam or in front of the Muziektheater. For gay and lesbian books, go to Boekhandel Vrolijk, 135 Paleisstraat, the largest gay and lesbian bookshop in Europe, or Vrowen in Druk, 5 Westermarkt, which sells second-hand and antiquarian books about and by women. Try also Intermale, 251 Spuistraat.

Clothing

Amsterdam has several department stores, the most prestigious of which is De Bijenkorf at 90 Damrak. It has several restaurants and cafés, and is a good place to relax between shopping and museum visits. Rokin, which extends from Damrak, is the location for other fine shops and department stores, including Maison de Bonneterie and Vroom & Dreesman. For designer labels, try P.C. Hooftstraat, Leidsestraat, Rokin and Van Baerlestraat; for high-street shops, go along Kalverstraat and into the Kalvertoren complex; just up the road is a Marks & Spencer.

Behind the Royal Palace is the elegant Magna Plaza shopping centre. For less conventional boutiques and speciality shops, try the side streets between the canals (Runstraat, Reestraat, Wolvenstraat), the streets around the Jordaan (Prinsenstraat), Damstraat and Sint-Antoniesbreestraat.

Jewellery

Jewellery shops all over town have eye-catching displays of modern and traditional pieces, some original and designed on the spot. But the fact that Amsterdam is a major diamond-cutting centre doesn't mean you'll get them cheap.

For handmade costume jewellery that is elegant and exotic, visit Christopher Clark (4 Molsteeg), and for sculptural designs in gold and silver, visit Anneke Schat, 20 Spiegelgracht or Hans Appenzeller, 1 Grimburgwal.

Porcelain and pottery

Cheap imitations of the familiar blue Delftware are sold all over town. The genuine article, always with a capital "D", is sold at Royal Delft's official retail branch, Holland Gallery De Munt, 12 Muntplein, and on Spiegelgracht.

Focke & Meltzer, with branches at 149 Gelderlandplein and the Okura Hotel (see page 220), have a good choice of porcelain, pottery and glass, and some attractive reproduction Delft tiles. For a huge range of antique tiles, try Eduard Kramer, 64 Nieuwe Spiegelstraat.

Gifts

Tulips and bulbs are always popular. If you fail to get them at the flower market, you can buy them at higher prices at the airport (see below). Other things typically Dutch are cigars (the best- known shop is Hajenius, 92 Rokin) and chocolates. For the latter, try Pompadour at 12 Huidenstraat, Jordino at 25 Haarlemmerdijk and Bonbon Jeannette in Centraal Station, which has a superb selection; Droste and Van Houten are popular brand names.

In terms of cheese, Edam and Gouda are household names but they come in a variety of types depending on their age, fat content and flavouring – jonge (young), belegen (medium) and oude (old). Leidsekaas is cheese made with cumin.

Other typical souvenirs are traditional Dutch clogs, and the ubiquitous fridge magnets depicting the city's architecture.

There is an enormous range of goods at Schiphol Airport. Apart from duty-free goods, there is an excellent food section, selling smoked Dutch eel and cheeses, and shops specialising in bulbs and seeds, flowers, Delftware, clothes and souvenirs. Although quite pricey, you can also find some unusual and affordable gifts here.

Tax Refunds

Non-EU residents are entitled to a refund of most of the 17.5 per-cent sales tax (VAT) levied on individual items costing in excess of €137. The leaflet Tax Free for Tourists, available at Schiphol Airport and the VVV office, explains the procedure and shop-keepers are always happy to help. For information, call Global Refund: (023) 524 1909.

Markets

All markets are held Monday to Saturday unless otherwise stated **"Floating" Flower Market**: Singel. Dazzling flower displays,

SEX SHOPS

A large percentage of those who visit Amsterdam are curious about the city's many sex shops, but the ones that you see in the Red Light District are so sleazy on the outside that even the most daring tourist is likely to hesitate. Yet once you are inside the atmosphere is low-key, with friendly, sensitive and knowledgeable staff.

Female & Partners at 100 Spuistraat sells erotic clothing and articles for women in a small shop just minutes from Dam Square. They carry the Marlies Dekkers line of lingerie, among others, which includes bras and panties creatively designed to put a little spice in your life, in basic black, white or red. There is also a variety of sex toys for sale. No need to feel embarrassed. The clientele is made up mainly of women or couples.

The next stop is usually the Condomerie (141 Warmoesstraat) which sells hundreds of condoms in a wide variety of colours, shapes and scents. Again, it is operated by a friendly, female staff. Other options are Mail & Female (489 Prinsengracht) and the Christine le Duc shops around the city.

many sold from barges. Some stalls will pack and export bulbs. Reasonable prices and worth seeing, even if you don't intend to buy.

Albert Cuypstraat: Large bustling general market with a wide choice of food, household goods, clothes, etc. *(see page 190).*

Boerenmarkt (Farmers' Market): Held Saturdays at Noorderkerkplein, with organic fruits, vegetables, fresh herbs, baked goods, cheeses, juices, and related wares from massage oil to ceramic pots.

Book Market: 10am–6pm Fridays on the Spui Square.

Oudemanhuispoort: Passageway with stalls selling antique books and prints.

Stamp Market: N.Z. Voorburgwal. Stamps and coins, held on Wednesday and Saturday.

Waterlooplein: Extensive flea market, Amsterdam's oldest, with a lot of junk and occasional bargains; clothes, books, records and antiques.

Diamond Factories

Amsterdam is a major international diamond centre with dozens of workshops where you can watch the cutting and polishing of the gems. Entrance is free and there is absolutely no obligation to buy. If you are tempted, bear in mind the import tax you might have to pay. The following factories operate free guided tours:

Amsterdam Diamond Centre
1–5 Rokin
Bonebakker & Zn
88/90 Rokin
Coster Diamonds
2–6 Paulus Potterstraat
Gassan Diamonds
173–175 Nieuwe Uilenburgerstraat
Stoeltie
13–17 Wagenstraat
Van Moppes Diamonds
2–6 Albert Cuypstraat

SPORT

Spectator Sports

Football

Amsterdam's Ajax is one of the top European clubs. Home matches are played at the Amsterdam ArenA, Bijlmermeer, in the southeastern part of the city (take the Metro to the Strandvliet exit). Tickets can be bought at the gate or booked in advance from the VVV or by writing to Ajax Travel, p/a Packages, PO Box 12522, 1100 AM Amsterdam (fax: 311 1945; e-mail: tickets@ ajax.nl). Groups of 10 or more can take a two-hour tour of the ArenA (tel: 311 1336 for reservations). The Ajax Museum (tel: 311 1444) is also worth visiting.

American Football

Local hotshots the Amsterdam Admirals, with cheerleaders in tow, get tough at the Amsterdam ArenA *(see above).*

Athletics

The Olympic Stadium hosts various athletic events. It's in Amsterdam Nieuw-Zuid at the end of tram lines 16 ad 24..

Baseball

The Amsterdam Pirates play honkbal (as baseball is known in Holland) at the Sportpark, 16 Jan van Galenstraat (tel: 684 8143) in the western Amsterdam Bos en Lommer district.

Participant Sports

Cycling

The Dutch are a nation of cyclists and the country is criss-crossed with cycle paths and routes. You can either hire a bike *(see page 215)* and set off independently, or opt for a bike excursion (includes bike hire) a cheese farm visit and boat rides. Information from VVV.

Golf

The greens closest to the city centre are at the Golf & Conference Centre Amstelborgh, 6 Borchlandweg, tel: 697 5000.

Ice Skating

If it's cold enough, you can skate on the canals or at a new skating rink at the Museumplein. There is year-round skating at the Jaap Edenbaan ice-skating rink, 64 Radioweg, tel: 694 9894.

Squash

Squash City, 6 Ketelmakerstraat, has squash courts, aerobics classes, showers and sauna. Tel: 626 7883 for information.

Swimming

De Mirandabad, 9 De Mirandalaan, has both indoor and outdoor pools. The Marnixbad, 9 Marnixplein, is an indoor pool with slides.

Watersports

Canoes, rowing boats and windsurfing boards can be hired in the Amsterdamse Bos. Canal bikes (similar to pedalos) can be hired at various points in the city.

OTHER ACTIVITIES

Brewery Tours

Brouwerij 't IJ
7 Funenkade
Tel: 622 8325
Located in an old public bath house and next to a prominent windmill. Open Wed–Sun 3–8pm. Brewery tours: Fri, Sat, Sun after 4pm by arrangement only, cost €2 including a drink. Real beer devotees may enjoy free tours on Fridays.

Amsterdams Brouwhuis Maximiliaan
6–8 Kloveniersburgwal
(near Nieuwmarkt)
Tel: 624 2778
Reservations: 626 6280
Situated in an old convent where the reverend ladies used to brew beer themselves. The fact that you can drink a beer in the brewing hall next to the copper kettles makes it all the more appealing *(see page 99)*. There is a very reasonable restaurant located in the old refectory. Open Tues–Thur noon–1am, Fri & Sat noon–2am and Sun noon–midnight. Brewery tours are by appointment only (phone or ask at the bar), cost €8 including drink, groups of up to 15.

Heineken Experience
78 Stadhouderskade
Tel: 523 9239
The former brewery building opened its doors as a brewing museum in 2001, and its guided tours involve a certain amount of beer consumption *(see page 189)*. Of course Heineken is still brewing, but has relocated its operation outside Amsterdam.

Proeflokalen (tasting rooms)
These are usually associated with spirits and distilleries and are, generally speaking, of the brown café genre and make excellent watering holes. Their original function was to serve as a tasting room before customers made their purchases – alas, no more.

Wijnand Fockink Proeflokaal
31 Pijlsteeg, 1012 HH
(next to the Krasnapolsky Hotel)
Tel: 639 2695.
Lovingly restored distillery that may be visited from 3–9pm daily. Inside you may expect to drink the numerous varieties and qualities of *jenevers* (Dutch gins) which vary from a light *jenever* to beautifully cask-matured nectar comparable to the finest single malt whiskies. The interior decor reflects its 17th-century splendour, including the traditional sand on the massively thick floorboards. Guided tours round the distillery by arrangement only.

City Walks

Brochures are available from the VVV and the Amsterdam Historical Museum detailing walks around the city and covering the Jordaan, Maritime Quarter, Jewish Amsterdam, famous shopping streets and Amsterdam School architecture, among other themes.

Tours

Travel agents organise city bus tours, canal cruises and excursions further afield. Within the city the most popular excursions are daytime and evening *rondvaart* canal cruises in modern glass-covered motor-launches *(see page 113)*. You can also take an organised tram ride around the city, starting from Centraal Station. City tours by coach take in the Koninklijk Palace, the Rijksmuseum, a diamond-cutting factory and other sights. It is cheaper to visit these yourself, but a tour is worth considering if time is limited and you don't know the city.

For excursions outside Amsterdam, the main operators are Holland International and Lindbergh Excursions *(see page 214)*. For those interested in personal guides who specialise in art, architecture, antiques, and even the Red Light District, get the *Amsterdam Information* booklet

at VVV offices. The booklet also includes information about special building tours of such landmarks as the Tuschinski cinema, ArenA football stadium, Beurs van Berlage and Concertgebouw.

Children's Activities

Tram trips, canal cruises, water pedalos, bicycle excursions outside the busy city environs, barrel-organs and mime shows are all likely to amuse the young. The **Vondelpark** has a good playground, duck ponds and free entertainment in summer. The **Amstelpark** provides pony rides and the **Amsterdamse Bos**, reached in summer by vintage trams, provides a huge expanse of parkland with lakes, swimming, riding, fishing, biking and canoes *(see page 193)*.

One of the most popular children's attractions is the NEMO **science museum** *(see page 182)*, where games and hands-on exhibitions allow children to explore the world of science and technology. Other favourites include **Madame Tussaud's** *(see page 82)*, the Children's Museum at the **Tropenmuseum** *(see page 175)*, the **Artis Zoo, Aquarium and Planetarium** *(see page 174)*, and the **Maritime Museum** *(see page 183)*. Also popular are the **children's farm** *(see page 186)* and the **Electric Tramline Museum** *(see page 194)*.

Smaller children will enjoy the **TunFun activity centre**, located underneath the busy traffic junction at Mr. Visserplein (the entrance is next to the Portuguese-Israelite Synagogue).

As an excursion for children, you can't beat **Madurodam** – a Dutch town in miniature complete with churches, castles, farms, ships and planes, followed, perhaps, by an afternoon on **Scheveningen beach**; just 45 minutes by train to The Hague (Den Haag) and then a 10-minute tram ride. Closer by is **Zaanse Schans** with authentic houses and windmills from the 1700s *(see page 199)*.

A-Z

DIRECTORY

A dmission Charges

Museums and galleries charge moderate entrance fees – typically €5 or 10. Some of the larger places have special deals for families. The Amsterdam Pass (see page 213) gives reduced entrance fees to the majority of museums and galleries in the city.

Young people under 24 can get reduced-rate admissions to most museums, though you may need to produce a passport as proof of your age. People aged over 65 are also entitled to discounts. On National Museum Weekend at the end of April, admission to some museums is free, and others charge reduced fees.

B udgeting for your Trip

If you're looking for a hotel with an acceptable minimum level of comfort, cleanliness and facilities, a reasonable starting point for the price of a double room is €60; in budget-class hotels, going up from there to around €100 should make a significant difference in quality. Canal-side hotels in the old centre tend to be more expensive, so you'll generally get more for your money elsewhere – but you won't get the canal view. For between €100 and €200 a whole range of hotels opens up, ranging from bland business-traveller places to characterful establishments looked after by loving owners. Beyond this, and certainly beyond €250,

you're moving into de-luxe territory, though you don't really arrive there in all its genuine-marble glory until €300 and above.

Food costs range from a couple of euros for a perfectly acceptable *broodje* (sandwich), through €10–20 for a two or three course meal at a traditional *eetcafé* (café with food) and €30–50 at a fine restaurant. From there, you can head up to the €100 mark and above, though the extra cost won't necessarily be justified in terms of taste.

Getting around by tram (and bus and Metro where appropriate) costs as little as about €7 a day. This is also the starting point for bike hire for a day, though you can expect to pay a few euros more at most places. Taxi fares for most journeys in the centre run from about €5–15. A taxi to the airport should cost around €35–45.

Business Hours

Normal shopping hours are 8.30am or 9am–6pm. Late-night shopping is Thursday until 9pm. Most shops close at 5pm on Saturday. All shops close for one half-day a week, usually Monday, when they open at 1pm. Many grocery stores, such as the Albert Heijn chain, are open most evenings until either 7pm or 9pm. Some shops have Sunday hours of 1–7pm. Many department stores and speciality shops in the city centre are also open on Sunday from noon to 5pm. Most banks and government offices are open 9am–5pm Monday to Friday.

Crime and Safety

Amsterdam is a centre of the drugs trade and much crime here is drugs-related. As a visitor, you are unlikely to be affected by big-time drugs-related crime, but you should take sensible precautions against becoming a victim of petty crime like pickpocketing and bag-snatching, and of the less common but more serious robberies with threats or violence. Keep a careful watch on wallets, bags and other valuables, especially on public transport, at busy transport nodes like Centraal Station and Schiphol Airport. And exercise some caution in certain areas after dark: the Red Light District – mostly safe but some of its narrow alleys may not be; deserted canal-sides; and Vondelpark.

In an emergency, call the police *(politie)* on 112. For non-emergencies, there are police stations around the city. Police headquarters is at 117 Elandsgracht, tel: 559 9111.

Customs

Personal possessions are not liable to duty and tax provided

CLIMATE

The Netherlands has a temperate climate, typical of north-western Europe. Extremes of heat and cold are rare, and the relatively long coastline and flat landscape results in frequent strong, chilly winds from the North Sea. Temperatures in the east of the country, away from the sea, are slightly lower in winter and higher in summer.

Amsterdam itself has a mild, maritime climate similar to that found in eastern England but with a little more rain, and slightly colder in winter. Average winter daytime temperatures are around 5°C (41°F), falling to 1°C (34°F) at night. When there is a cold spell, however, temperatures can plummet to –10°C (14°F) and canals freeze over. Summers are quite warm: the July afternoon average is 22°C (72°F), falling to around 13°C

(55°F) at night. Occasional heat-waves see temperatures up to 30°C (86°F) and beyond.

You can expect rain at any time of year. Spring is generally the driest time and a favourite for tulip enthusiasts. The advantages of a visit in winter are the cut-price hotel prices and package deals, plus the fact that museums and galleries are pleasantly uncrowded.

Mean daily maxima

	Jan	Feb	Mar	Apr	May	Jun	Jul	Aug	Sep	Oct	Nov	Dec
Max	4	5	8	13	18	21	22	22	19	14	9	5
Min	-1	-1	1	4	8	11	13	13	13	10	7	3	1

Mean nightly minima

TEMPERATURE (°C)

	Jan	Feb	Mar	Apr	May	Jun	Jul	Aug	Sep	Oct	Nov	Dec
	68	53	44	49	52	58	77	87	72	72	70	64

PRECIPITATION IN MM

you are staying for less than six months and you intend to take them out of the country again. There is no restriction on the amount of currency that you can bring into the Netherlands. Among prohibited or restricted goods are plants, flowers, weapons and recreational drugs.

Duty-free shopping is no longer available to travellers within the European Union. For travel within the EU, customs restrictions on alcohol, cigarettes and some other items no longer apply, although there are guide levels designed to prevent illegal trading.

Despite this, travellers departing from Schiphol Airport to destinations in and out of the EU may still take advantage of reduced prices on all goods except for alcoholic beverages and tobacco. In a unique action, the airport and the shop-owners decided to band together to pay the sales tax themselves; in this way the prices for perfume, electronic equipment, cameras and other items remain at duty-free levels. Alcohol

and tobacco are still available for sale, but at prices comparable to normal shops in the city. Travellers to the Canary Islands (Spain) and the Channel Islands (UK) are not affected by the ruling.

Disabled Travellers

The Royal Association for Disability and Rehabilitation (RADAR) has information on planning holidays, transport and equipment for rent, and accommodation. Their address is Unit 12, City Forum, 250 City Rd, London EC1V 8AF, tel: (020) 7250 3222.

Information is also available from the VVV-Amsterdam *(see page 234)* which gives advice on the accessibility of hotels, restaurants, museums and other places of interest with disabled facilities. The Uitbureau on Leidseplein has a brochure on the accessibility of theatres, concert halls etc., but it's written in Dutch.

Most of the major museums and galleries have access for wheelchairs, although the city in general, with its cobbled streets and wealth of steep narrow staircases, is not ideal, and you should check before booking into a hotel whether it has a lift, as some staircases can be almost as steep as ladders.

E lectricity

The standard for electricity in Holland is 220 volts AC. Hotels may have a 110-volt or 120-volt outlet for shavers.

Embassies & Consulates

Consulates in Amsterdam
Canada, 7 Sophialaan
Tel: 311 1600
UK, 44 Koningslaan
Tel: 676 4343
US, 19 Museumplein
Tel: 575 5309

Embassies (in The Hague)
Australia, 4 Carnegielaan
Tel: (070) 310 8200
Ireland, 9 Dr. Kuyperstraat
Tel: (070) 363 0993
New Zealand, 10 Carnegielaan
Tel: (070) 346 9324
South Africa, 40 Wassenaarseweg. Tel: (070) 392 4501
UK, 10 Lange Voorhout
Tel: (070) -427 0427
US, 102 Lange Vorhout
Tel: (070) 310 9209

These offices are generally open 8.30am–4pm (some consular offices are open only in the morning) and are closed on public holidays of their country.

Entry Requirements

Visitors from the European Union, the US, Canada, Australia,

EMERGENCY NUMBERS

- **Police, Fire, Ambulance**
  tel: 112
- **General Doctors' and Dental Service** tel: 592 3434.
  (For urgent medical or dental treatment; open 24 hours.)

New Zealand and most other European countries require only a valid passport. Citizens of most other countries must obtain a visa in advance from Dutch embassies or consulates in their home countries.

G ay & Lesbian Travellers

Amsterdam has plenty to offer gay travellers. There are special hotels, restaurants, bars, bookshops, shops, nightclubs, cinemas and plenty more.

The best point of reference and information is undoubtedly the national gay and lesbian organisation, the COC. Regardless of one's tastes, this institution provides something for everyone, is a key source for Amsterdam gay information and a non-profit organisation there to help gay people, be their needs social, legal or medical. The COC's big social night is Friday which attracts up to 600 gays and lesbians. The evening starts at 8pm for the youth section (16 years upwards), the café opens its doors at 10pm, and the disco starts at 11pm, with festivities continuing until 4am. Saturday night is exclusively for women but follows pretty much the same pattern. Sunday is multicultural night, open to all, and closes at the much earlier time of 12.30am. The COC is a large complex housing numerous halls including a small theatre where some English productions are played. In addition to these activities there are six leather and S&M parties a year, which have become something of an international event. Of interest to English speakers is the Wednesday English-speaking group from 8–10pm where one can discuss all aspects of gay life in Amsterdam.

The Man to Man Gay Guide, available at Vrolijk Gay and Lesbian Bookshop, is full of useful information. A list of books for lesbian readers is available on request at the bookshop.

The Amsterdam Columbia Fun Map user-friendly street map

giving details of all gay and lesbian bars, restaurants, hotels, beauty salons, shops, cinemas and anything of gay/lesbian relevance. It's available from the COC and other gay bookshops:
COC: 14 Rozenstraat, 1016 NX, tel: 623 4596.
Vrolijk Gay and Lesbian Bookshop: 135 Paleisstraat, tel: 623 5142.

H ealth & Medical Care

No health certificates or vaccinations are required for European Union citizens. EU citizens who have obtained an E111 form from their local post office before departure are entitled to free treatment by a doctor and free prescribed medicines. This insurance is not comprehensive and won't cover you, for example, for holiday cancellation or the cost of repatriation. For full cover, take out separate medical insurance.

Medical services

The most central hospital in Amsterdam is the Onze Lieve Vrouwe Gasthuis, le (first) 279 Oosterparkstraat, tel: 599 9111. The main hospital is the Academisch Medisch Centrum (AMC), 9 Meibergdreef, tel: 566 3333. Both hospitals have an outpatients department and an emergency casualty ward.

The medical services in the Netherlands are good. People with middle-to-high incomes usually have private insurance, while the rest of the population falls under the National Health or Ziekenfonds. People go to a general practitioner (huisarts) for check-ups and general ailments. Visitors who require medical treatment can ask at their hotel for the name of a local GP.

For emergency services, the two hospitals (ziekenhuizen) listed above provide excellent care. As long as one is medically insured, services are rendered and are billed at a later date to your home address.

Pharmacies

Pharmacies *(apotheken)* are normally open Monday to Friday 9am–5.30pm or 6pm. Weekend and late-night pharmacies operate on a rotating basis. If you have a general question about your state of health, a pharmacist will generally suggest an over-the-counter remedy. A list of out-of-hours pharmacies is posted on the front of every *apotheek*.

Internet

Each internet café has its own ambience, so choose accordingly. Some have scanners, colour printers and other extras.

The easyEverything chain has two Internet cafés: at 33 Damrak (tel: 320 8082), open daily 7.30am–11pm; and at 22 Reguliersbreestraat (tel: 320 6291), open 24 hours a day. The Internet Café, 11 Martelaarsgracht (tel: 627 1052), is open Sunday–Thursday 9am–1am, Friday–Saturday 9am–3am. An increasing number of hotels also offer Internet access.

For useful websites on Amsterdam see page 234.

Lost Property

Report loss or theft of valuables to the police immediately as most insurance policies insist on a police report. The main police station is at 117 Elandsgracht, tel: 559 9111. For items lost on public transport, contact the GVB Head Office, 108–114 Prins Hendrikkade, tel: 551 4911. Loss of passports should be reported immediately to the police and your consulate *(see page 231).*

The Lost Property Office is at 18 Stephensonstraat, tel: 559 3005, or you can also contact the main police station.

Maps

The GVB office in front of Centraal Station provides free public transport route maps. The Insight Fleximap to Amsterdam is detailed and easy to use, with a full street index, and its laminated finish means that getting wet in the frequent Amsterdam rain is not a problem.

Media

Newspapers and magazines

The main national newspapers are *NRC Handelsblad*, the most respected paper, the more left-wing *De Volkskrant*, and *De Telegraaf*, on the political right. English newspapers arrive on the same day they are published and are widely available. The monthly English-language *Amsterdam Day by Day* gives listings and reviews of events, available from VVV offices. Brown café noticeboards are another source of information on events.

The *Uitkrant*, available at the Uitburo on the Leidseplein, is a free monthly publication which, although in Dutch, is easily readable for concert venues and dates of performances. Pick up their English brochure, *Culture in Amsterdam*, at their offices at Kleine 21 Gartmanplantsoen, tel: 0900-0191, for reservations to events. There are also brochures available from the VVV – Amsterdam Winter and Summer Arts Adventures – costing €2.50. These are part of the "language is no problem" performances and exhibitions.

Television and radio

On cable TV you can watch Britain's BBC channels, plus Sky, CNN, NBC and various other international networks. English-language films are frequently shown on Dutch TV channels, undubbed. On the radio, you can tune into the BBC World Service, BBC Radio 4 and Sky Radio.

Money

The unit of currency in the Netherlands (and in most other countries of the European Union) is the euro (€). A euro is divided into 100 cents. Euro notes come in denominations of 5, 10, 20, 50, 100, 200 and 500; coins are 1 cent, 2 cents, 5 cents, 10 cents, 20 cents, €1 and €2.

Changing money

The best rates of exchange are at national banks; beware high commission rates at hotels. Major credit cards and eurocheques are accepted in all main hotels, restaurants and shops.·

The GWK (Grenswisselkantoren NV) is a national financial institution where you can exchange any currency and also use credit cards or travellers' cheques. The GWK exchange office inside Centraal Station is open long hours: Mon–Sat 7am–10.30pm, Sun 9am–10.30pm. Change is also available at post offices (at good rates) and banks.
There can be a considerable difference in commission charged between the various institutions and at the different times of night or day.

There are automatic cash-dispensers all over the city. Most can be accessed by foreign credit cards and charge cards, or cash cards with the Cirrus or Plus symbol. GWK and other currency exchange outlets also accept major credit cards.

Credit cards

Credit cards are accepted at hotels, restaurants, shops, car hire companies and airlines. MasterCard, American Express, Diners Club, Eurocard, Visa and JCB are all recognised, plus many more.

Tipping

Tips are included in taxi fares and prices in restaurants and bars, so all that is required is to leave some small change if you think the service warrants it – but service personnel won't object to receiving a tip and have become used to the fact that many visitors (in contrast

PUBLIC HOLIDAYS

- **1 January** New Year's Day
- **March/April** Good Friday, Easter Sunday and Monday
- **30 April** Queen's Day
- **May** Ascension Day (sixth Thursday after Easter)
- **May/June** Whit Monday (eighth Monday after Easter)
- **25/26 December** Christmas Day, Boxing Day

to their fellow citizens) do tip. In most restaurants, a tip of 10 percent will be considered generous, or at least adequate.

P ostal Services

Most post offices are open Monday to Friday, 9am–5pm; the main branch, behind the Palace at Singel 250–6, is open until 8pm on Thursday evenings and 9am–1pm on Saturdays. Stamps are available from post offices, tobacconists, and some newsstands and stationery shops.

Poste restante facilities are available at main post offices – you need a passport to collect your mail. You can also send a fax and make long-distance calls at post offices (buying a telephone card), and make photocopies.

R eligious Services

There are places to worship for most denominations in Amster-

dam, and they are held in a variety of historic and unique venues.

Catholic Services
Sint Nicolaaskerk
73 Prins Hendrikkade
High Mass, Sundays 10.30am
Obrechtkerk
28 Jacob Obrechtstraat
High Mass, Sundays 9.30 and 11am
De Papegaai
58 Kalverstraat
Sundays 10.30am and 12.15pm

Reformed Services
The Anglican Church
42 Groenburgwal
Sundays 10.30am
English Reformed Church/ Presbyterian/Church of Scotland
48 Begijnhof
Sundays 10.30am
Jewish Services
Portugees-Israëlitische Synagoge (Orthodox) 1 Mr Visserplein
Saturdays 9am

S tudent Travellers

Young people under 24 are entitled to reduced-rate admissions to most museums, though a passport may be required as proof of age. The magazine *Amsterdam Day by Day*, available at local book shops and VVV offices is crammed with information on current exhibitions and all cultural events.

The local student campus restaurants are called Mensas and anyone can eat there. Food is filling and cheap but served only Monday to Friday lunch and dinner. Two popular ones are Mensa Agora Universitair Restaurant 11 Roeterstraat (near the Artis Zoo) and Mensa Atrium Universitair Restaurant in the city centre at 237 Oudezijds Achterburgwal.

T elephones

Amsterdam telephone numbers generally have seven digits. When dialling an Amsterdam number from outside the city, the area code to use is '020' (or '20' from outside the Netherlands). Most telephone boxes take phonecards (€5, €12.50, €25 and €50), which you can buy in post offices, large stores and cafés. Some take coins (5, 10, 20, 50 cents or €1).

To dial a number outside the Netherlands, first dial 00 (international access number), then the country code, the area code and the subscriber's number. For information about phone numbers within the Netherlands, tel: 0900 8008; for information about phone numbers abroad, tel: 0900 8418.
To use phonecards dial the following access numbers:
AT&T: 0900 022 9111.
MCI: 0800 022 9122
Sprint: 0800 022 9119
British Telecom: 0800 022 9944
Canada Direct: 0800 022 9116

If you bring your mobile phone with you, remember that if you are calling a local number it is necessary to dial the international access code (eg "00" from the UK) followed by the code for the Netherlands (31) and Amsterdam (20), and therefore calls are expensive. This is because you are still operating through your service provider at home.

Time Zone

The Netherlands is one hour ahead of Greenwich Mean Time (GMT). If it is noon in Amsterdam, it is also noon in Paris, Rome and Berlin, 11am in London, 6am in New York, Montreal and Boston, 5am in Chicago, 3am in Los Angeles and San Francisco, and 9pm in Sydney. From the last weekend in March to the last weekend in October, the clocks are advanced one hour – this corresponds to the rest of the EU and with Daylight Savings Time in North America.

Toilets

Public toilets in Amsterdam are few and far between, and the more or less open-to-view urinals – for men only – are pretty grim. But there are plenty of cafés and fast-food restaurants where you can use the toilet either free or for a charge of 25–50 cents. Hotels, in particular those with busy lobbies (so you won't be recognised as an interloper), are a resource that needn't be overlooked, and their toilets are invariably clean.

Tourist Information

The main tourist office (VVV) is opposite Centraal Station at 10 Stationsplein, tel: 0900 400 4040, or 551 2525 (call centre) (www.visitamsterdam.nl), open daily 9am–5pm. There is another office inside the station at platform 2, open Mon–Sat 8am–8pm, Sun 9am–5pm, and a

VVV bureau at 104 Leidsestraat, open Sun–Wed 9am–5pm, Thurs–Sat until 8pm.

There is a tourist information office at the airport, which is useful if you have not already booked your accommodation. The booklet *What's On in Amsterdam* lists events in the city. Other guides can also be bought at the VVV.

The GVB Tickets and Information office, also at Stationsplein, alongside the dock to your left as you exit, tel: 0900 9292 (50 cents per minute), provides information and ticket sales for local and city public transport. Open Monday–Friday 7am–9pm, Saturday and Sunday 8am–9pm.

Useful Addresses

Netherlands Board of Tourism USA and Canada
355 Lexington Avenue 19th Floor
New York, NY 10017
Tel: (212) 370 7360
Fax: (212) 370 9507
E-mail: info@goholland.com
www.goholland.com
Netherlands Board of Tourism UK and Ireland
PO Box 30783,
London WC2B 6DH
Tel: (020) 7539 7950
Brochure-line Tel: 0906-871 7777
Fax: (020) 7828-7941
E-mail: hollandinfo-uk@nbt.org.uk
www.goholland.com

Travel Agents

American Express
66 Damrak
Tel: 504 8780

Amsterdam Travel Service and Tours
(specialists for British travellers)
10 Dam
Tel: 627 6236;
UK office: Bridge House,
55–59 High Road, Broxbourne,
Herts EN10 7DT
Tel: (01992) 456 056
Holland International
33a Prins Hendrikkade
Tel: 625 3035
Lindbergh Excursions
26 Damrak
Tel: 622 2766

Websites

The first place to turn to for information on Amsterdam is the VVV Amsterdam/Amsterdam Tourist Board's own comprehensive website www.visitamsterdam.nl, which has plenty of travel-related information and news from the city: attractions, sights and places of interest; hotels and restaurants, guided tours; walking routes; shopping; and more. It's all promotional and uncritical, of course, but it's still full of useful information. For a wider vista on Holland, there's the Netherlands Board of Tourism's site www.visitholland.com, which does a similar job on a wider scale. Two good, independent sites are www.amsterdamhotspots.nl, which, as the name suggest, covers the hottest places for eating, drinking, smoking (hash), dancing, and much more; and for restaurant reviews see www.dinner-in-amsterdam.nl

For details on internet access in Amsterdam see page 232.

Women Travellers

Public transport is mostly busy until midnight, which means there should be little danger of being alone aboard a bus or a tram at night; and many trams have a conductor as well as a driver. Many Amsterdam women get around by bike – for safety, most carry shoulder bags, with the strap crossed over the shoulder, and the clasp facing inwards.

L ANGUAGE

UNDERSTANDING THE LANGUAGE

Dutch pronunciation

Eavesdropping on any Dutch conversation, you could be forgiven for thinking that Dutch people constantly need to clear their throat! This Germanic language regularly uses a guttural consonant similar to the "ch" in the Scottish word "loch". In Dutch terms this is known as the "soft g", although the "hard g" sounds almost the same – if you look at Dutch words that begin with a "g", then you can reasonably assume the word starts with that infamous "ch". If you wish to greet someone with a *goedemorgen* (good morning); pronouncing the first or second "g" without the "ch" sound will identify you as German. Don't worry about being wrongly identified though; any attempt you may make at speaking Dutch will be received as a compliment. To this end, here are a few tips on Dutch pronunciation:

Consonants

As a rule, the "hard consonants" such as t, k, s and p are pronounced almost the same as in English, but sometimes a little softer. For example, the Dutch would refer to little as "liddle". *j* is pronounced as a y *(ja* meaning yes is pronounced *ya)* *v* is pronounced as f *(vis* meaning fish is pronounced *fiss)*

je is pronounced as *yer* *tje* is pronounced as *ch (botje* meaning little bone is pronounced *botchyer)*

Vowels

ee is pronounced as *ay (nee* meaning no is pronounced *nay)* *oo* is pronounced as *o (hoop* meaning hope is also pronounced as *hope)* *ij* is pronounced as *eay (ijs* meaning ice cream is pronounced *ace)* *a* is pronounced as *u (bank* also meaning bank is pronounced as *bunk).*

Dutch Words & Phrases

How much is it? *Hoeveel is het?* (or) *Hoeveel kost dit?*
What is your name? *Wat is uw naam?*
My name is... *Mijn naam is ... Ik heet ...*
Do you speak English? *Spreekt u Engels?*
I am English *Ik ben Engelsman*
...American*...Amerikaan*
I don't understand *Ik begrijp het niet*
Please speak more slowly *Kunt u langzamer praten, alstublieft*
Can you help me? *Kunt u mij helpen?*
I'm looking for... *Ik zoek...*
Where is...? *Waar is...?*
I'm sorry *Excuseer/Pardon*

I don't know *Ik weet het niet*
No problem *Geen probleem*
Have a good day! *Prettige dag nog!*
That's it *Precies*
Here it is *Het is hier*
There it is *Het is daar*
Let's go *Kom/We zijn weg*
See you tomorrow *Tot morgen*
See you soon *Tot straks!*
At what time? *Hoe laat?*
When? *Wanneer?*
What time is it? *Hoe laat is het?*
yes *ja*
no *neen*
please *alstublieft*
thank you *dank u*
...(very much) *...(wel)*
you're welcome *graag gedaan*
excuse me *excuseer/pardon*
hello *hallo*
goodbye *tot ziens*
good evening *Goeden avond*
here *hier*
there *daar*
today *vandaag*
yesterday *gisteren*
tomorrow *morgen*
now *nu*
later *later*
right away *direct/onmiddellijk*
this morning *vanmorgen*
this afternoon *deze namiddag*
this evening *vanavond*

On the Road

Where is the spare wheel? *Waar is het reservewiel?*

TRANSPORT

ACCOMMODATION

ACTIVITIES

A – Z

LANGUAGE

Where is the nearest garage?
Waar is de dichtstbijzijnde garage?
Our car has broken down *Onze auto is in panne*
I want to have my car repaired *Ik wil mijn auto laten herstellen*
the road to... *de straat naar...*
left *links*
right *rechts*
straight on *rechtstreeks*
far/near *ver/nabij*
opposite *tegenover*
beside *naast*
car park *de parking*
over there *daar*
at the end *aan het eind*
on foot *te voet*
by car *met de auto*
town map *het stadplan*
road map *de (wegen) kaart*
street *de straat*
square *het plein*
give way *geef voorrang*
dead end *doodlopende straat*
no parking *verboden te parkeren*
motorway *de autosnelweg*
toll *de tol*
speed limit *de snelheids-beperking*
petrol *de benzine*
diesel *de diesel*
water/oil *water/olie*
puncture *een lekke band*
wipers *ruitewissers*

Shopping

Where is the nearest bank?
Waar is de dichtstbijzijnde
...post office? *postkantoor?*
I'd like to buy... *Ik zou graag (or) kopen*
How much is it? *Hoeveel is het? (or) Hoeveel kost het?*
Do you take credit cards? *Neemt u crediet kaarten?*
Have you got? *Hebt u...?*
I'll take it *Ik neem het*
I'll take this one/that one *Ik neem dit/deze*
What size is it? *Welke maat is het?*
Anything else? *Iets anders?*
size *de maat*
cheap *goedkoop*
expensive *duur*
enough *genoeg*
too much *te veel*

a piece *een stuk*
each *per stuk*
bill *de rekening*
chemist *de apotheek*
bakery *de bakkerij*
bookshop *de boekhandel*
delicatessen *delicatessen*
department store *het warenhuis*
fishmonger *de viswinkel*
grocery *de kruidenier*
tobacconist *de tabakwinkel*
market *de markt*
supermarket *de supermarkt*
junk shop *brocante/antiquiteiten*

Sightseeing

town *de stad*
old town *de oude stad*
abbey *de abdij*
cathedral *de kathedraal*
church *de kerk*
keep *de slottoren*
mansion *het herenhuis*
hospital *het ziekenhuis*
town hall *het stadhuis*
nave *het schip*
stained glass *het glasraam*
staircase *de trap*
tower *de toren*
walk *de tour*
country house/castle *het kasteel*
museum *het museum*
art gallery *de galerie*
exhibition *de tentoonstelling*
tourist information office *het bureau voor toerisme (VVV)*
free *gratis*
open *open*
closed *gesloten*
every day *elke dag*
all year *het hele jaar*
all day *de hele dag*
swimming pool *het zwembad*
to book *reserveren/boeken*

Emergencies

Help! *Help!*
Call a doctor *Bel een dokter*
Call an ambulance *Bel een ziekenwagen*
Call the police *Bel de politie*
Call the fire brigade *Bel de brandweer*
Where is the nearest telephone? *Waar is de dichtstbijzijnde telefoon?*

Where is the nearest hospital?
Waar is het dichtstbijzijnde ziekenhuis?
I am sick *Ik ben ziek*
I have lost my passport/purse *Ik ben mijn paspoort/ portemonnee kwijt/verloren*

Telephoning

How do I make an outside call?
Hoe krijg ik een buitenlijn?
I want to make an international (local) call *Ik wil naar het buitenland bellen*
What is the dialling code? *Wat is het zonenummer/ landnummer?*
I'd like an alarm call for 8 o'clock tomorrow morning *Ik wil om 8 uur gewekt worden*
Who's calling? *Met wie spreek ik?*
Hold on, please *Blijf aan de lijn, alstublieft*
The line is busy *De lijn is in gesprek*
I have dialled the wrong number *Ik heb een verkeerd nummer gedraaid*

Eating Out

breakfast *het ontbijt*
lunch *lunch/middageten*
dinner *diner/avondeten*
meal *de maaltijd*
first course *het voorgerecht/entrée*
main course *het hoofdgerecht*
drink included *drank inbegrepen*
wine list *de wijnkaart*
the bill *de rekening*
fork *het vork*
knife *het mes*
spoon *de lepel*
plate *het bord*
glass *het glas*
napkin *het servet*
ashtray *de asbak*
I am a vegetarian *Ik ben vegetarier*
I am on a diet *Ik volg een dieet*
What do you recommend? *Wat beveelt u aan?*
I'd like to order *Ik wil bestellen*
That is not what I ordered *Dit is niet wat ik besteld heb*
Is service included? *Is de dienst inbegrepen?*

MENU DECODER

Breakfast & Snacks
boter butter
boterham bread with butter
brood bread
broodjes rolls
eieren eggs
...met spek bacon and eggs
...met ham ham and eggs
spiegeleieren fried eggs
roerei scrambled eggs
zacht gekooktei soft-boiled
    eggs
kaas cheese
honing honey
confitur jam
pannekoek pancake
peper pepper
joghurt yoghurt
zout salt
suiker sugar

Vlees/Meat
biefstuk steak
brochette kebab
carbonnade casserole of beef,
    beer and onions
eend duck
eendenborst breast of duck
escargot/slak snail
gebraad roast
gegrild grilled
gegrild vlees grilled meat
gehakt minced meat
gevuld stuffed
goedgebakken well done
ham ham
kalfsvlees veal
kalkoen turkey
kikkerbillen frog's legs
kip chicken
konijn rabbit
kuiken young chicken
lams vlees lamb
lamskotelet lamb chop
lendestuk sirloin
lever liver
niertjes kidneys
spek small pieces of bacon,
    often added to salads
stoofpot casserole of beef and
vegetables
varkens vlees pork

Vis/Fish
ansjovis anchovies
calamars/inktvis squid

daurade sea bream
forel trout
garnaal shrimp
haring herring
heilbot halibut
kabeljauw cod
koolvis hake
kreeft lobster
langoestine large prawns
limande lemon sole
lotte monkfish
mosselen mussels
oester oyster
paling eel
rogge skate
schaaldier shellfish
sint-jakobsschelp scallops
tonijn tuna
zeebaars sea bass
zeevruchten seafood
zalm salmon

Groenten/Vegetables
aardappel potato
ajuin/ui onion
artisjok artichoke
asperge asparagus
aubergine eggplant
augurk gherkin
avocado avocado
biet turnip
bloemkool cauliflower
boon dried bean
champignon mushroom
cantharel wild mushroom
(dooierzwam) chips potato
    crisps
courgette zucchini
erwten peas
frieten chips French fries
gemengde sla mixed leaf salad
groene bonen green beans
groene sla green salad
komkommer cucumber
kool cabbage
linzen lentils
look garlic
mais corn
noot/walnoot nut walnut
paprika bell pepper
peterselie parsley
prei leek
radijs radish
rauw raw
rijst rice
selder celery

spinazie spinach
tomaat tomato
witloof chicory
witte peen parsnip

Vruchter/Fruit
aardbei strawberry
ananas pineapple
appel apple
citroen lemon
druiven grapes
framboos raspberry
kers cherry
limoen lime
mango mango
meloen melon
perzik peach
peer pear
pruim prune
vijg fig

Puddings
gebak/taart cake
slagroom whipped cream

Dranken/Drinks
bier beer
...een fles bottled
...van het vat on tap
koffie coffee
...met melk of room with milk or
    cream
...decafeine decaffeinated
...zwart/espresso
    black/espresso
filterkoffie filtered
koud cold
limonade fizzy lemonade
citroensap lemon juice
sinaasappelsap orange juice
vers fresh
warme chocolademelk hot
    chocolate
huiswijn house wine
melk milk
mineraalwater mineral water
karaf pitcher
water/wijn water/wine
rood red
schuimwijn sparkling wine
zacht sweet
thee tea
...kruidenthee herb infusion
...kamille camomile
wit white
met ijs with ice

TRANSPORT ACCOMMODATION ACTIVITIES A-Z LANGUAGE

FURTHER READING

History and Politics

Amsterdam – A Brief Life in the City by Geert Mak, Harvill Press (1999).
Traces the city's progress from a little town of merchants and fishermen into a thriving metropolis.
The Diary of a Young Girl by Anne Frank, Doubleday, New York (1995)/Viking (1997).
Few books have been as widely read or as influential as the diary of Anne Frank.
The Dutch Revolt by Geoffrey Parker, Peregrine Books (Penguin Group) (1988).
A brilliant picture of the character of the Dutch in their revolt against the Spanish overlords during the Eighty Years War (1568–1648).
The Embarrassment of Riches by Simon Schama, University of California Press (1988).
An academic but very readable insight into culture and society during Holland's Golden Age.
The Tulip by Anna Pavord, Bloomsbury (1999).
Not just a horticultural examination of an extraordinary flower, but also a fantastic piece of sociological and historical research.

Art and Architecture

Dutch Art and Architecture 1600–1800 by Jakob Rosenberg et al, Penguin, (1988).
A standard work, first published in 1966, rewritten by popular demand, with new insights. especially into the works of Hals and Rembrandt. Richly illustrated but in monochrome.
Dutch Painting by R.H. Fuchs, Oxford University Press (1978; now reprinted).

A condensed though comprehensive overview of Dutch painting from the Middle Ages to the present.
The Van Gogh File by Ken Wilkie, Souvenir Press (1990).
A journalist and Van Gogh enthusiast travels in the footsteps of Van Gogh. Along the way, he uncovers intriguing insights into the artist's life.
Painters of Amsterdam: Four Centuries of Cityscapes by Carole Denninger-Schreuder, Thoth Publishers (2000).
Ms Denninger-Schreuder did have a little "assistance" with this beautiful book – from Rembrandt, Van Gogh and Mondrian, to name but a few.
Amsterdam by Martin Kers and Willem Wilmink, Inmerc/Schipper Art Productions (1991).
Martin Kers has given the city a luminous, other-worldly quality in this book of photographs.

The Dutch People

The British and the Dutch by K.H.D. Haley, George Philip, (1988).
Political and cultural relations through the ages. A clear, readable study of the love/hate relationship between the two countries.
The Low Sky: Understanding the Dutch by Han Vander Horst, Scriptum/Nuffic Books (1996).
This thoughtful book investigates below the surface to explore modern Holland's dilemmas and taboos.
The Undutchables by Colin White and Laurie Boucke, White & Boucke Publishing (1995).
An irreverent, often accurate, though cliché-ridden, observation of the Dutch and their habits.

Other Insight Guides

Insight Guide: The Netherlands, captures the essence of the Netherlands with incisive text and memorable photography. *Insight Pocket Guide: Amsterdam* includes tailor-made itineraries and personal recommendations from a local host. The **Compact Guides** to the **Netherlands** and **Amsterdam** are the perfect on-the-spot companions. The **Insight Fleximap Amsterdam** provides detailed street maps with full indexing in a tough, laminated plastic finish – perfect for keeping out the rain.

FEEDBACK

We do our best to ensure the information in our books is as accurate and up-to-date as possible. The books are updated on a regular basis, using local contacts who painstakingly add, amend and correct as required. However, some mistakes and omissions are inevitable and we are ultimately reliant on our readers to put us in the picture.
We would welcome your feedback on any details related to your experiences using the book "on the road". We will acknowledge all contributions, and we'll offer an Insight Guide to the best letters received.

Please write to us at:
Insight Guides
PO Box 7910
London SE1 1WE
United Kingdom
Or send email to:
insight@apaguide.co.uk

AMSTERDAM STREET ATLAS

The key map shows the area of Amsterdam covered by the atlas section. An index of street names and places of interest shown on the maps can be found on the following pages. For each entry there is a page number and grid reference.

Map Legend

Motorway with Junction	⊖ Border Crossing	Motorway
Motorway (under construction)	✈ Airport	Dual Carriageway
Dual Carriageway	✝ Church (ruins)	Main Roads
Main Road	✝ Monastery	
Secondary Road	🏰 Castle (ruins)	Minor Roads
Minor road	∴ Archaeological Site	
Track	∩ Cave	Footpath
International Boundary	★ Place of Interest	Railway
Province Boundary	🏛 Mansion/Stately Home	Pedestrian Area
National Park/Reserve	☼ Viewpoint	Important Building
Ferry Route	⚑ Beach	Park

Ⓜ	Metro
🚌	Bus Station
❶	Tourist Information
✉	Post Office
⛪	Cathedral/Church
☾	Mosque
✡	Synagogue
⛫	Statue/Monument
∐	Tower
⚓	Lighthouse

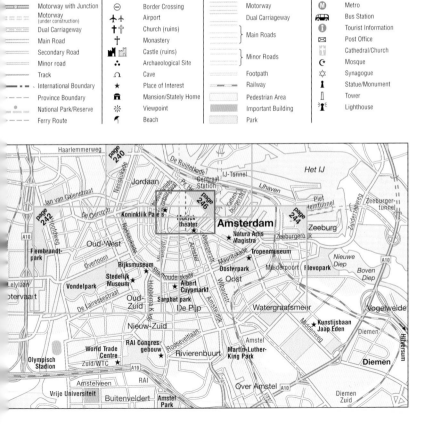

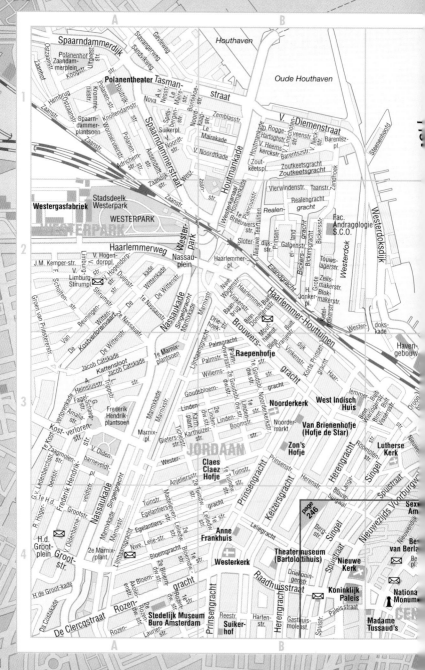

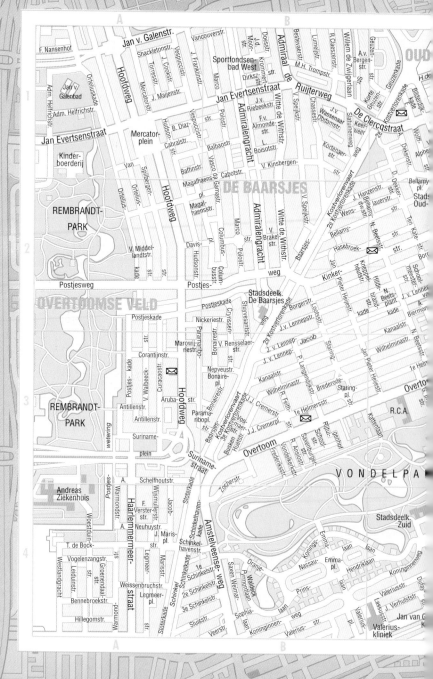

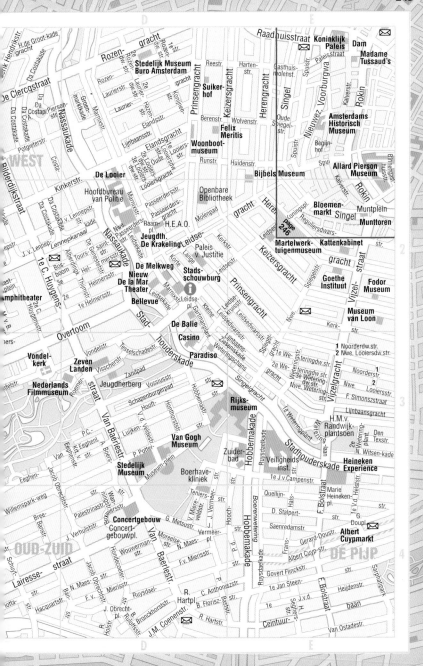

Raadhuisstraat
Koninklijk Paleis
Dam
Madame Tussaud's
Rozen-
gracht
Stedelijk Museum
Buro Amsterdam
Reestr.
Harten-
str.
Gasthuis-
molenst.
Paleisstraat
Spuistr.
Kalverstr.
Rokin
De Clercqstraat
Prinsengracht
Keizersgracht
Herengracht
Singel
Nieuwez. Voorburgwa
Suiker-
hof
Rozen-
str.
Laurierstr.
Berenstr.
Wolvenstr.
Oude
Spiegel-
str.
Amsterdams
Historisch
Museum
WEST
Groen-
marktkade
Nassaukade
Da Costapl.
Piersen-
str.
Laurier-
Elandstr.
Lijnbaanstr.
Elandsgracht
Felix
Meritis
Woonboot-
museum
Runstr.
Huidenstr.
Begijn-
hof
Spui
Allard Pierson
Museum
De Looier
Hoofdbureau
van Politie
Passeerdersstr.
Passeerders-
gracht
Loorsgracht
Bijbels Museum
gracht
Heren
Openbare
Bibliotheek
Koningspl.
Bloemen-
markt
Singel
Muntplein
Munttoren
Da Costakade
Nwe.
Passeerdersstr.
Raam-
str.
Molenpad
Regulierdwars-
Leidse
H.E.A.O.
Jeugdth.
De Krakeling
Leidse-
Kerkstr.
Paleis
v. Justitie
Lange
Keizersgracht
Martelwerk-
tuigenmuseum
Kattenkabinet
page
246
De Melkweg
Nieuw
De la Mar
Theater
Stads-
schouwburg
Prinsengracht
Nwe.
Goethe
Instituut
Vijzelstraat
Fodor
Museum
amphitheater
Bellevue
Leidse-
pl.
Kerk-
Museum
van Loon
De Balie
Casino
Paradiso
Overtoom
Stad
houderskade
Leidsekruisstr.
Spiegel
gracht
1 Noorderdw.str.
2 Nwe. Looiersdw.str.
Vondel-
kerk
Zeven
Landen
Vondelstr.
Tesselschadest.
Visscherstr.
Zandpad
Singelgracht
2e We-
teringdw.str.
1e We-
teringdw.str.
1
Noorderstr.
1
Nwe.
Looiers-
str.
Nederlands
Filmmuseum
Jeugdherberg
Vossiusstr.
Schapenburgerpad
Hooft-
Hobbemastr.
Rijks-
museum
Weteringschans
Weteringplant
Vijzelgracht
F. Simonszstraat
Lijnbaansgracht
P.C.
Van Baerlestr.
Luijken-
P. Potter
Van Gogh
Museum
Hobbemakade
Zuider-
bad
Stadhouderskade
H.M.v.
Randwijk-
plantsoen
N. Witsen-kade
Den
Texstr.
Stedelijk
Museum
Museum-plein
Boerhave-
kliniek
Veiligheids
inst.
Ruysdaelkade
Heineken
Experience
Willemspark-weg
Bree-
str.
Palestrinastr.
Teniers-
str.
V. Miere-
veldstr.
J. V. Vermeer-
str.
1e J.v.Campenstr.
Quellijnstr.
Hals-
str.
D. Stalpert-
Marie
Heineken-
pl.
F. Bolstraat
v.d. Helstr.
str.
OUD-ZUID
Concertgebouw
Concert-
gebouwpl.
J. Verhulststr.
G. Metsustr.
Hooch-
Moreelse-
str.
N. Maes-
Vermeer-
pl.
Saenredamstr.
Frans
Gerard-Dou-str.
G.
Doupl.
Albert
Cuypmarkt
Lairesse-
straat
Van Baerlestr.
Wouwerman-
str.
Jacob Obrechtstr.
N. Maes-str.
Miereisstr.
F.v. Mierisstr.
Ruysdael-
str.
Hobbema-
Albert Cuyp-str.
Govert Flinckstr.
F. Bolstraat
DE PIJP
Sarphatipark
Heijdenstr.
Hacquartstr.
J. Obrecht-
pl.
Bronckhorststr.
R.
Hartpl.
C. Anthonisz.str.
B. Florisz.str.
1e Jan Steen-
str.
1e
J.v.d.
Sweelinckstr.
Ceintuur-
baan
Van Ostadestr.

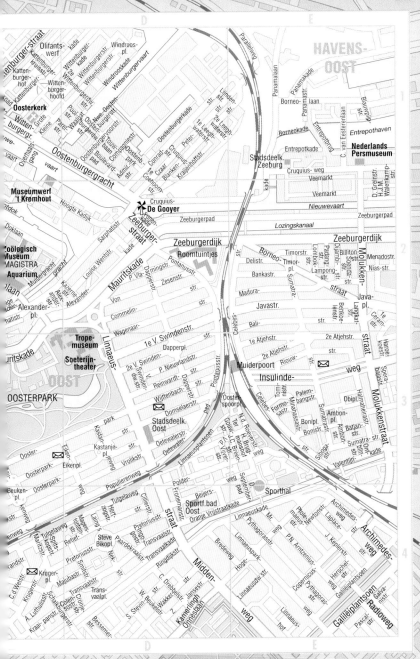

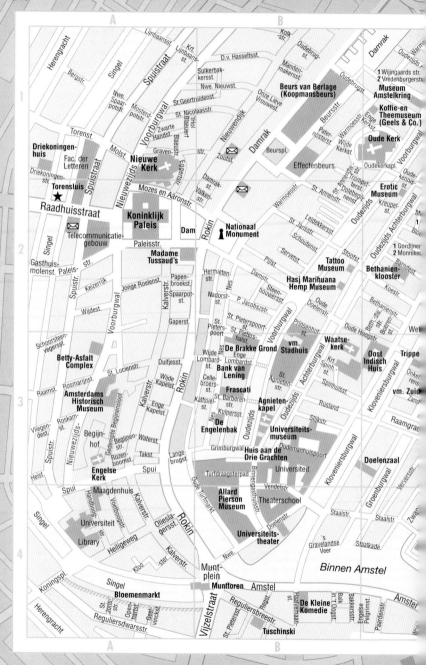

Schreierstoren

Oudezijds Kolk

nkje (uisje) st.

Gelderse kade

Smids- st.

Kromme Waal

Binnenkant

Oosterdokskade

Stedelijk Museum

Oosterdokskade

Oosterdok

Gelderse- st.

Waals-

Waals-

Scheepvaarthuis
Hoofdkant.
GVBA

Binnenkant

Buiten Bantammerstr.

Prins Hendrikkade

Binnen Bantammerstr.

Nwe.

Nwe.

Amsterdams
Marionetten
Theater

'eilandsgracht

Binnenkant

Schipperstr.

Brandewijnstr.

Recht Boomssloot

Ridder- str.

Jonkerstr.

Montelbaanstr.

Oude Waal

Kalkmarkt

Lange K.dw.str.

Koningsstr.

Keizerstr.

Dijkstr.

Dijk dw.str.

Kl.
Kl. Kleersloot

Booms-
sloot

Krt. Konings-
str.

Krt. Koningsstr.

Krt. Konings
dw.str.

Montelbaans-
toren

Rapen-

's Gravenhekje

Prins Hendrikkade

Paperstr.

NIEUWMARKT

J.B.
Siebbeleshof

Krom

Oudeschans

Krt. Keizers
dw.str.

Oudeschans

Kazelsstr.

Oudeschans

Oosters-
kade

Rapenburg

Foeliestraat

Nwe. Foeliestraat

noekjesstr.

Krt.
Oudeschans

Oudeschans

Oudeschans

Schoekjesstr.

Houtkopers-
burgwal

Nwe. Batavierstr.

Uilenburgerstr.

burgwal

Nwe.
Grachtje

Foelie-dw.
str.

Schipperstr.

Rapenburger-
pl.

Oudeschans

Nwe.

Uilenburgergracht

Uilenburgerstr.

Valkenburgerstr.

Rapenburgerpl.

Anne Frank- str.

Entrepotdok

Jodenhouttuinen

Jodenbree-

Houtkopers-
dw.str.

Uilenburg-
gerstr.

Amsterdamse
Hoogeschool
voor de Kunsten

um Het
ndthuis
nd Experience

Waterloo-

str.

Rapenburgstr.

Mozes en
Aäronkerk

Rapenburgstr.

Nationaal
Vakbonds-
museum

Vlooienmarkt

pl.

Mr.
Visserplein

Nieuwe Herengracht

WERTHEIM-
PARK

Plantage Parklaan

H. Polaklaan

ams Peil (NAP)

Muiderstraat

Moederhuis

Muziek-
theater

Waterlooplein

Turfst.

De Dokwerker

J. D.
Meijerpl.

Portuguees-
Isra'litische
Synagoge

Plantage
Universiteit

Plantage Parklaan

Middenlaan

ol.
nboot

Joods
Historisch
Museum

Nwe. Amstel-str.

Weesperstraat

WATERLOOPLEIN

Dr. D.M. Stuijspad

HORTUS
BOTANICUS

Hollandsche
Schouwburg

wbrug

Hortusplantseon

STREET INDEX

ART & PHOTO CREDITS

Action Press/Rex Features 41
Akg-images London 20L, 30, 40, 146
Alamy 77
Amsterdam Historical Museum 17, 19, 24, 25, 88, 206T
The Art Archive 157
Jan Van Arkel/Foto Natura 193T
Dave Bartruff/Corbis 185
H. Berkhout/Foto Natura 159T, 191
A Bloomfield/Trip 133
Bodo Bondzio 10/11, 35, 58, 130, 142
Tibor Bognar/Trip 95, 136, 156
Dirk Buwalda 179
Jamie Carstairs/Trip 61, 106, 131, 204
Cephas Picture Library 195, 208
Escape 39, 134
Mary Evans Picture Library 26, 28, 84, 186
Lee Foster 152
Anne Frank House 118R, 120
Guglielmo Galvin 3, 9B, 22, 50, 82T, 88T, 90T, 106T, 111, 113T, 116T, 119T, 123T, 132R, 135, 148T, 169T, 181T, 194T
Glyn Genin 1, 2/3, 4, 6T, 6B, 7C, 8T, 9T, 38, 85T, 86T, 92T, 96T, 97, 98, 103R, 104, 104T, 105T, 108, 108T, 112, 114T, 116, 121T, 122, 123, 125, 128, 132L, 139T, 143, 153L, 164L/R, 165, 166T, 168, 169, 170, 171, 172, 173, 174, 175T, 178, 180, 181L/R, 182, 182T, 183, 184, 185T, 187, 188, 189
Michel Gotin 91L, 176, 202T
Manfred Gottschalk 206
Grandadam/The Picture Box 55

David Hanson/Stone/Getty Images 71
Robert Harding Picture Library 12/13
Robert Harding Picture Library/Alamy 92
D&J Heaton 198
Hans Hofer 23
Phillip Hollis/Alamy 44
Van der Norma Horst/The Picture Box 192L
Jan Butchofsky-Houser/HouserStock 42/43
M.J.Kielty/Cephas 163, 180T, 190T, 200T
Lyle Lawson 27, 153R, 196/197
Tom Le Bas 140T, 140, 141T, 142T, 172T, 173T
Mauritshuis Den Haag 150T
Bert Muller/Foto Natura 99
Richard Nowitz 80, 83, 83T, 86, 89, 103L, 109, 114/115, 162
Philips International B.V. 49
Lesley Player 14, 37L, 51, 52, 53, 76, 94, 96, 102T, 131T, 139
Pictures Colour Library 54, 70/71, 132T, 144/145, 147
The Picture Box back cover centre, 5, 45, 56, 57, 66, 67L/R, 124, 134T, 158, 231
Popperfoto/Alamy 193
Eddy Posthuma de Boer 21, 29, 48, 101, 107, 126, 138T, 153T, 154, 155L, 164T, 186T
Christine Osborne/COP 46, 59, 60, 81T, 85, 101T, 202
University Museum de Agnietenkapel 102
G.P. Reichelt 141
Rex Features 79T
Paul Van Riel 81R, 87, 100, 113, 121, 137, 138, 171T, 207

Rijksmuseum 16, 148, 149, 150, 177
Helene Rogers/Trip 37R, 81L
Ellen Rooney 64, 65, 119, 127
David Simson 47
Gordon Singer 82,105, 167T
Spaarnestad Foto 118L
Stedelijk Museum 155R
SuperStock 68/69
Swim Ink/Corbis 201
B. Tanaka/Taxi/Getty Images 110
B Turner/Trip 79
Bill Wassman 129, 181L, 199, 203T, 207T, 209
George Wright 99T, 117
Gregory Wrona 8L, 210, 210T, 165T, 205T
Volkmar Janicke back cover left & bottom
Inge Yspeert/Foto Natura 192R
Kim Zwarts/Cobra 194

Picture Spreads

Pages 62/63
Top row, left to right: Lesley Player, Glyn Genin/Apa
Bottom row: Glyn Genin, Gregory Wrona, Eduard Bergman, Glyn Genin
Pages 160/161
Top row: both Glyn Genin
Bottom row: Glyn Genin, Glyn Genin, Glyn Genin, H Berkhout/Foto Natura

Map production: Stephen Ramsay and Laura Morris

GENERAL INDEX

Amsterdam Transport

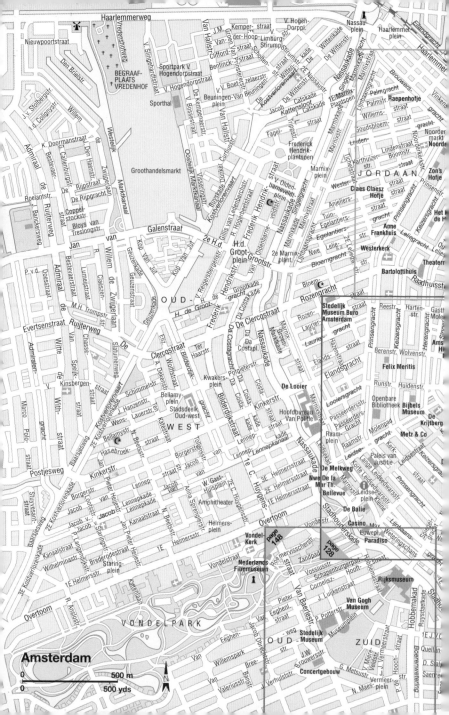